THE POCKET BOOK
OF QUOTATIONS
will help you to:

- Select an appropriate quotation on almost any subject.

- Locate a quotation when you know the name of the author.

- Discover the title of the book from which a quotation is taken.

- Find the author's name when you already know the words of a quotation.

- Learn when the author was born and when he died.

These and many other reference aids are yours when you use this compact and valuable book.

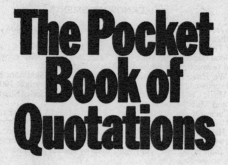

The Pocket Book of Quotations

EDITED BY HENRY DAVIDOFF

POCKET BOOKS

New York   London   Toronto   Sydney   Tokyo

ACKNOWLEDGMENTS

Thanks are due to the following music publishers for permission to include certain lyrics in this book:

"A Hot Time In The Old Town Tonight," "My Mother Was A Lady," "Nobody," "In The Good Old Summer Time" and "Take Back Your Gold" copyrighted and used by special permission of Edward B. Marks Music Corp.

"Yes! We Have No Bananas," copyright 1923 by Skidmore Music Co. Inc., copyright renewed. By permission. "School Days," copyright 1906, 1907 by Gus Edwards Music Co. Inc., copyright renewed. By permission of Shapiro, Bernstein & Co. Inc. and Mills Music Inc.

"The Curse Of An Aching Heart," copyright 1913 Leo Feist, Inc. Copyright renewal 1941 Leo Feist, Inc. Used by special permission of copyright proprietor.

"Hail! Hail! The Gang's All Here," copyright 1917 Leo Feist, Inc. Copyright renewal 1945 Leo Feist, Inc. Used by special permission of copyright proprietor.

"The Band Played On," copyright, used by special permission of Harms, Inc.

POCKET BOOKS, a division of Simon & Schuster Inc.
1230 Avenue of the Americas, New York, N.Y. 10020

ISBN: 0-671-60386-8

First Pocket Books printing September 1942

46 45 44 43 42 41 40 39

POCKET and colophon are trademarks of
Simon & Schuster Inc.

Printed in the U.S.A.

INTRODUCTORY
NOTE

~~~~~~

THIS NEW COLLECTION contains the cream of the quotations which have become famous the world over. In the case of those that appeared first in a foreign language the original wording has been given as well as an English version.

It should be kept in mind that *famous* quotations are not necessarily the *best* from a literary point of view. Otherwise, the editor would not have included, as he did, some of the ravings of Hitler and Mussolini. Nor do the many popular songs included in this collection mark a high-water line in literary expression, yet some of them have become part of the language.

In order to make it easy for the reader to find what he may be looking for, the list of topics or categories under which the quotations are arranged has been given in full at the beginning, with the page numbers on which they appear. Thus hundreds of subjects and themes from "Absence" to "Zeus" will be found arranged alphabetically. In addition, at the end of the book, there is a complete index of the authors quoted—with dates of birth and death—and the pages on which quotations from them occur. In a few instances, as is the case with Shakespeare and the Bible, the references are too numerous to be listed.

—THE EDITOR

TABLE OF
CONTENTS

Contents

Contents

Contents

✦ T ✦

The Pocket
Book of
Quotations

ABSENCE

Absence makes the heart grow fonder,
Isle of Beauty, Fare thee well!
—THOMAS H. BAYLY, *Isle of Beauty*

ACCIDENTS

Accidents will occur in the best-regulated families; and
in families not regulated by that pervading influence which
sanctifies while it enhances the—a—I would say, in short,
by the influence of Woman, in the lofty character of
Wife. . . . —DICKENS, *David Copperfield*

ADAM

Whilst Adam slept, Eve from his side arose:
Strange his first sleep should be his last repose.
—ANON., *The Consequences*

Adam the goodliest man of men since born
His sons, the fairest of her daughters Eve.
—MILTON, *Paradise Lost, IV*

In Adam's fall
We sinnèd all. —*New England Primer*

Adam and Eve had many advantages, but the principal
one was, that they escaped teething.
—MARK TWAIN, *Pudd'nhead Wilson's Calendar*

ADULTERY

What men call gallantry, and gods adultery,
Is much more common where the climate's sultry.
                                    —BYRON, *Don Juan, I*

ADVERSITY

Sweet are the uses of adversity;
Which, like the toad, ugly and venomous,
Wears yet a precious jewel in his head.
                        —SHAKESPEARE, *As You Like It, II, I*

AGE

Grow up as soon as you can. It pays. The only time you
really live fully is from thirty to sixty.
                            —HERVEY ALLEN, *Anthony Adverse*

Grow old along with me!
The best is yet to be,
The last of life for which the first was made:
                            —R. BROWNING, *Rabbi Ben Ezra*

As a white candle in a holy place,
So is the beauty of an aged face.
                        —JOSEPH CAMPBELL, *The Old Woman*

We do not count a man's years, until he has nothing else
to count.   —EMERSON, *Society and Solitude*

That age is best which is the first,
    When youth and blood are warmer;
But being spent, the worse, and worst
    Times, still succeed the former.
                            —HERRICK, *To the Virgins*

Your old men shall dream dreams, your young men shall
see visions.   —OLD TESTAMENT, *Joel, II, 28*

Crabbed age and youth cannot live together.
> —SHAKESPEARE, *The Passionate Pilgrim*

I have lived long enough; my way of life
Is fall'n into the sear, the yellow leaf:
> —SHAKESPEARE, *Macbeth, V, 3*

When you are old and gray and full of sleep,
And nodding by the fire, take down this book.
> —W. B. YEATS, *When You Are Old*

ALE

And malt does more than Milton can
To justify God's ways to man.
> —A. E. HOUSMAN, *A Shropshire Lad*

Dost thou think, because thou art virtuous, there shall be
no more cakes and ale?
> —SHAKESPEARE, *Twelfth Night, II, 3*

Back and side go bare, go bare:
Both foot and hand go cold;
But, belly, God send thee good ale enough,
Whether it be new or old.
> —JOHN STILL (?), *Gammer Gurton's Needle*

ALLAH

Praise be to Allah, the Lord of creation,
The merciful, the compassionate
Ruler of the Day of Judgment
Help us, lead us in the path. > —MAHOMET, *Koran, I*

ALLIANCES

Peace, commerce and honest friendship with all nations
—entangling alliances with none.
> —JEFFERSON, *First Inaugural Address*

ALLITERATION

Who oft but without success, have pray'd
For Apt Alliteration's Artful Aid.
> —CHARLES CHURCHILL, *Prophecy of Famine*

An Austrian army, awfully arrayed,
Boldly by battery besieged Belgrade;
Cossack commanders cannonading come,
Dealing destruction's devastating doom;
(*Etc., to the letter* Z.)
> —A. A. WATTS, *The Siege of Belgrade*

AMBITION

All ambitions are lawful except those which climb upward on the miseries or credulities of mankind.
> —JOSEPH CONRAD, *A Personal Record*

I would rather be the first man here than the second in Rome.   —JULIUS CAESAR (according to Plutarch)

I had Ambition, by which sin
The angels fell;
I climbed and, step by step, O Lord,
Ascended into Hell.   —W. H. DAVIES, *Ambition*

Cromwell, I charge thee, fling away ambition:
By that sin fell the angels;
> —SHAKESPEARE, *Henry VIII, III, 2*

AMERICA

America! America!
God shed His grace on thee.
> —KATHARINE L. BATES, *America the Beautiful*

O, Columbia, the gem of the ocean,
The home of the brave and the free,

The shrine of each patriot's devotion,
    A world offers homage to thee.
            —THOMAS A. BECKET (an English actor, 1843)

Westward the course of empire takes its way;
    The four first acts already past,
A fifth shall close the drama with the day:
    Time's noblest offspring is the last.
                    —GEORGE BERKELEY, Bishop of Cloyne,
On the Prospect of Planting Arts and Learning in America
                                        (1745)

Bring me men to match my mountains,
Bring me men to match my plains,
Men with empires in their purpose,
And new eras in their brains.
                    —S. W. Foss, *The Coming American*

Hail, Columbia! happy land!
            —JOSEPH HOPKINSON, *Hail, Columbia* (1789)

The land of the free and the home of the brave.
            —FRANCIS SCOTT KEY, *The Star-Spangled Banner*

Intellectually I know that America is no better than any
other country; emotionally I know she is better than every
other country.   —SINCLAIR LEWIS, Speech

Thou, too, sail on, O Ship of State!
Sail on, O Union, strong and great!
            —LONGFELLOW, *The Building of the Ship*

It will never be possible for any length of time for any
group of the American people, either by reason of wealth
or learning or inheritance or economic power, to retain any

mandate, any permanent authority to arrogate to itself the political control of American public life.

—Franklin D. Roosevelt, Address, June, 1936

The American people never carry an umbrella. They prepare to walk in eternal sunshine.

—Alfred E. Smith, Speech

My country, 'tis of thee,
Sweet land of liberty,
Of thee I sing;

—Samuel Francis Smith, *America* (1831)

The United States is not a nation of people which in the long run allows itself to be pushed around.

—Dorothy Thompson, *On the Record*

America is God's Crucible, the great Melting-Pot where all the races of Europe are melting and reforming . . .

—Israel Zangwill, *The Melting-Pot, I*

AMERICAN

I am not a Virginian, but an American.

—Patrick Henry, Speech, Sept. 5, 1774

I am willing to love all mankind except an American.

—Samuel Johnson (Boswell, *Life, III*)

. . . who reads an American book? or goes to an American play? or looks at an American picture or statue? . . .

—Sydney Smith, *Edinburgh Review* (Jan. 1820)

Some Americans need hyphens in their names because only part of them has come over.

—Woodrow Wilson, Address, May 16, 1914

ANCESTRY

The Jukes were an old family too.
—LILLIAN HELLMAN, *The Children's Hour*

i have often noticed that
ancestors never boast
of the descendants who boast
of ancestors i would rather
start a family than finish
one blood will tell but
often it tells too much
—DON MARQUIS, *a roach of the taverns*

The man who has not anything to boast of but his illus-
trious ancestors is like a potato—the only good belonging to
him is underground.
—SIR THOMAS OVERBURY, *Characters* (1614)

ANGEL

How many angels can dance on the point of a very fine
needle without jostling each other?
—ISAAC D'ISRAELI, *Curiosities of Literature*
(on an idea in Thomas Aquinas)

Look homeward, Angel, now, and melt with ruth.
—MILTON, *Lycidas*

Be not forgetful to entertain strangers: for thereby some
have entertained angels unawares.
—NEW TESTAMENT, *Hebrews, XIII, 2*

And flights of angels sing thee to thy rest!
—SHAKESPEARE, *Hamlet, V, 2*

ANGER

I was angry with my friend;
I told my wrath, my wrath did end.

I was angry with my foe;
I told it not, my wrath did grow.
>—WILLIAM BLAKE, *A Poison Tree*

ANIMALS

I think I could turn and live with animals, they are so placid and self-contained.
>—WALT WHITMAN, *Song of Myself*

APPEASEMENT

My good friends, this is the second time in our history that there has come back from Germany to Downing Street peace with honour. . . . I believe it is peace for our time.
>—NEVILLE CHAMBERLAIN, Address on return from Munich, Sept., 1938

APRIL

Oh, to be in England
Now that April's there.
>—R. BROWNING, *Home Thoughts from Abroad*

April is the cruelest month, breeding
Lilacs out of the dead land, mixing
Memory and desire, stirring
Dull roots with spring rain.
>—T. S. ELIOT, *The Waste Land*

April, April,
Laugh thy girlish laughter;
Then, the moment after,
Weep thy girlish tears!   —WILLIAM WATSON, *Song*

ARGUMENT

Myself when young did eagerly frequent
Doctor and Saint, and heard great argument
   About it and about; but evermore
Came out by the same door wherein I went.
>—OMAR KHAYYÁM, *Rubáiyát* (FitzGerald trans.)

I am not arguing with you—I am telling you.
   —J. McN. WHISTLER, *Gentle Art of Making Enemies*

ARMAMENTS

The Saviour came. With trembling lips
He counted Europe's battleships.
"Yet millions lack their daily bread.
So much for Calvary!" he said.
                —NORMAN GALE, *The Second Coming*

ARROW

I shot an arrow into the air,
It fell to earth, I knew not where;

· · · · · · ·

I breathed a song into the air,

· · · · · · ·

Long long afterward in an oak
I found the arrow still unbroke;
And the song, from beginning to end,
I found again in the heart of a friend.
                —LONGFELLOW, *The Arrow and the Song*

ART

All passes. Art alone
   Enduring stays to us.
The Bust outlasts the throne,—
   The Coin, Tiberius.   —AUSTIN DOBSON, *Ars Victrix*

Art is long and time is fleeting.
                —LONGFELLOW, *A Psalm of Life*

Art lies in concealing art.
(*Ars est celare artem.*)   —OVID, *Art of Love*

All art is but imitation of nature.
(Omnis ars naturae imitatio est.)
—SENECA, *Epistle to Lucilius*

ASPIRATION

What I aspired to be,
And was not, comforts me.
—R. BROWNING, *Rabbi Ben Ezra*

The shades of night were falling fast,
As through an Alpine village passed
A youth, who bore, 'mid snow and ice,
A banner with the strange device,
Excelsior!   —LONGFELLOW, *Excelsior*

ATHEISM

The fool hath said in his heart, There is no God.
—OLD TESTAMENT, *Psalms, XIV, 1*

My atheism, like that of Spinoza, is true piety towards
the universe and denies only gods fashioned by men in
their own image, to be servants of their human interests.
—GEORGE SANTAYANA, *Soliloquies in England*

AUTUMN

The melancholy days are come, the saddest of the year,
Of wailing winds, and naked woods, and meadows
brown and sear.
—WILLIAM C. BRYANT, *The Death of the Flowers*

When chill November's surly blast
Made fields and forests bare.
—ROBERT BURNS, *Man Was Made to Mourn*

BABBITT

His name was George F. Babbitt, and . . . he was nim-
ble in the calling of selling houses for more than people
could afford to pay.   —SINCLAIR LEWIS, *Babbitt* (1922)

BABY

Where did you come from, baby dear?
Out of the Everywhere into the here . . .
—GEORGE MACDONALD, *At the Back of the North Wind*

Out of the mouth of babes and sucklings hast thou ordained strength.   —OLD TESTAMENT, *Psalms, VIII, 2*

Sweetest li'l' feller, everybody knows;
Dunno what you call him, but he's mighty lak' a rose.
—FRANK L. STANTON, *Mighty Lak' a Rose*

BASEBALL

These are the saddest of possible words:
  "Tinker to Evers to Chance."
Trio of bear cubs, and fleeter than birds,
  Tinker and Evers and Chance.
—FRANKLIN P. ADAMS, *Baseball's Sad Lexicon*

There was ease in Casey's manner as he stepped into his
  place,
There was pride in Casey's bearing and a smile on
  Casey's face,
      . . . .
But there is no joy in Mudville—mighty Casey has struck
  out.   —E. L. THAYER, *Casey at the Bat*

BEAUTY

What is lovely never dies,
But passes into other loveliness.
—THOMAS BAILEY ALDRICH, *A Shadow of the Night*

There is no excellent beauty that hath not some strange-
ness in the proportion. —FRANCIS BACON, *Essays: Of Beauty*

If you get simple beauty and naught else,
You get about the best thing God invents.
—R. BROWNING, *Fra Lippo Lippi*

She walks in beauty, like the night
    Of cloudless climes and starry skies;
And all that's best of dark and bright
    Meet in her aspect and her eyes;
                    —BYRON, *She Walks in Beauty*

Lord of the far horizons,
    Give us the eyes to see
Over the verge of the sundown
    The beauty that is to be.
                —BLISS CARMAN, *Lord of the Far Horizons*

She is not fair to outward view
    As many maidens be:
Her loveliness I never knew
    Until she smiled on me: —HARTLEY COLERIDGE, *Song*

I slept and dreamed that life was beauty.
I woke—and found that life was duty;
Was my dream, then, a shadowy lie?
Toil on, sad heart, courageously,
And thou shalt find thy dream shall be
A noonday light and truth to thee.
                —ELLEN STURGIS HOOPER, *Beauty and Duty*

Beauty for some provides escape,
Who gain a happiness in eyeing
The gorgeous buttocks of the ape
Or autumn sunsets exquisitely dying.
                —ALDOUS HUXLEY, *The Ninth Philosopher's Song*

The beauty of things was born before eyes and
    sufficient to itself; the heart-breaking beauty
Will remain when there is no heart to break for it.
                —ROBINSON JEFFERS, *Credo*

A thing of beauty is a joy for ever:
Its loveliness increases; it will never
Pass into nothingness.   —KEATS, *Endymion*

"Beauty is truth, truth beauty,"—that is all
  Ye know on earth, and all ye need to know.
                      —KEATS, *Ode on a Grecian Urn*

Beauty is that Medusa's head
Which men go armed to seek and sever.
It is most deadly when most dead,
And dead will stare and sting forever.
                      —ARCHIBALD MACLEISH, *Beauty*

Beauty is Nature's coin, must not be hoarded,
But must be current, and the good thereof
Consists in mutual and partaken bliss . . .
                      —MILTON, *Comus*

As the lily among thorns, so is my love among the
daughters.   —OLD TESTAMENT, *Song of Solomon, II, 2*

Beauty is excrescence, superabundance, random ebul-
lience, and sheer delightful waste to be enjoyed in its own
high right.
  —DONALD CULROSS PEATTIE, *An Almanac for Moderns*

Helen, thy beauty is to me
  Like those Nicæan barks of yore,
That gently, o'er a perfumed sea,
  The weary, wayworn wanderer bore
  To his own native shore.   —POE, *To Helen*

She was good as she was fair,
  None, none on earth above her!

As pure in thought as angels are:
  To know her was to love her.
                        —SAMUEL ROGERS, *Jacqueline*

Remember that the most beautiful things in the world
are the most useless; peacocks and lilies, for example.
                        —JOHN RUSKIN, *The Stones of Venice, I*

What is beautiful is good and who is good will soon
also be beautiful.   —SAPPHO, *Fragments, 101*

            . . . her beauty made
The bright world dim, and everything beside
Seemed like the fleeting image of a shade.
                        —SHELLEY, *The Witch of Atlas*

Beauty is a short-lived reign.
                  —SOCRATES (quoted by Diogenes Laertius)

BED

Early to bed and early to rise,
Makes a man healthy, wealthy, and wise.
                —FRANKLIN, *Poor Richard's Almanac* for 1735

In winter I get up at night
And dress by yellow candle-light.
In summer, quite the other way,
I have to go to bed by day.
                —R. L. STEVENSON, *The Land of Counterpane*

BEE

Where the bee sucks, there suck I;
In a cowslip's bell I lie.
                        —SHAKESPEARE, *The Tempest, V, 1*

How doth the busy little bee
  Improve each shining hour,

And gather honey all the day
   From every opening flower!
                    —ISAAC WATTS, *Against Idleness*

BELIEF

A man must not swallow more beliefs than he can digest.
                    —HAVELOCK ELLIS, *The Dance of Life*

Blessed are they that have not seen, and yet have believed.   —NEW TESTAMENT, *John, XX, 29*

Lord, I believe; help thou mine unbelief.
                    —NEW TESTAMENT, *Mark, IX, 24*

For, dear me, why abandon a belief
Merely because it ceases to be true?
Cling to it long enough, and not a doubt
It will turn true again, for so it goes.
                    —ROBERT FROST, *The Black Cottage*

Believing where we cannot prove.
                    —TENNYSON, *In Memoriam*

I believe because it is impossible.
(Credo quia impossibile.)—TERTULLIAN, *De Carne Christi*

BELLS

Those evening bells! those evening bells!
How many a tale their music tells!
Of youth and home, and that sweet time
When last I heard their soothing chime.
                    —THOMAS MOORE, *Those Evening Bells*

Keeping time, time, time,
   In a sort of Runic rhyme,
To the tintinnabulation that so musically wells
   From the bells, bells, bells . . .   —POE, *The Bells*

BIRDS

> I saw with open eyes
> Singing birds sweet
> Sold in the shops
> For the people to eat,
> Sold in the shops of
> Stupidity Street.   —RALPH HODGSON, *Stupidity Street*

BIRTH

> Naked came I out of my mother's womb, and naked shall
> I return thither: —OLD TESTAMENT, *Job, I, 21*

> Why is it that we rejoice at a birth and grieve at a
> funeral? Is it because we are not the person concerned?
>   —MARK TWAIN, *Pudd'nhead Wilson's Calendar*

> Our birth is but a sleep and a forgetting:
> The Soul that rises with us, our life's Star,
>   Hath had elsewhere its setting,
>   And cometh from afar:
>   Not in entire forgetfulness,
>   And not in utter nakedness,
> But trailing clouds of glory do we come
>   From God who is our home:
>   —WORDSWORTH, *Intimations of Immortality*

BLESSING

> "God bless us every one!" said Tiny Tim, the last of all.
>   —DICKENS, *A Christmas Carol*

> Blessed is he that cometh in the name of the Lord.
>   —NEW TESTAMENT, *Matthew, XXIII, 39*

> I had most need of blessing, and "Amen"
> Stuck in my throat.   —SHAKESPEARE, *Macbeth, II, 2*

BLINDNESS

Oh, say! what is that thing call'd light,
   Which I must ne'er enjoy?
What are the blessings of the sight?
   Oh, tell your poor blind boy.
                    —COLLEY CIBBER, *The Blind Boy*

When I consider how my light is spent,
   Ere half my days, in this dark world and wide,
   And that one talent, which is death to hide,
Lodg'd with me useless, though my soul more bent
To serve therewith my Maker, and present
   My true account, lest he, returning, chide;
                    —MILTON, *Sonnet: On His Blindness*

They be blind leaders of the blind. And if the blind lead
the blind, both shall fall into the ditch.
                    —NEW TESTAMENT, *Matthew, XV, 14*

BLISS

It was a dream of perfect bliss,
Too beautiful to last.   —T. H. BAYLY, *It Was a Dream*

"BLUES"

I hate to see the evenin' sun go down,
I hate to see the evenin' sun go down,
'Cause my baby done gone an' lef' this town:
   Feelin' tomorrer jes' like I feel today,
   Feelin' tomorrer jes' like I feel today,
   I'll pack my trunk an' make my get-away.
                    —W. C. HANDY, *St. Louis Blues*

De railroad bridge 's
A sad song in de air.
Ever' time de trains pass
I wants to go somewhere.
                    —LANGSTON HUGHES, *Homesick Blues*

BOBOLINK

Merrily swinging on briar and weed,
    Near to the nest of his little dame,
Over the mountain-side or mead,
    Robert of Lincoln is telling his name:
        Bob-o-link, bob-o-link
        Spink, spank, spink;
                —WILLIAM C. BRYANT, *Robert of Lincoln*

BODY

For the body at best
    Is a bundle of aches,
Longing for rest;
    It cries when it wakes.
                —EDNA ST. VINCENT MILLAY, *Moriturus*

If anything is sacred the human body is sacred.
        —WALT WHITMAN, *I Sing the Body Electric*

BOLDNESS

He either fears his fate too much,
    Or his deserts are small,
That dares not put it to the touch,
    To gain or lose it all.
                —JAMES GRAHAM, Marquis of Montrose,
                        I'll Never Love Thee More

And dar'st thou then
To beard the lion in his den,
The Douglas in his hall?   —SCOTT, *Marmion*

I dare do all that may become a man;
Who dares do more is none.
                —SHAKESPEARE, *Macbeth, I, 7*

BOOKS

Some books are to be tasted, others to be swallowed, and some few to be chewed and digested: . . .
—BACON, *Essays: Of Studies*

When I am dead, I hope it may be said:
"His sins were scarlet, but his books were read."
—HILAIRE BELLOC, *On His Books*

Blessings upon Cadmus, the Phoenicians, or whoever it was that invented books. —CARLYLE, *Letter to R. Mitchell*

There is no frigate like a book
    To take us lands away,
Nor any coursers like a page
    Of prancing poetry.—EMILY DICKINSON, *Poems, I, 99*

To produce a mighty book, you must choose a mighty theme. No great and enduring volume can ever be written on the flea, though many there be that have tried it.
—HERMAN MELVILLE, *Moby Dick*

A good book is the precious life-blood of a master-spirit, embalmed and treasured up on purpose to a life beyond life.   —MILTON, *Areopagitica*

Of making many books there is no end.
—OLD TESTAMENT, *Ecclesiastes, XII, 12*

Camerado, this is no book,
Who touches this, touches a man, . . .
—WALT WHITMAN, *So Long*

There is no such thing as a moral or an immoral book. Books are well written or badly written. That is all.
—OSCAR WILDE, *The Picture of Dorian Gray*

BOOTS

Boots—boots—boots—boots—movin' up and down again!
There's no discharge in the war!   —KIPLING, *Boots*

BORROWING

Neither a borrower nor a lender be:
For loan oft loses both itself and friend,
And borrowing dulls the edge of husbandry.
                              —SHAKESPEARE, *Hamlet, I, 3*

BOSTON

And this is the good old Boston,
  The home of the bean and the cod,
Where the Lowells talk only to Cabots,
  And the Cabots talk only to God.
          —J. C. BOSSIDY, *On the Aristocracy of Harvard*

Boston runs to brains as well as to beans and brown
bread. But she is cursed with an army of cranks whom
nothing short of a strait-jacket or a swamp-elm will ever
control.   —W. C. BRANN, *The Iconoclast*

BOURBONS

They have learned nothing and forgotten nothing.
(*Ils n'ont rien appris, ni rien oublié.*)
                          —TALLEYRAND, (ascribed to him
                              by Chevalier de Parat, 1796)

BOY

God bless all little boys who look like Puck,
  With wide eyes, wider mouths and stickout ears,
Rash little boys who stay alive by luck
  And heaven's favor in this world of tears.
              —ARTHUR GUITERMAN, *Blessing on Little Boys*

The boy stood on the burning deck,
  Whence all but him had fled;
The flame that lit the battle's wreck
  Shone round him o'er the dead.
          —FELICIA D. HEMANS, *Casabianca*

I remember, I remember
The fir-trees dark and high;
I used to think their slender tops
Were close against the sky:
It was a childish ignorance,
But now 'tis little joy
To know I'm farther off from heav'n
Than when I was a boy.
       —THOMAS HOOD, *I Remember, I Remember*

Across the fields of yesterday
  He sometimes comes to me,
A little lad just back from play—
  The lad I used to be.   —T. S. JONES, JR., *Sometimes*

When I was a beggarly boy,
  And lived in a cellar damp,
I had not a friend nor a toy,
  But I had Aladdin's lamp.   —J. R. LOWELL, *Aladdin*

The smiles and tears of boyhood's years,
  The words of love then spoken.
      —THOMAS MOORE, *Oft in the Stilly Night*

When that I was and a little tiny boy,
  With hey, ho, the wind and the rain;
A foolish thing was but a toy,
  For the rain it raineth every day.
       —SHAKESPEARE, *Twelfth Night, V, 1*

What are little boys made of, made of?
What are little boys made of?
Snips and snails and puppy-dog tails,
And such are little boys made of.
                    —SOUTHEY, *What All the World Is Made Of*

Blessings on thee, little man,
Barefoot boy, with cheek of tan!
With thy turned-up pantaloons,
And thy merry whistled tunes.
                    —WHITTIER, *The Barefoot Boy*

BRAVE

How sleep the brave, who sink to rest
By all their country's wishes bless'd!

. . . .

By fairy hands their knell is rung;
By forms unseen their dirge is sung.
            —WILLIAM COLLINS, *Ode Written in the Year 1746*

BREAD

O God! that bread should be so dear,
    And flesh and blood so cheap!
                    —THOMAS HOOD, *The Song of the Shirt*

Man shall not live by bread alone.
                    —NEW TESTAMENT, *Matthew, IV, 4*

Cast thy bread upon the waters: for thou shalt find it
after many days.   —OLD TESTAMENT, *Ecclesiastes, XI, 1*

The poet's fate is here in emblem shown,
He asked for bread and he received a stone.
                    —SAMUEL WESLEY, *On Butler's Monument*

BREVITY

Since brevity is the soul of wit,
And tediousness the limbs and outward flourishes,
I will be brief.   —SHAKESPEARE, *Hamlet, II, 2*

BROOK

I chatter, chatter as I flow
  To join the brimming river,
For men may come and men may go,
  But I go on for ever.   —TENNYSON, *The Brook*

BROTHER

Am I my brother's keeper?
                    —OLD TESTAMENT, *Genesis, IV, 9*

BROTHERHOOD

Brotherhood is not just a Bible word. Out of comradeship can come and will come the happy life for all. The underdog can and will lick his weight in the wildcats of the world.   —HEYWOOD BROUN, *The Fifty-first Birthday*

Then none was for a party;
  Then all were for the state;
Then the great man helped the poor,
  And the poor man loved the great:
Then lands were fairly portioned;
  Then spoils were fairly sold:
The Romans were like brothers
  In the brave days of old.
              —MACAULAY, *Lays of Ancient Rome: Horatius*

BROWN, JOHN

I, John Brown, am now quite certain that the crimes of this guilty land will never be purged away but with Blood.
    —JOHN BROWN, *Last Statement*, Dec. 2, 1859

John Brown's body lies a-mouldering in the grave,
  His soul goes marching on!
                        —C. S. HALL, *John Brown's Body*

John Brown of Osawatomie, they led him out to die;
And lo! a poor slave-mother with her little child pressed
  nigh.   —WHITTIER, *Brown of Osawatomie*

BRUTALITY

The conviction of the justification of using even most
brutal weapons is always dependent on the presence of a
fanatical belief in the necessity of the victory of a revolutionary new order on this globe.
                        —ADOLF HITLER, *Mein Kampf*

BUGLE

Blow, bugle, blow, set the wild echoes flying,
Blow, bugle; answer, echoes, dying, dying, dying.
                        —TENNYSON, *The Princess*

BUILD

He builded better than he knew;—
The conscious stone to beauty grew.
                        —EMERSON, *The Problem*

In the elder days of Art,
  Builders wrought with greatest care
Each minute and unseen part;
  For the Gods see everywhere.
                        —LONGFELLOW, *The Builders*

BULLFIGHT

It is impossible to believe the emotional and spiritual
intensity and pure, classic beauty that can be produced by
a man, an animal, and a piece of scarlet serge draped over
a stick.   —ERNEST HEMINGWAY, *Death in the Afternoon*

BUSINESS

Seest thou a man diligent in his business? He shall stand before kings; he shall not stand before mean men.
—OLD TESTAMENT, *Proverbs, XXII, 29*

We demand that big business give people a square deal.
—THEODORE ROOSEVELT, Letter

That which is everybody's business is nobody's business.
—IZAAK WALTON, *The Compleat Angler*

CAESAR

Render therefore unto Caesar the things which are Caesar's and unto God the things that are God's.
—NEW TESTAMENT, *Matthew, XXII, 21*

Imperious Caesar, dead and turn'd to clay,
Might stop a hole to keep the wind away.
—SHAKESPEARE, *Hamlet, V, 1*

Hail, Caesar, those who are about to die salute thee!
(*Ave, Caesar, morituri te salutant!*)
—Salutation of Roman Gladiators, according to SUETONIUS

CALUMNY

Be thou as chaste as ice, as pure as snow, thou shalt not escape calumny.   —SHAKESPEARE, *Hamlet, III, 1*

CANDLE

My candle burns at both ends;
    It will not last the night;
But, ah, my foes, and, oh, my friends—
    It gives a lovely light!
—EDNA ST. VINCENT MILLAY, *A Few Figs from Thistles*

Neither do men light a candle, and put it under a bushel, but on a candlestick, and it giveth light unto all that are in the house.   —NEW TESTAMENT, *Matthew, V, 15*

CANDOR

I want that glib and oily art,
To speak and purpose not.
    —SHAKESPEARE, *King Lear, I, 1*

I think it good plain English, without fraud,
To call a spade a spade, a bawd a bawd.
    —JOHN TAYLOR ("The Water Poet"), *A Kicksey Winsey*

CAPITALISM

Capitalism did not arise because capitalists stole the land or the workmen's tools, but because it was more efficient than feudalism. It will perish because it is not merely less efficient than socialism, but actually self-destructive.
    —J. B. S. HALDANE, *I Believe*

Capital, created by labor of the worker, oppresses the worker by undermining the small proprietor and creating an army of the unemployed.   —NIKOLAI LENIN

Capital is only the fruit of labor, and could never have existed if labor had not first existed.
    —ABRAHAM LINCOLN, First Annual Message to Congress
        (Dec. 3, 1861)

Capitalist production begets, with the inexorability of a law of nature, its own negation.   —KARL MARX, *Capital*

CARE

Ye banks and braes o' bonnie Doon,
    How can ye bloom sae fresh and fair?
How can ye chant, ye little birds,
    And I sae weary fu' o' care?   —BURNS, *Bonnie Doon*

And the night shall be filled with music,
  And the cares, that infest the day,
Shall fold their tents, like the Arabs,
  And as silently steal away.
                    —LONGFELLOW, *The Day Is Done*

CARTHAGE

Carthage must be destroyed!
(*Delenda est Carthago!*)
          —MARCUS CATO (from Plutarch, *Life of Cato*)

CAT

When I play with my cat, who knows whether I do not
make her more sport than she makes me?
                    —MONTAIGNE, *Essays, II*

I like little Pussy, her coat is so warm,
And if I don't hurt her, she'll do me no harm.
                    —JANE TAYLOR, *I Like Little Pussy*

CAVALIER

Marching along, fifty-score strong,
Great-hearted gentlemen, singing this song.
                    —R. BROWNING, *Cavalier Tunes*

CAVELL, EDITH

O gentle hands that soothed the soldier's brow
And knew no service save of Christ's the Lord!
Thy country now is all humanity.
                    —G. E. WOODBERRY, *Edith Cavell*

CHANCE

Chance is perhaps the pseudonym of God when He did
not want to sign.
                    —ANATOLE FRANCE, *The Garden of Epicurus*

Under the bludgeonings of chance
  My head is bloody, but unbowed.
                    —W. E. HENLEY, *Invictus*

A million million spermatozoa,
  All of them alive:
Out of their cataclysm but one poor Noah
  Dare hope to survive.
And among that billion minus one
  Might have chanced to be
Shakespeare, another Newton, a new Donne—
  But the One was Me.
            —ALDOUS HUXLEY, *Fifth Philosopher's Song*

CHANGE

Nothing of him that doth fade
But doth suffer a sea-change
Into something rich and strange.
                    —SHAKESPEARE, *The Tempest, I, 2*

The old order changeth, yielding place to new
And God fulfils himself in many ways,
Lest one good custom should corrupt the world.
                    —TENNYSON, *The Passing of Arthur*

Things do not change; we change. —THOREAU, *Walden*

CHANTICLEER

And hark! how clear bold chanticleer,
Warmed with the new wine of the year,
Tells all in his lusty crowing!
            —J. R. LOWELL, *The Vision of Sir Launfal*

While the cock with lively din
Scatters the rear of darkness thin,
And to the stack, or the barn door,
Stoutly struts his dames before.   —MILTON, *L'Allegro*

Some say that ever 'gainst that season comes
Wherein our Saviour's birth is celebrated,
The bird of dawning singeth all night long.
—SHAKESPEARE, *Hamlet, I, 1*

CHAOS

And the earth was without form and void; and darkness
was upon the face of the deep.
—OLD TESTAMENT, *Genesis, I, 2*

CHARACTER

Don't *say* things. What you *are* stands over you the
while, and thunders so that I cannot hear what you say
to the contrary. —EMERSON, *Social Aims*

Character is what you are in the dark.
—DWIGHT L. MOODY, *Sermons*

Fame is what you have taken,
  Character's what you give;
When to this truth you waken,
  Then you begin to live.
—BAYARD TAYLOR, *Improvisations*

CHARITY

Alas! for the rarity
Of Christian charity
  Under the sun! —THOMAS HOOD, *The Bridge of Sighs*

With malice toward none; with charity for all.
—LINCOLN, Second Inaugural Address, March 4, 1865

They take the paper and they read the headlines,
So they've heard of unemployment and they've heard of
  breadlines,

And they philanthropically cure them all
By getting up a costume charity ball.
                —OGDEN NASH, *Pride Goeth Before a Raise*

Though I speak with the tongues of men and of angels,
and have not charity, I am become as sounding brass or a
tinkling cymbal. —NEW TESTAMENT, *I Corinthians, XIII, 1*

And now abideth faith, hope, charity, these three; but
the greatest of these is charity.
                —NEW TESTAMENT, *I Corinthians, XIII, 13*

Verily I say unto you, Inasmuch as ye have done it unto
one of the least of these my brethren, ye have done it unto
me.   —NEW TESTAMENT, *Matthew, XXV, 40*

If a body's ever took charity, it makes a burn that don't
come out.   —JOHN STEINBECK, *The Grapes of Wrath*

Let the man who has and doesn't give
Break his neck, and cease to live!
Let him who gives without a care
Gather rubies from the air.
                —JAMES STEPHENS, *In the Imperative Mood*

Behold, I do not give lectures or a little charity,
When I give I give myself.
                —WALT WHITMAN, *Song of Myself*

CHARLES II

Here lies our sovereign lord the king,
    Whose word no man relies on;
He never says a foolish thing,
    Nor ever does a wise one.
        —JOHN WILMOT, EARL OF ROCHESTER, *Epitaph for
        Charles II* (while the latter was still alive)

CHASTITY

Who can find a virtuous woman? For her price is far
above rubies.   —OLD TESTAMENT, *Proverbs, XXXI, 10*

If she seem not chaste to me,
What care I how chaste she be?
  —SIR WALTER RALEIGH, *Shall I, Like a Hermit, Dwell?*

My chastity's the jewel of our house,
Bequeathed down from many ancestors.
        —SHAKESPEARE, *All's Well That Ends Well, IV, 2*

CHAUCER

Dan Chaucer, well of English undefiled,
On Fame's eternal beadroll worthy to be filed.
        —EDMUND SPENSER, *The Faerie Queene, IV*

CHEATING

Don't steal; thou'lt never thus compete
Successfully in business. Cheat.
        —AMBROSE BIERCE, *The Devil's Dictionary*

We know that there are chiselers. At the bottom of every
case of criticism and obstruction we have found some
selfish interest, some private axe to grind.
        —FRANKLIN D. ROOSEVELT, Speech, 1936

CHEERING

Don't cheer, boys; the poor devils are dying.
  —CAPT. JOHN W. PHILIP, At the battle of Santiago, 1898

CHICAGO

Hog-butcher for the World,
Tool-maker, Stacker of Wheat,
Player with Railroads and the Nation's Freight-handler;
Stormy, husky, brawling,
City of Big Shoulders.   —CARL SANDBURG, *Chicago*

CHILD

When I was a child, I spake as a child, I understood as a child, I thought as a child; but when I became a man, I put away childish things.
—NEW TESTAMENT, *I Corinthians, XIII, 11*

Train up a child in the way he should go; and when he is old, he will not depart from it.
—OLD TESTAMENT, *Proverbs, XXII, 6*

How sharper than a serpent's tooth it is
To have a thankless child!
—SHAKESPEARE, *King Lear, I, 4*

A child should always say what's true
And speak when he is spoken to,
And behave mannerly at table;
At least as far as he is able.
—R. L. STEVENSON, *The Whole Duty of Children*

I do not love him because he is good, but because he is my little child.
—RABINDRANATH TAGORE, *The Crescent Moon*

Gentle Jesus, meek and mild,
Look upon a little child,
Pity my simplicity,
Suffer me to come to Thee.
—CHARLES WESLEY, *Gentle Jesus*

The child is father of the man.
—WORDSWORTH, *My Heart Leaps Up*

CHILDHOOD

How dear to this heart are the scenes of my childhood,
When fond recollection recalls them to view;

The orchard, the meadow, the deep-tangled wildwood,
   And every loved spot which my infancy knew.
         —SAMUEL WOODWORTH, *The Old Oaken Bucket*

CHILDREN

Between the dark and the daylight,
   When the night is beginning to lower,
Comes a pause in the day's occupations,
   That is known as the Children's Hour.
               —LONGFELLOW, *The Children's Hour*

Suffer little children to come unto me, and forbid them
not; for of such is the kingdom of God.
               —NEW TESTAMENT, *Mark, X, 14*

It is very nice to think
The world is full of meat and drink,
With little children saying grace
In every Christian kind of place.
               —R. L. STEVENSON, *A Thought*

Let dogs delight to bark and bite,
   For God hath made them so;
Let bears and lions growl and fight,
   For 'tis their nature too.

But, children, you should never let
   Such angry passions rise;
Your little hands were never made
   To tear each other's eyes.
         —ISAAC WATTS, *Against Quarreling and Fighting*

"CHINEE"

Which I wish to remark,
   And my language is plain,
That for ways that are dark
   And for tricks that are vain,

The heathen Chinee is peculiar,
   Which the same I would rise to explain.
      —BRET HARTE, *Plain Language from Truthful James*

CHIVALRY

But the age of chivalry is gone; that of sophisters, economists, and calculators has succeeded.
—EDMUND BURKE, *Reflections on the French Revolution*

CHOICE

God offers to every mind its choice between truth and repose.   —EMERSON, *Essays: Intellect*

''CHORTLE''

Oh, frabjous day! Callooh! Callay!
He chortled in his joy.
      —LEWIS CARROLL, *Through the Looking-Glass*

CHRIST

There is a green hill far away,
   Without a city wall,
Where the dear Lord was crucified,
   Who died to save us all.
      —CECIL FRANCES ALEXANDER, *There Is a Green Hill*

The vision of Christ that thou dost see
Is my vision's greatest enemy.
Thine is the friend of all Mankind,
Mine speaks in Parables to the blind.
      —WILLIAM BLAKE, *The Everlasting Gospel*

The best of men
That e'er wore earth about him was a sufferer;
A soft, meek, patient, humble, tranquil spirit,
The first true gentleman that ever breathed.
      —THOMAS DEKKER, *The Honest Whore, I, 1, 12*

Thou hast conquered, O Galilean!
(*Vicisti, Galilaee!*)
>   —EMPEROR JULIAN, Dying words (apocryphal)

Then came Jesus forth, wearing the crown of thorns and
the purple robe. And Pilate saith unto them, Behold the
man! (*Ecce homo*)   —NEW TESTAMENT, *John, XIX, 5*

All history is incomprehensible without Christ.
>   —ERNEST RENAN, *Life of Jesus*

Must then Christ perish in torment in every age to save
those that have no imagination?
>   —BERNARD SHAW, *Saint Joan*, Epilogue

I fled Him, down the nights and down the days;
  I fled Him, down the arches of the years;
I fled Him, down the labyrinthine ways
  Of my own mind; and in the midst of tears
I hid from Him, and under running laughter.
>   —FRANCIS THOMPSON, *The Hound of Heaven*

CHRISTIAN

Onward, Christian soldiers!
  Marching as to war,
With the Cross of Jesus
  Going on before.
>   —S. BARING-GOULD, *Onward, Christian Soldiers*

Christian, what of the night?—
I cannot tell; I am blind;
I halt and hearken behind
If haply the hours will go back
And return to the dear dead light, . . .
>   —SWINBURNE, *A Watch in the Night*

CHRISTIANITY

Christianity taught men that love is worth more than intelligence.   —JACQUES MARITAIN, *I Believe*

I call Christianity the one great curse, the one enormous and innermost perversion, the one great instinct of revenge, for which no means are too venomous, too underhand, too underground and too petty—I call it the one immortal blemish of mankind.   —NIETZSCHE, *The Antichrist*

CHRISTMAS

God rest you merry, gentlemen,
    Let nothing you dismay,
For Jesus Christ, our Saviour,
    Was born upon this day.   —ANON., Old Carol

'Most all the time, the whole year round, there ain't no
    flies on me,
But jest 'fore Christmas I'm as good as I kin be!
                    —EUGENE FIELD, *Jest 'fore Christmas*

I heard the bells on Christmas Day
Their old familiar carols play,
    And wild and sweet
    The words repeat
Of peace on earth, good-will to men.
                    —LONGFELLOW, *Christmas Bells*

'Twas the night before Christmas, when all through the
    house
Not a creature was stirring, not even a mouse.
                    —C. C. MOORE, *A Visit from St. Nicholas*

Hark the herald angels sing,
Glory to the new-born King;

Peace on earth, and mercy mild,
God and sinners reconciled.
                    —CHARLES WESLEY, *Christmas Hymns*

CHURCH

Wherever God erects a house of prayer,
The Devil always builds a chapel there;
And 'twill be found upon examination,
The latter has the largest congregation.
            —DANIEL DEFOE, *The True-Born Englishman*

Some to church repair
Not for the doctrine, but the music there.
                    —POPE, *Essay on Criticism, II*

CIRCE

Who knows not Circe,
The daughter of the Sun, whose charmed cup
Whoever tasted, lost his upright shape,
And downward fell into a groveling swine.
                    —MILTON, *Comus*

CIRCLE

He drew a circle that shut me out—
Heretic, rebel, a thing to flout.
But Love and I had the wit to win.
We drew a circle that took him in.
                    —EDWIN MARKHAM, *Outwitted*

CIRCUS

Bread and circus games.
(Panem et circenses.)   —JUVENAL, *Satires, X*

CITY

To one who has been long in city pent,
    'Tis very sweet to look into the fair
    And open face of heaven,—   —KEATS, *Sonnet*

As one who long in populous city pent,
Where houses thick and sewers annoy the air.
                              —MILTON, *Paradise Lost, IX*

Fields and trees teach me nothing, but the people in a
city do.   —SOCRATES (*Plato,* Phaedrus)

CIVILIZATION

Civilization means a society based upon the opinion of
civilians. It means that violence, the rule of warriors and
despotic chiefs, the conditions of camps and warfare, of
riot and tyranny, give place to parliaments where laws are
made, and independent courts of justice in which over long
periods those laws are maintained.
            —WINSTON CHURCHILL, *Blood, Sweat and Tears*

Civilization is a progress from an indefinite, incoherent
homogeneity toward a definite, coherent heterogeneity.
                        —HERBERT SPENCER, *First Principles*

CLEVELAND, GROVER

They love him, gentlemen, and they respect him, not
only for himself, but for his character, for his integrity and
judgment and iron will; but they love him most for the
enemies he has made.
                    —GEN. EDWARD S. BRAGG, Speech, 1884

CLEVER

Be good, sweet maid, and let who can be clever.
                            —CHARLES KINGSLEY, *A Farewell*

CLOUD

Be still, sad heart! and cease repining;
Behind the clouds is the sun still shining.
                              —LONGFELLOW, *The Rainy Day*

I bring fresh showers for the thirsting flowers,
    From the seas and the streams;
I bear light shade for the leaves when laid
    In their noonday dreams.   —SHELLEY, *The Cloud*

I wandered lonely as a cloud
That floats on high o'er vales and hills.
    —WORDSWORTH, *Poems of the Imagination, 12*

"COCK ROBIN"

Who killed Cock Robin?
    "I," said the Sparrow,
    "With my bow and arrow,
I killed Cock Robin."
    —ANON., *The Death and Burial of Cock Robin*

COLISEUM

"While stands the Coliseum, Rome shall stand;
When falls the Coliseum, Rome shall fall;
And when Rome falls—the world."
    —BYRON, *Childe Harold, IV*

COMMUTER

Commuter—one who spends his life
In riding to and from his wife;
A man who shaves and takes a train,
And then rides back to shave again.
    —E. B. WHITE, *The Commuter*

COMPANIONS

I have had playmates, I have had companions,
In my days of childhood, in my joyful schooldays—
All, all are gone, the old familiar faces.
    —CHARLES LAMB, *The Old Familiar Faces*

Associate yourself with men of good quality if you esteem
your own reputation; for 'tis better to be alone than in bad
company.   —GEORGE WASHINGTON, *Rules of Civility*

COMPARISONS

. . . Hyperion to a satyr, Thersites to Hercules, mud to marble, dunghill to diamond, a singed cat to a Bengal tiger, a whining puppy to a roaring lion.

—JAMES G. BLAINE, referring to Roscoe Conkling
in a Speech, 1886

COMPENSATION

Evermore in the world is this marvellous balance of beauty and disgust, magnificence and rats.

—EMERSON, *Conduct of Life*

COMPLAINING

The wheel that squeaks the loudest
Is the one that gets the grease.

—JOSH BILLINGS, *The Kicker*

I am a lone lorn creetur . . . and everythink goes contrairy with me.   —DICKENS, *David Copperfield*

Nothing to do but work,
   Nothing to eat but food,
Nothing to wear but clothes
   To keep one from going nude.

—BEN F. KING, *The Pessimist*

COMPROMISE

From compromise and things half done,
   Keep me with stern and stubborn pride;
And when at last the fight is won,
   God, keep me still unsatisfied.

—LOUIS UNTERMEYER, *Prayer*

CONCEIT

He was like the cock who thought the sun had risen to hear him crow.   —GEORGE ELIOT, *Adam Bede*

CONDUCT

Conduct is three-fourths of our life and its largest concern. —MATTHEW ARNOLD, *Literature and Life*

Do all the good you can,
In all the ways you can,
In all the places you can,
At all the times you can,
To all the people you can,
As long as ever you can.
—JOHN WESLEY, *Rules of Conduct*

CONQUEROR

I came, I saw, I conquered.
(*Veni, vidi, vici.*)
—JULIUS CAESAR, Letter to Amantius, 47 B.C.

See the conquering hero comes!
Sound the trumpets, beat the drums!
—THOMAS MOREL, Text for Handel's *Judas Maccabeus*

CONSCIENCE

Conscience is God's presence in man.
—SWEDENBORG, *Arcana Coelesta*

Thus conscience does make cowards of us all;
And thus the native hue of resolution
Is sicklied o'er with the pale cast of thought.
—SHAKESPEARE, *Hamlet, III, 1*

The conscience of the dying belies their lives.
—VAUVENARGUES, *Réflexions*

CONSERVATIVE

A conservative is a man who is too cowardly to fight and too fat to run. —ELBERT HUBBARD, *Epigrams*

CONSISTENCY

A foolish consistency is the hobgoblin of little minds, adored by little statesmen and philosophers and divines.
—EMERSON, *Essays: Self-Reliance*

Gineral C. is a dreffle smart man;
 He's ben on all sides thet give places or pelf;
But consistency still wuz a part of his plan,—
 He's been true to *one* party,—an' thet is himself.
—J. R. LOWELL, *Biglow Papers*

CONSTANCY

I am constant as the northern star,
Of whose true-fix'd and resting quality
There is no fellow in the firmament.
—SHAKESPEARE, *Julius Caesar, III, 1*

CONSTITUTION

What's the Constitution between friends?
—TIMOTHY J. CAMPBELL, to Pres. Cleveland, 1885

You will find no justification in any of the language of the Constitution for delay in the reforms which the mass of the American people now demand.
—FRANKLIN D. ROOSEVELT, Address, 1939

CONTENT

But if I'm content with a little,
Enough is as good as a feast.
—ISAAC BICKERSTAFFE, *Love in a Village*

When we have not what we like, we must like what we have. —BUSSY-RABUTIN, Letter to Mme. de Sévigné

CONTRADICTION

Do I contradict myself?
Very well then I contradict myself.

(I am large, I contain multitudes.)
> —WALT WHITMAN, *Song of Myself*

COOKS

God sends meat and the devil sends cooks.
> —THOMAS DELONEY, *Works* (1600)

We may live without poetry, music and art;
We may live without conscience and live without heart;
We may live without friends, we may live without books,
But civilized man cannot live without cooks.
> —OWEN MEREDITH, *Lucile, 1*

The cook was a good cook, as cooks go; and as cooks go
she went.   —"SAKI" (H. H. MUNRO), *Reginald*

COQUETTE

In the School of Coquettes
  Madam Rose is a scholar;—
Oh, they fish with all nets
In the School of Coquettes!
When her brooch she forgets
'Tis to show a new collar.   —AUSTIN DOBSON, *Circe*

There's language in her eye, her cheek, her lip,
Nay, her foot speaks; her wanton spirits look out
At every joint and motive of her body.
> —SHAKESPEARE, *Troilus and Cressida, IV, 5*

COSMOPOLITAN

I am not an Athenian nor a Greek, but a citizen of the
world.   —SOCRATES (quoted by Plutarch)

COUNTRY

Our country! in her intercourse with foreign nations may
she always be in the right; but our country, right or wrong!
> —STEPHEN DECATUR, Toast, April, 1816

Our country is the world—our countrymen are all mankind.
—WILLIAM LLOYD GARRISON, Motto of *The Liberator*, 1830

Our country is wherever we are well off.
—MILTON, Letter, 1666 *(cf.* Latin: *Ubi bene, ibi patria.)*

My country is the world, and my religion is to do good.
—THOMAS PAINE, *Rights of Man*

COUNTRY AND TOWN

God made the country and man made the town.
—COWPER, *The Task*

The country is lyric,—the town dramatic. When mingled they make the most perfect musical drama.
—LONGFELLOW, *Kavanagh*

COURAGE

What though the field be lost?
All is not lost; th' unconquerable will,
And study of revenge, immortal hate,
And courage never to submit or yield.
—MILTON, *Paradise Lost, 1*

COURT AND COURTIER

Lordlings and witlings not a few,
Incapable of doing aught,
Yet ill at ease with nought to do.
—WALTER SCOTT, *Bridal of Triermain*

The two maxims of any great man at court are, always to keep his countenance, and never to keep his word.
—SWIFT, *Thoughts on Various Subjects*

O happy they that never saw the court,
Nor ever knew great men but by report.
—JOHN WEBSTER, *The White Devil, V, 6*

COW

> I never saw a purple cow,
>   I never hope to see one;
> But, I can tell you, anyhow,
>   I'd rather see than be one.
>   —GELETT BURGESS, *The Purple Cow*

> The friendly cow all red and white,
>   I love with all my heart:
> She gives me cream with all her might
>   To eat with apple-tart. —R. L. STEVENSON, *The Cow*

COWARD

> God Almighty hates a quitter.
>   —GEN. SAMUEL FESSENDEN,
>   at the Republican Convention, 1896

> Art thou afeared
> To be the same in thine own act and valour
> As thou art in desire? Wouldst thou have that
> Which thou esteem'st the ornament of life,
> And live a coward in thine own esteem?
>   —SHAKESPEARE, *Macbeth, I, 7*

> Cowards die many times before their deaths;
> The valiant never taste of death but once.
>   —SHAKESPEARE, *Julius Caesar, II, 2*

> He was a coward to the strong:
> He was a tyrant to the weak.
>   —SHELLEY, *Rosalind and Helen*

CREDIT (Public)

He smote the rock of the national resources, and abundant streams of revenue gushed forth. He touched the dead corpse of public credit, and it sprang upon its feet.
                    —DANIEL WEBSTER, On Alexander Hamilton (1831)

CREDITOR

A creditor is worse than a master; for a master owns only your person, a creditor owns your dignity, and can belabour that. —VICTOR HUGO, *Les Misérables*

CREDULITY

Ye who listen with credulity to the whispers of fancy, and pursue with eagerness the phantoms of hope; ...
—SAMUEL JOHNSON, *Rasselas*

CREED

Whose life laughs through and spits at their creed,
Who maintain thee in word, and defy thee in deed!
—R. BROWNING, *Holy-Cross Day*

My creed is this:
  Happiness is the only good.
  The place to be happy is here.
  The time to be happy is now.
  The way to be happy is to make others so.
—ROBERT G. INGERSOLL, *Motto*

Shall I ask the brave soldier who fights by my side
In the cause of mankind, if our creeds agree?
—THOMAS MOORE, *Come Send Round the Wine*

Orthodoxy is my doxy; heterodoxy is another man's doxy.
—WILLIAM WARBURTON, To Lord Sandwich

CRIME

And who are the greater criminals—those who sell the instruments of death, or those who buy them and use them?
—ROBERT E. SHERWOOD, *Idiot's Delight*

YANK: Sure! Lock me up! Put me in a cage! Dat's de on'y answer yuh know. G'wan, lock me up!
POLICEMAN: What you been doin'?

YANK: Enough to gimme life for! I was born, see? Sure
dat's de charge. Write it in de blotter. I was born,
get me? —EUGENE O'NEILL, *The Hairy Ape*

CRISIS

These are the times that try men's souls.
—THOMAS PAINE, *The American Crisis*

CRITICISM

Criticism is a disinterested endeavour to learn and propa-
gate the best that is known and thought in the world.
—MATTHEW ARNOLD, *Essays in Criticism*

Reviewers are usually people who would have been
poets, historians, biographers, if they could: they have
tried their talents at one or the other, and have failed;
therefore they turn critics.
—S. T. COLERIDGE, *Lectures: Shakespeare and Milton*

The good critic is he who narrates the adventures of his
soul among masterpieces.
—ANATOLE FRANCE, *La Vie littéraire*

'Tis hard to say if greater want of skill
Appears in writing or in judging ill.
—POPE, *Essay on Criticism*

CROSS

Under this standard shalt thou conquer.
(*In hoc signo vinces.*)
—EMPEROR CONSTANTINE, Motto assumed by him,
A.D. 312

CROWN

Uneasy lies the head that wears a crown.
—SHAKESPEARE, *Henry IV, II, III, 1*

CRUELTY

I must be cruel, only to be kind.
—SHAKESPEARE, *Hamlet, III, 4*

Come you spirits . . .
And fill me from the crown to the toe, top-full
Of direst cruelty! make thick my blood;
. . . Come to my woman's breasts,
And take my milk for gall, you murdering ministers!
—SHAKESPEARE, *Macbeth, I, 5*

CULTURE

Culture is "to know the best that has been said and
thought in the world."
—MATTHEW ARNOLD, *Literature and Dogma*

In the room the women come and go
Talking of Michelangelo.
—T. S. ELIOT, *The Love Song of J. Alfred Prufrock*

CUPID

Cupid and my Campaspe play'd
At cards for kisses; Cupid paid:
—JOHN LYLY, *Alexander and Campaspe*

But Cupid is a downy cove,
Wot it takes a lot to hinder,
And if you shuts him out o' the door,
Vy he valks in at the vinder,
—J. R. PLANCHÉ, *The Discreet Princess*

This wimpled, whining, purblind wayward boy;
This senior-junior, giant-dwarf, Dan Cupid.
—SHAKESPEARE, *Love's Labour's Lost, III, 1*

CURFEW

The curfew tolls the knell of parting day.
—GRAY, *Elegy Written in a Country Churchyard*

England's sun was slowly setting o'er the hilltops far
  away,
Filling all the land with beauty at the close of one sad
  day.

. . . .

Now I'm old I will not falter,—Curfew it must ring to-
  night.

. . . .

And she breathed in husky whisper:—"Curfew must not
  ring to-night."
     —ROSA H. THORPE, *Curfew Must Not Ring To-night*

CURSE

Let fever sweat them till they tremble
Cramp rack their limbs till they resemble
  Cartoons by Goya:
Their daughters sterile be in rut,
May cancer rot their herring gut,
The circular madness on them shut,
  Or paranoia.   —W. H. AUDEN, *On This Island*

He cursed him at board, he cursed him in bed;
From the sole of his foot to the crown of his head;
He cursed him in sleeping, that every night
He should dream of the devil, and wake in a fright;
He cursed him in eating, he cursed him in drinking,
He cursed him in coughing, in sneezing, in winking;
He cursed him in sitting, in standing, in lying;
He cursed him in walking, in riding, in flying;
He cursed him in living, he cursed him in dying!—
     —R. H. BARHAM, *The Jackdaw of Rheims*

I shall curse you with book and bell and candle.
     —SIR THOMAS MALORY, *Morte d'Arthur*

Weary se'n-nights nine times nine
Shall he dwindle, peak and pine.
                    —SHAKESPEARE, *Macbeth, I, 3*

All the infections that the sun sucks up
From bogs, fens, flats, on Prosper fall, and make him
By inch-meal a disease.
                    —SHAKESPEARE, *The Tempest, II, 2*

May the strong curse of crossed affections light
Back on thy bosom with reflected blight!
And make thee in thy leprosy of mind
As loathsome to thyself as to mankind!
                —SHELLEY, *To the Lord Chancellor* (Weldon)

Cursed be the social wants that sin against the strength
    of youth!
Cursed be the social lies that warp us from the living
    truth!
Cursed be the sickly forms that err from honest Nature's
    rule!
Cursed be the gold that gilds the straiten'd forehead
    of the fool!
                    —TENNYSON, *Locksley Hall*

CUSTOM

But to my mind, though I am native here
And to the manner born, it is a custom
More honour'd in the breach than the observance.
                    —SHAKESPEARE, *Hamlet, I, 4*

CYNIC

A man who knows the price of everything and the value
of nothing.   —OSCAR WILDE, *Lady Windermere's Fan, III*

DAMN

Damn with faint praise, assent with civil leer,
And without sneering teach the rest to sneer.
—POPE, *Epistle to Dr. Arbuthnot*

DANCING

On with the dance! let joy be unconfin'd;
No sleep till morn, when Youth and Pleasure meet
To chase the glowing Hours with flying feet.
—BYRON, *Childe Harold, III*

They are waiting on the shingle- will you come and join
    the dance?
Will you, won't you, will you, won't you, will you join
    the dance?
Will you, won't you, will you, won't you, won't you join
    the dance?   —LEWIS CARROLL, *Alice in Wonderland*

Dancing is the loftiest, the most moving, the most beautiful of the arts, because it is no mere translation or abstrac-
tion from life; it is life itself.
—HAVELOCK ELLIS, *The Dance of Life*

Come and trip it as ye go,
On the light fantastic toe.   —MILTON, *L'Allegro*

Come unto these yellow sands,
    And then take hands:
Courtsied when you have, and kiss'd
    (The wild waves whist.)
Foot it featly here and there;
And, sweet sprites, the burthen bear.
—SHAKESPEARE, *The Tempest, I, 2*

"DANNY DEEVER"

"What are the bugles blowin' for?" said Files-on-Parade.
"To turn you out, to turn you out," the Colour-Sergeant
    said.

. . . .

An' they're hangin' Danny Deever in the mornin'.
—KIPLING, *Danny Deever*

DARKNESS

The sun's rim dips; the stars rush out:
At one stride comes the dark.
—S. T. COLERIDGE, *The Ancient Mariner*

No light, but rather darkness visible.
—MILTON, *Paradise Lost, I*

DARLING

Tenderly bury the fair young dead,
    Pausing to drop on his grave a tear;
Carve on the wooden slab at his head,
    "Somebody's darling slumbers Here!"
—MARIE R. LA COSTE, *Somebody's Darling*

DAWN

Night's candles are burnt out, and jocund day
Stands tip-toe on the misty mountain-tops.
—SHAKESPEARE, *Romeo and Juliet, III, 5*

And down the long and silent street,
The dawn, with silver-sandalled feet,
Crept like a frightened girl.
—OSCAR WILDE, *The Harlot's House*

DAY

Think that day lost whose low descending sun
Views from thy hand no worthy action done.
—ANON. (about 1690)

Well, this is the end of a perfect day,
    Near the end of a journey too;

But it leaves a thought that is big and strong,
    With a wish that is kind and true.
                        —CARRIE J. BOND, *A Perfect Day*

My days are swifter than a weaver's shuttle.
                        —OLD TESTAMENT, *Job, VII, 6*

How troublesome is day!
It calls us from our sleep away;
It bids us from our pleasant dreams awake,
It sends us forth to keep or break
Our promises to pay.
    —THOMAS LOVE PEACOCK, *How Troublesome Is Day*

But the tender grace of a day that is dead
Will never come back to me.
                        —TENNYSON, *Break, Break, Break*

DEAD

Marley was dead: to begin with ... Old Marley was as
dead as a door-nail.   —DICKENS, *A Christmas Carol*

Let the dead bury their dead.
                        —NEW TESTAMENT, *Matthew, VIII, 22*

When I am dead, my dearest,
    Sing no sad songs for me;
Plant thou no roses at my head,
    Nor shady cypress tree:
Be the green grass above me
    With showers and dewdrops wet;
And if thou wilt, remember,
    And if thou wilt, forget.   —CHRISTINA ROSSETTI, *Song*

DEATH

Strew on her roses, roses,
    And never a spray of yew.

In quiet she reposes:
  Ah! would that I did too.
                    —MATTHEW ARNOLD, *Requiescat*

O Death! the poor man's dearest friend—
The kindest and the best.
                    —BURNS, *Man Was Made to Mourn*

Da spreeng ees com'; but oh, da joy
  Eet is too late!
He was so cold, my leetla boy,
  He no could wait.   —T. A. DALY, *Da Leetla Boy*

Afraid? Of whom am I afraid?
Not Death, for who is He?
The porter of my father's lodge
As much abasheth me.
                    —EMILY DICKINSON, *Time and Eternity*

Death be not proud, though some have called thee
Mighty and dreadful, for thou art not so,
For, those, whom thou think'st, thou dost overthrow,
Die not, poor death, nor yet canst thou kill me . . .
  . . . death, thou shalt die.
                    —JOHN DONNE, *Holy Sonnets, X*

Account ye no man happy till he die.
                    —EURIPIDES, *Daughters of Troy*

The little toy dog is covered with dust,
  But sturdy and staunch he stands;
And the little toy soldier is red with rust,
  And his musket moulds in his hands;
Time was when the little toy dog was new,
  And the soldier was passing fair;
And that was the time when our Little Boy Blue
  Kissed them and put them there.
                    —EUGENE FIELD, *Little Boy Blue*

Can storied urn or animated bust
　Back to its mansion call the fleeting breath?
Can Honour's voice provoke the silent dust,
　Or Flattery soothe the dull cold ear of Death?
　　　　—GRAY, *Elegy Written in a Country Churchyard*

When life is woe,
And hope is dumb,
The World says, "Go!"
The Grave says, "Come!"
　　　　—ARTHUR GUITERMAN, *Betel-Nuts*

One more Unfortunate,
　Weary of breath,
Rashly importunate
　Gone to her death!
Take her up tenderly,
　Lift her with care;
Fashioned so slenderly,
　Young, and so fair!
　　　　—THOMAS HOOD, *The Bridge of Sighs*

Our very hopes belied our fears,
　Our fears our hopes belied;
We thought her dying when she slept,
　And sleeping when she died.
　　　　—THOMAS HOOD, *The Death-Bed*

Pale Death, with impartial step, knocks at the poor man's
cottage and the palaces of kings.
(*Pallida Mors aequo pulsat pede . . .*)
　　　　—HORACE, *Odes, I, 4*

With rue my heart is laden
　For golden friends I had,
For many a rose-lipt maiden
　And many a lightfoot lad.
　　　　—A. E. HOUSMAN, *A Shropshire Lad*

Ah, what avails the sceptred race,
  Ah, what the form divine!
What every virtue, every grace!
  Rose Aylmer, all were thine.
Rose Aylmer, whom these wakeful eyes
  May weep, but never see,
A night of memories and sighs
  I consecrate to thee.   —W. S. LANDOR, *Rose Aylmer*

There is a Reaper, whose name is Death,
  And with his sickle keen,
He reaps the bearded grain at a breath,
  And the flowers that grow between.
       —LONGFELLOW, *The Reaper and the Flowers*

I am dying, Egypt, dying,
  Ebbs the crimson life-tide fast,
And the dark Plutonian shadows
  Gather on the evening blast.
—W. H. LYTLE, *Antony and Cleopatra* (the first line is
                  from Shakespeare)

Around, around the sun we go:
The moon goes round the earth.
We do not die of death:
We die of vertigo.
      —ARCHIBALD MACLEISH, *Mother Goose's Garland*

But O the heavy change, now thou art gone,
Now thou art gone and never must return!
          —MILTON, *Lycidas*

So we must part, my body, you and I
  Who've spent so many pleasant years together.
'Tis sorry work to lose your company
  Who clove to me so close.
      —COSMO MONKHOUSE, *Any Soul to Any Body*

And grant me, when I face the grisly Thing,
One haughty cry to pierce the gray Perhaps!
O let me be a tune-swept fiddlestring
That feels the Master Melody—*and snaps!*
—J. G. NEIHARDT, *Let Me Give Out My Years*

O death, where is thy sting? O grave, where is thy victory?   —NEW TESTAMENT, *I Corinthians, XV, 54*

For dust thou art, and unto dust shalt thou return.
—OLD TESTAMENT, *Genesis, III, 19*

There the wicked cease from troubling; and there the weary be at rest.   —OLD TESTAMENT, *Job, III, 17*

I sometimes think that never blows so red
The Rose as where some buried Caesar bled;
   That every Hyacinth the Garden wears
Dropped in her Lap from some once lovely head.
—OMAR KHAYYÁM, *Rubáiyát* (FitzGerald trans.)

O eloquent, just, and mighty Death! whom none could advise, thou hast persuaded; what none hath dared, thou hast done; . . . thou hast drawn together all the far-stretched greatness, all the pride, cruelty, and ambition of man, and covered it over with these two narrow words, *Hic jacet!*
—SIR WALTER RALEIGH, *History of the World, V*

Out of the chill and the shadow,
   Into the thrill and the shrine;
Out of the dearth and the famine,
   Into the fulness divine.
—MARGARET E. SANGSTER, *Going Home*

Like the dew on the mountain,
   Like the foam on the river,

Like the bubble on the fountain,
   Thou art gone, and for ever!
                    —WALTER SCOTT, *The Lady of the Lake*

I have a rendezvous with Death
At some disputed barricade. . . .
And I to my pledged word am true,
I shall not fail that rendezvous.
   —ALAN SEEGER, *I Have a Rendezvous with Death*

. . . . death,
The undiscovered country, from whose bourn
No traveller returns.   —SHAKESPEARE, *Hamlet, III, 1*

Fear no more the heat o' the sun
   Nor the furious winter's rages;
Thou thy worldly task hast done,
   Home art gone and ta'en thy wages.
                    —SHAKESPEARE, *Cymbeline, IV, 2*

Golden lads and girls all must,
As chimney-sweepers, come to dust.
                    —SHAKESPEARE, *Cymbeline, IV, 2*

After life's fitful fever, he sleeps well;
Treason has done his worst: nor steel nor poison,
Malice domestic, foreign levy, nothing
Can touch him further. —SHAKESPEARE, *Macbeth, III, 2*

The weariest and most loathed worldly life
That age, ache, penury, and imprisonment
Can lay on nature, is a paradise
To what we fear of death.
                    —SHAKESPEARE, *Measure for Measure, III, 1*

Come away, come away, death,
   And in sad cypress let me be laid;

Fly away, fly away, breath:
  I am slain by a fair cruel maid.
My shroud of white, stuck all with yew,
  O, prepare it!
My part of death, no one so true
  Did share it.   —SHAKESPEARE, *Twelfth Night, II, 4*

Death is here and death is there,
Death is busy everywhere,
All around, within, beneath,
Above is death—and we are death.
                              —SHELLEY, *Death* (1820)

Sunset and evening star,
  And one clear call for me!
And may there be no moaning of the bar
  When I put out to sea.

· · · · · · · · · ·

I hope to see my Pilot face to face
  When I have crost the bar.
                           —TENNYSON, *Crossing the Bar*

She lived unknown, and few could know
  When Lucy ceased to be;
But she is in her grave, and, oh,
  The difference to me!
—WORDSWORTH, *She Dwelt Among the Untrodden Ways*

DECEIT

You can fool some of the people all of the time, and all of
the people some of the time, but you cannot fool all of the
people all the time.
—LINCOLN, (A. K. McClure: *Lincoln's Yarns and Stories*)

O, what a tangled web we weave,
When first we practice to deceive!
                         —WALTER SCOTT, *Marmion, VI*

DECISION

> Once to every man and nation comes the moment to
>   decide,
> In the strife of Truth and Falsehood, for the good or
>   evil side;   —J. R. LOWELL, *The Present Crisis*

DEEDS

> Great things are done when men and mountains meet;
> This is not done by jostling in the street.
>   —WILLIAM BLAKE, *Gnomic Verses, I*

> Something attempted, something done,
> Has earned a night's repose:
>   —LONGFELLOW, *The Village Blacksmith*

> If it were done when 'tis done, then 'twere well
> It were done quickly.   —SHAKESPEARE, *Macbeth, I, 7*

> How far that little candle throws its beams!
> So shines a good deed in a naughty world.
>   —SHAKESPEARE, *Merchant of Venice, V, 1*

> The vilest deeds like poison weeds
>   Bloom well in prison-air:
> It is only what is good in Man
>   That wastes and withers there:
>   —OSCAR WILDE, *The Ballad of Reading Gaol*

DEFENSE

> We build and defend not for our generation alone. We
> defend the foundations laid by our fathers. We build a life
> for generations yet unborn. We defend and we build a way
> of life, not for America alone, but for all mankind.
>   —FRANKLIN D. ROOSEVELT, Fireside Chat, May, 1940

> Millions for defense but not one cent for tribute.
>   —CHARLES C. PINCKNEY, 1796

DEFIANCE

Lay on, Macduff,
And damn'd be him that first cries "Hold, enough!"
—SHAKESPEARE, *Macbeth*, V, 7

DELUGE

After us the deluge!
—MME. DE POMPADOUR, To Louis XV

DEMOCRACY

. . . that government of the people, by the people, for the people, shall not perish from the earth.
—LINCOLN, Gettysburg Address

On the whole, with scandalous exceptions, Democracy has given the ordinary worker more dignity than he ever had.   —SINCLAIR LEWIS, *It Can't Happen Here*

Democracy is a kingless regime infested by many kings who are sometimes more exclusive, tyrannical, and destructive than one, if he be a tyrant.
—BENITO MUSSOLINI, *Fascism*

Not only our future economic soundness but the very soundness of our democratic institutions depends on the determination of our Government to give employment to idle men.
—FRANKLIN D. ROOSEVELT, Radio address, April, 1938

The world must be made safe for democracy.
—WOODROW WILSON, Address to Congress, April, 1917

DESIRE

There are two tragedies in life. One is not to get your heart's desire. The other is to get it.
—BERNARD SHAW, *Man and Superman*, IV

The desire of the moth for the star,
    Of the night for the morrow,
The devotion to something afar
    From the sphere of our sorrow.
        —SHELLEY, *One Word Is too Often Profaned*

DESTINY

No man of woman born,
Coward or brave, can shun his destiny.
        —HOMER, *Iliad*, VI (Bryant trans.)

This generation of Americans has a rendezvous with
destiny.   —FRANKLIN D. ROOSEVELT, Address, 1936

If God in His wisdom have brought close
    The day when I must die,
That day by water or fire or air
My feet shall fall in the destined snare
    Wherever my road may lie.
        —D. G. ROSSETTI, *The King's Tragedy*

DEVIL

Forthwith the Devil did appear,
For name him, and he's always near.
        —MATTHEW PRIOR, *Hans Carvel*

The devil can cite Scripture for his purpose.
        —SHAKESPEARE, *Merchant of Venice*, I, 3

The prince of darkness is a gentleman.
        —SHAKESPEARE, *King Lear*, III, 4

DICTATORSHIP

Dictatorship—a fetish worship of one man—is a passing
phase. A state of society where men may not speak their

minds, where children denounce their parents to the police
... such a state of society cannot long endure.

—WINSTON CHURCHILL, *Blood, Sweat and Tears*

The Fuehrer is the Party and the Party is the Fuehrer.
Just as I feel myself only as a part of the Party, the Party
feels itself only as a part of me.

—ADOLF HITLER, At Nazi Congress, 1935

... the ultimate failures of dictatorship cost humanity
far more than any temporary failures of democracy.

—FRANKLIN D. ROOSEVELT, Address, 1937

DIGNITY

Perhaps the only true dignity of man is his capacity to
despise himself.

—GEORGE SANTAYANA, *Introduction to ... Spinoza*

Too coy to flatter, and too proud to serve,
Thine be the joyless dignity to starve.

—TOBIAS SMOLLETT, *Advice*

No race can prosper till it learns that there is as much
dignity in tilling a field as in writing a poem.

—BOOKER T. WASHINGTON, *Up from Slavery*

DINING

He may live without books,—what is knowledge but
    grieving?
He may live without hope,—what is hope but deceiving?
He may live without love,—what is passion but pining?
But where is the man that can live without dining?

—OWEN MEREDITH, *Lucile, I*

DINNERTIME

As the Texas darky said: "Dinner-time fur some folks;
but just twelve o'clock fur me!"

—IRVIN S. COBB, *Paths of Glory*

DISAPPOINTMENT

Oh! ever thus from childhood's hour,
    I've seen my fondest hopes decay;
I never lov'd a tree or flower,
    But 'twas the first to fade away.
I never nurs'd a dear gazelle,
    To glad me with its soft black eye,
But when it came to know me well,
    And love me, it was sure to die.
                    —Thomas Moore, *Lalla Rookh*

DISCRETION

When you have got an elephant by the hind leg, and he is trying to run away, it's best to let him run.
—Abraham Lincoln, Remark to C. A. Dana, April 14, 1865

He that fights and runs away
May live to fight another day.
But he that is in battle slain
Will never rise to fight again.
                    —J. Ray, *History of the Rebellion* (1749)

The better part of valour is discretion.
                    —Shakespeare, *Henry IV, I, V, 4*

DISEASE

We classify disease as error, which nothing but Truth or Mind can heal. —Mary Baker Eddy, *Science and Health*

DISILLUSION

There's not a joy the world can give like that it takes
    away,
When the glow of early thought declines in feeling's dull
    decay;
'Tis not on youth's smooth cheek the blush alone, which
    fades so fast,

But the tender bloom of heart is gone, ere youth itself is
    past.   —BYRON, *Stanzas for Music*

Oh, what a dusty answer gets the soul
When hot for certainties in this our life!
           —GEORGE MEREDITH, *Modern Love*

DISLIKE

I do not love thee, Doctor Fell:
The reason why I cannot tell;
But this I know, and know full well:
I do not love thee, Doctor Fell.
      —THOMAS BROWN, Impromptu translation of
                      Martial's epigram

DISOBEDIENCE

Of Man's first disobedience, and the fruit
Of that forbidden tree whose mortal taste
Brought death into the World, and all our woe,
With loss of Eden, . . .   —MILTON, *Paradise Lost, I, 1*

DISTANCE

Distance lends enchantment to the view.
        —T. CAMPBELL, *The Pleasures of Hope*

DOCTOR

When people's ill, they comes to I,
   I physics, bleeds, and sweats 'em;
Sometimes they live, sometimes they die.
   What's that to I? I lets 'em.
        —DR. J. C. LETTSOM, *On Himself*

Physician, heal thyself. —NEW TESTAMENT, *Luke, IV, 23*

But when the wit began to wheeze,
   And wine had warm'd the politician,

Cur'd yesterday of my disease,
   I died last night of my physician.
           —PRIOR, *The Remedy Worse Than the Disease*

DOG

A dog starved at his master's gate
Predicts the ruin of the state.
           —BLAKE, *Auguries of Innocence*

If there is no God for thee
Then there is no God for me.
           —ANNA H. BRANCH, *To a Dog*

You're only a dog, old fellow; a dog, and you've had
   your day;
But never a friend of all my friends has been truer than
   you alway.   —J. S. CUTLER, *Roger and I*

Old dog Tray's ever faithful,
   Grief cannot drive him away;
He's gentle, he is kind; I'll never, never find
   A better friend than old dog Tray.
           —STEPHEN C. FOSTER, *Old Dog Tray*

And in that town a dog was found,
   As many dogs there be,
Both mongrel, puppy, whelp, and hound,
   And curs of low degree.
           —GOLDSMITH, *Elegy on the Death of a Mad Dog*

I'm a lean dog, a keen dog, a wild dog, and lone;
I'm a rough dog, a tough dog, hunting on my own;
I'm a bad dog, a mad dog, teasing silly sheep;
I love to sit and bay the moon, to keep fat souls from
   sleep.   —IRENE R. MacLEOD, *Lone Dog*

A living dog is better than a dead lion.
>   —OLD TESTAMENT, *Ecclesiastes, IX, 4*

I am his Highness' dog at Kew;
Pray tell me, sir, whose dog are you?
>   —POPE, Engraved on the collar of a dog
>   which he gave to His Royal Highness

If you pick up a starving dog and make him prosperous,
he will not bite you. That is the principal difference between a dog and a man.
>   —MARK TWAIN, *Pudd'nhead Wilson's Calendar*

DOLLAR

The Almighty Dollar, that great object of universal devotion.   —WASHINGTON IRVING, *Wolfert's Roost*

DOUBT

O Lord—if there is a Lord; save my soul—if I have a soul.
Amen.   —ERNEST RENAN, *Prayer of a Skeptic*

I am cabin'd, cribb'd, confined, bound in
To saucy doubts and fears.
>   —SHAKESPEARE, *Macbeth, III, 4*

There lives more faith in honest doubt,
Believe me, than in half the creeds.
>   —TENNYSON, *In Memoriam*

Ever insurgent let me be,
Make me more daring than devout;
From sleek contentment keep me free,
And fill me with a buoyant doubt.
>   —LOUIS UNTERMEYER, *A Prayer*

DOVE

Oh that I had wings like a dove! for then would I fly
away and be at rest.   —OLD TESTAMENT, *Psalms, IV, 6*

DREAM

If there were dreams to sell,
Merry and sad to tell,
And the crier rung his bell,
　　What would you buy?
　　　　　　—THOMAS LOVELL BEDDOES, *Dream-Pedlary*

I dreamt that I dwelt in marble halls,
With vassals and serfs at my side.
　　　　　　—ALFRED BUNN, *The Bohemian Girl*

A damsel with a dulcimer
In a vision once I saw:
It was an Abyssinian maid,
And on her dulcimer she played,
Singing of Mount Abora.
　　　　　　—S. T. COLERIDGE, *Kubla Khan*

Dreamer of dreams, born out of my due time,
Why should I strive to set the crooked straight?
　　　　　　—WILLIAM MORRIS, *The Earthly Paradise*

And all my days are trances,
　　And all my nightly dreams
Are where thy gray eye glances
　　And where thy footstep gleams—
In what ethereal dances
　　By what eternal streams.   —POE, *To One in Paradise*

To sleep: perchance to dream; ay there's the rub;
For in that sleep of death what dreams may come,

When we have shuffled off this mortal coil,
Must give us pause.   —SHAKESPEARE, *Hamlet, III, 1*

I arise from dreams of thee
In the first sweet sleep of night,
When the winds are breathing low,
And the stars are shining bright.
                    —SHELLEY, *Lines to an Indian Air*

A pleasing land of drowsy head it was,
Of dreams that wave before the half-shut eye;
And of gay castles in the clouds that pass,
For ever flushing round a summer sky.
                    —THOMSON, *The Castle of Indolence*

Two gates the silent house of Sleep adorn:
Of polished ivory this, that of transparent horn:
True visions through transparent horn arise;
Through polished ivory pass deluding lies.
                    —VIRGIL, *Aeneid, VI* (Dryden trans.)

But I, being poor, have only my dreams;
I have spread my dreams under your feet;
Tread softly, for you tread on my dreams.
                    —W. B. YEATS, *The Cloths of Heaven*

DRESS

A sweet disorder in the dress
Kindles in clothes a wantonness.
                    —HERRICK, *Delight in Disorder*

Whenas in silks my Julia goes,
Then, then, methinks how sweetly flows
The liquefaction of her clothes!
                    —HERRICK, *Upon Julia's Clothes*

Still to be neat, still to be drest,
As you were going to a feast;
Still to be powder'd, still perfumed:
> —BEN JONSON, *Epicoene, I, 1*

Where's the man could ease a heart
Like a satin gown?
> —DOROTHY PARKER, *The Satin Dress*

Costly thy habit as thy purse can buy,
But not express'd in fancy; rich, not gaudy;
For the apparel oft proclaims the man.
> —SHAKESPEARE, *Hamlet, I, 3*

The tulip and the butterfly
Appear in gayer coats than I:
Let me be dressed fine as I will,
Flies, worms, and flowers exceed me still.
> —ISAAC WATTS, *Against Pride in Clothes*

DRINKING

If all be true that I do think,
There are five reasons we should drink;
Good wine—a friend—or being dry—
Or lest we should be by and by—
Or any other reason why.
> —HENRY ALDRICH, Latin epigram of the 16th century

Inspiring bold John Barleycorn,
What dangers thou canst make us scorn!
Wi' tippenny, we fear nae evil;
Wi' usquebae, we'll face the devil!
> —BURNS, *Tam O' Shanter*

Bacchus' blessings are a treasure,
Drinking is the soldier's pleasure:

Rich the treasure, sweet the pleasure,
    Sweet is pleasure after pain.
                        —DRYDEN, *Alexander's Feast*

Come, landlord, fill the flowing bowl until it does run
    over,
Tonight we will all merry be—tomorrow we'll get sober.
                —JOHN FLETCHER, *The Bloody Brother, II, 2*

Could man be drunk forever
    With liquor, love, or fights,
Lief should I rouse at morning
    And lief lie down at nights.
                        —A. E. HOUSMAN, *A Shropshire Lad*

If ever I marry a wife,
    I'll marry a landlord's daughter,
For then I may sit in the bar,
    And drink cold brandy and water.
                        —CHARLES LAMB (impromptu)

Wreath the bowl
    With flowers of soul,
The brightest Wit can find us;
    We'll take a flight
    Tow'rds heaven to-night,
And leave dull earth behind us.
                        —THOMAS MOORE, *Wreath the Bowl*

What did the Governor of North Carolina say to the
Governor of South Carolina?
    "It's a long time between drinks."
—GOV. JOHN M. MOREHEAD (quoted by Stevenson in *The
    Wrong Box,* and by Kipling in *The Light That Failed*)

Candy
Is dandy

But liquor
Is quicker.   —OGDEN NASH, *Reflection on Ice-Breaking*

Drink! for you know not whence you came, nor why;
Drink! For you know not why you go, nor where.
　　　　—OMAR KHAYYÁM, *Rubáiyát* (FitzGerald trans.)

And let me the canikan clink;
　A soldier's but a man;
　A life's but a span;
Why, then, let a soldier drink.
　　　　　　　　　—SHAKESPEARE, *Othello, II, 3*

O God, that men should put an enemy in their mouths to
steal away their brains! that we should, with joy, pleasance,
revel and applause, transform ourselves into beasts!
　　　　　　　　　—SHAKESPEARE, *Othello, II, 3*

Fifteen men on the Dead Man's Chest—
　Yo—ho—ho and a bottle of rum!
Drink and the devil had done for the rest—
　Yo—ho—ho and a bottle of rum!
　　　　　　　　—STEVENSON, *Treasure Island*

I cannot eat but little meat,
　My stomach is not good;
But sure I think that I can drink
　With him that wears a hood.
　　　　　—JOHN STILL, *Gammer Gurton's Needle*

DRINKING (Toast)

Here's to your good health and your family's good
health. May you live long and prosper.
　　　　　—JOSEPH JEFFERSON, *Rip Van Winkle*

Here's to the maiden of bashful fifteen;
　Here's to the widow of fifty;

Here's to the flaunting, extravagant quean;
And here's to the housewife that's thrifty.
—R. B. Sheridan, *School for Scandal*, III, 3

DRUNKENNESS

Not drunk is he who from the floor
Can rise alone, and still drink more;
But drunk is he who prostrate lies,
Without the power to drink or rise.
—T. L. Peacock, *Misfortunes of Elphin*

I went to Frankfort, and got drunk
With that most learn'd professor, Brunck;
I went to Worms, and got more drunken
With that more learn'd professor, Ruhnken.
—Richard Porson, *Facetiae Cantabrigienses*

DUTY

So nigh is grandeur to our dust,
So near to God is man,
When Duty whispers low, *Thou must*,
The youth replies, *I can.*   —Emerson, *Voluntaries*

I slept and dreamed that life was Beauty;
I woke, and found that life was Duty.
—Ellen S. Hooper, *Beauty and Duty*

England expects every man to do his duty.
—Lord Nelson, Signal at Trafalgar, 1805

Stern Daughter of the Voice of God!
O Duty! if that name thou love,
Who art a light to guide, a rod
To check the erring, and reprove;
—Wordsworth, *Ode to Duty*

Not snow nor rain nor heat nor gloom of night stays these couriers from the swift completion of their appointed rounds.   MOTTO OF THE U. S. POSTAL SERVICE

EARTH

The poetry of earth is never dead; . . .
The poetry of earth is ceasing never.
                    —KEATS, *On the Grasshopper and Cricket*

One generation passeth away, and another generation cometh; but the earth abideth for ever.
                    —OLD TESTAMENT, *Ecclesiastes, I, 4*

EAST

Ship me somewheres east of Suez, where the best is like
    the worst,
Where there aren't no Ten Commandments an' a man
    can raise a thirst.   —KIPLING, *Mandalay*

Oh, East is East, and West is West, and never the twain
    shall meet,
Till Earth and Sky stand presently at God's great Judg-
    ment Seat.   —KIPLING, *The Ballad of East and West*

EASTER

In the bonds of Death He lay
    Who for our defence was slain;
But the Lord is risen to-day.
    Christ hath brought us life again,
Wherefore let us all rejoice,
Singing loud, with cheerful voice,
    Hallelujah!
                    —MARTIN LUTHER, *In the Bonds of Death*

"Christ the Lord is risen to-day,"
Sons of men and angels say:

Raise your joys and triumphs high;
Sing, ye heavens, and earth, reply.
>   —CHARLES WESLEY, *Christ the Lord Is Risen*

EATING

Let us eat and drink; for to-morrow we shall die.
>   —OLD TESTAMENT, *Isaiah, XXII, 13*

Other men live to eat, while I eat to live.
>   —SOCRATES (quoted by Diogenes Laertius)

ECHO

Sweet Echo, sweetest Nymph, that liv'st unseen
    Within thy airy shell,
By slow Meander's margent green,
    And in the violet-embroidered vale.
>   —MILTON, *Comus*

Our echoes roll from soul to soul,
And grow for ever and for ever.
>   —TENNYSON, *The Princess*

EDUCATION

Nothing in education is so astonishing as the amount of
ignorance it accumulates in the form of inert facts.
>   —HENRY ADAMS, *The Education of Henry Adams*

What's a' your jargon o' your schools,
Your Latin names for horns and stools;
If honest Nature made you fools.
>   —BURNS, *First Epistle to J. Lapraik*

Better build schoolrooms for "the boy,"
Than cells and gibbets for "the Man."
>   —ELIZA COOK, *A Song for the Ragged Schools*

EGOISM

I find no sweeter fat than sticks to my own bones.
—WALT WHITMAN, *Song of Myself*

ELOQUENCE

While listening senates hang upon thy tongue,
Devolving through the maze of Eloquence
A roll of periods, sweeter than her song.
—THOMSON, *The Seasons: Autumn*

ENEMY

If thine enemy hunger, feed him; if he thirst, give him
drink: for in so doing thou shalt heap coals of fire on his
head.   —NEW TESTAMENT, *Romans, XII, 20*

We have met the enemy and they are ours.
—OLIVER HAZARD PERRY: After battle of Lake Erie, 1813

I choose my friends for their good looks, my acquaint-
ances for their good characters, and my enemies for their
good intellects. A man cannot be too careful in the choice
of his enemies. —OSCAR WILDE, *The Picture of Dorian Gray*

ENGLAND

I will not cease from mental fight,
    Nor shall my sword sleep in my hand,
Till we have built Jerusalem
    In England's green and pleasant land.
—WILLIAM BLAKE, *Milton*

If I should die, think only this of me:
That there's some corner of a foreign field
That is forever England.
—RUPERT BROOKE, *The Soldier*

Oh, to be in England
Now that April's there, . . .
—R. BROWNING, *Home Thoughts from Abroad*

Men of England! who inherit
Rights that cost your sires their blood.
> —THOMAS CAMPBELL, *Men of England*

England is the paradise of women, the purgatory of men, and the hell of horses.
> —JOHN FLORIO, *Second Frutes* (1591)

What have I done for you,
  England, my England?
What is there I would not do,
  England, my own?
> —W. E. HENLEY, *England, My England*

Oh England is a pleasant place for them that's rich and high,
But England is a cruel place for such poor folks as I.
> —CHARLES KINGSLEY, *The Last Buccaneer*

God of our fathers, known of old,
  Lord of our far-flung battle-line,
Beneath whose awful Hand we hold
  Dominion over palm and pine—
Lord God of Hosts, be with us yet,
Lest we forget—lest we forget!
> —KIPLING, *The Recessional*

Old England still throbs with the muffled fire
  Of a Past she can never forget:
And again shall she banner the world up higher;
  For there's life in the Old Land yet.
> —GERALD MASSEY, *Old England*

This blessed plot, this earth, this realm, this England.
> —SHAKESPEARE, *Richard II, II, 1*

I thank the goodness and the grace
  Which on my birth have smiled,

And made me, in these Christian days,
  A happy English child.
    —ANN AND JANE TAYLOR, *A Child's Hymn of Praise*

When Britain first, at Heaven's command,
  Arose from out the azure main,
This was the charter of the land
  And guardian angels sung this strain—
"Rule, Britannia! Britannia rules the waves!
Britons never shall be slaves."
                    —THOMSON, *Rule, Britannia*

I traveled among unknown men
  In lands beyond the sea;
Nor, England! did I know till then
  What love I bore to thee.
    —WORDSWORTH, *I Travelled Among Unknown Men*

ENGLISHMAN

He is an Englishman!
  For he himself has said it,
  And it's greatly to his credit,
That he is an Englishman!
  For he might have been a Roosian,
  A French or Turk or Proosian,
Or perhaps Itali-an.
  But in spite of all temptations
  To belong to other nations,
He remains an Englishman!
                —W. S. GILBERT, *H.M.S. Pinafore, II*

EPIGRAM

What is an epigram? A dwarfish whole,
Its body brevity, and wit its soul.
            —S. T. COLERIDGE, In the *London Morning Post*

EPITAPHS

Underneath this sable hearse
Lies the subject of all verse:
Sidney's sister, Pembroke's mother:
Death, ere thou hast slain another,
Fair, and learn'd, and good as she,
Time shall throw a dart at thee.
—WILLIAM BROWNE, *On the Countess Dowager
of Pembroke*

Here lies a most beautiful lady,
Light of step and heart was she;
I think she was the most beautiful lady
That ever was in the West Country.
—WALTER DE LA MARE, *An Epitaph*

Let there be no inscription upon my tomb. Let no man
write my epitaph. I am here ready to die. . . . Let my character and motives repose in obscurity and peace, till other
times and other men can do them justice.
—ROBERT EMMET, Speech at his trial, 1803

He lies below, correct in cypress wood,
And entertains the most exclusive worms.
—DOROTHY PARKER, *The Very Rich Man*

Under the wide and starry sky,
Dig the grave and let me lie.
Glad did I live and gladly die,
    And I laid me down with a will.
This be the verse you grave for me:
*Here he lies where he longed to be;
Home is the sailor, home from the sea,
    And the hunter home from the hill.*
—R. L. STEVENSON, *Requiem*

EQUALITY

We hold these truths to be self-evident, that all men are created equal; that they are endowed by their creator with certain unalienable rights; that among these are life, liberty and the pursuit of happiness.

—THOMAS JEFFERSON, *The Declaration of Independence*

I celebrate myself, and sing myself,
And what I assume you shall assume,
For every atom belonging to me as good belongs to you.
—WALT WHITMAN, *Song of Myself*

ERROR

Truth, crushed to earth, shall rise again;
Th' eternal years of God are hers;
But Error, wounded, writhes in pain,
And dies among his worshippers.
—WILLIAM C. BRYANT, *The Battle-Field*

Errors, like straws, upon the surface flow;
He who would search for pearls must dive below.
—DRYDEN, *All for Love*, Prologue

Good nature and good sense must ever join;
To err is human, to forgive divine.
—POPE, *Essay on Criticism*

Error is the force that welds men together; truth is communicated to men only by deeds of truth.
—TOLSTOY, *My Religion*

ETERNITY

I saw Eternity the other night
Like a great ring of pure and endless light.
—HENRY VAUGHAN, *The World*

EUROPE

Better fifty years of Europe than a cycle of Cathay.
—TENNYSON, *Locksley Hall*

EVENING

Now fades the glimmering landscape on the sight,
And all the air a solemn stillness holds.
—GRAY, *Elegy Written in a Country Churchyard*

EVIDENCE

Some circumstantial evidence is very strong, as when
you find a trout in the milk.
—THOREAU, *Journal*, Nov., 1850

EVIL

For every evil under the sun,
There is a remedy, or there is none;
If there be one, try and find it,
If there be none, never mind it.
—W. C. HAZLITT, *English Proverbs*

Evil is wrought by want of Thought
As well as want of Heart.
—THOMAS HOOD, *The Lady's Dream*

The evil that men do lives after them;
The good is oft interred with their bones.
—SHAKESPEARE, *Julius Caesar, III, 1*

Evil [more accurately: *Shame*] to him who evil thinks.
(*Honi soit qui mal y pense.*)
MOTTO OF THE ORDER OF THE GARTER

EVOLUTION

A fire-mist and a planet,
A crystal and a cell,

A jellyfish and a saurian,
  And caves where the cave men dwell;
Then a sense of law and beauty,
  And a face turned from the clod—
Some call it Evolution,
  And others call it God.
                —W. H. CARRUTH, *Each in His Own Tongue*

When you were a tadpole and I was a fish,
In the Paleozoic time,
And side by side on the ebbing tide,
We sprawled through the ooze and slime.
                —LANGDON SMITH, *Evolution*

This survival of the fittest, which I have here sought to
express in mechanical terms, is that which Mr. Darwin has
called "natural selection, or the preservation of favoured
races in the struggle for life."
                —HERBERT SPENCER, *Principles of Biology*

EXAMPLE

Lives of great men all remind us
  We can make our lives sublime,
And, departing, leave behind us
  Footprints on the sands of time.
                —LONGFELLOW, *A Psalm of Life*

EXCESS

To gild refined gold, to paint the lily,
To throw a perfume on the violet,
To smooth the ice, or add another hue
Unto the rainbow, or with taper-light
To seek the beauteous eye of heaven to garnish,
Is wasteful and ridiculous excess.
                —SHAKESPEARE, *King John, IV, 2*

EXILE

The world was all before them, where to choose
Their place of rest, and Providence their guide:
They, hand in hand, with wand'ring steps and slow,
Through Eden took their solitary way.
                    —MILTON, *Paradise Lost* (last lines)

EXPERIENCE

A sadder and a wiser man
He rose the morrow morn.
                    —S. T. COLERIDGE, *The Ancient Mariner*

Thou shalt know by experience how salt the savor is of
other's bread, and how sad a path it is to climb and de-
scend another's stairs.
(*Tu proverai si come sa di sale
Lo pane altrui, e com' è duro calle
Lo scendere e il salir per l'altrui scale.*)
                    —DANTE, *Paradise, XVII*

Experience keeps a dear school, yet Fools will learn in no
other.   —FRANKLIN, *Poor Richard's Almanac* for 1743

Nor deem the irrevocable Past,
    As wholly wasted, wholly vain,
If, rising on its wrecks, at last
    To something nobler we attain.
                    —LONGFELLOW, *The Ladder of St. Augustine*

EXPERT

An expert is one who knows more and more about less
and less. —NICHOLAS M. BUTLER, Commencement address

EYES

Her eyes the glow-worm lend thee,
The shooting stars attend thee;
    And the elves also,

Whose little eyes glow
Like the sparks of fire, befriend thee.
> —HERRICK, *The Night-Piece, to Julia*

Drink to me only with thine eyes,
    And I will pledge with mine;
Or leave a kiss but in the cup,
    And I'll not look for wine.   —BEN JONSON, *To Celia*

Where did you get your eyes so blue?
Out of the sky as I came through.
—GEORGE MACDONALD, *At the Back of the North Wind*

The light that lies
In women's eyes,
Has been my heart's undoing.
> —THOMAS MOORE, *The Time I've Lost in Wooing*

FACE

There is a garden in her face,
Where roses and white lilies grow;
A heavenly paradise is that place,
Wherein all pleasant fruits do flow.
There cherries grow, which none may buy,
Till "Cherry ripe" themselves do cry.
> —THOMAS CAMPION, *Cherry Ripe*

"Say, boys! if you give me just another whiskey I'll be
    glad,
And I'll draw right here a picture of the face that drove
    me mad."   —H. A. D'ARCY, *The Face Upon the Floor*

There's no art
To find the mind's construction in the face.
> —SHAKESPEARE, *Macbeth, I, 4*

If I should die to-night,
My friends would look upon my quiet face
Before they laid it in its resting place,
And deem that death had left it almost fair.
　　　—ARABELLA E. SMITH, *If I Should Die To-night*

FAILURE

In the lexicon of youth, which Fate reserves
For a bright manhood, there is no such word
As—fail!　　　　　—BULWER-LYTTON, *Richelieu, III, 1*

They never fail who die
In a great cause: the block may soak their gore;
Their heads may sodden in the sun; their limbs
Be strung to city gates and castle walls—
But still their spirit walks abroad.
　　　　　—BYRON, *Marino Faliero, II, 2*

And nothing to look backward to with pride,
And nothing to look forward to with hope.
　　　—ROBERT FROST, *The Death of the Hired Man*

They went forth to battle, but they always fell.
　　　　—JAMES MACPHERSON (OSSIAN), *Cath-loda*

I sing the hymn of the conquered, who fall in the battle
　of life,
The hymn of the wounded, the beaten who died over-
　whelmed in the strife.　　　—W. W. STORY, *Io Victis*

FAIRIES

Up the airy mountains,
　Down the rushy glen,
We daren't go a-hunting
　For fear of little men;
Wee folk, good folk,
　Trooping all together;

Green jacket, red cap,
   And white owl's feather!
                    —WILLIAM ALLINGTON, *The Fairies*

When the first baby laughed for the first time, his laugh
broke into a million pieces, and they all went skipping
about. That was the beginning of fairies.
                    —J. M. BARRIE, *The Little White Bird*

Where the bee sucks, there suck I:
In the cowslip's bell I lie;
There I couch when owls do cry.
On the bat's back I do fly
After summer merrily.
                    —SHAKESPEARE, *The Tempest, V, 1*

FAITH

The reason why birds can fly and we can't is simply
that they have perfect faith, for to have faith is to have
wings.   —J. M. BARRIE, *The Little White Bird*

Faith without works is dead.
                    —NEW TESTAMENT, *James, II, 20*

I have fought a good fight, I have finished my course,
I have kept the faith. —NEW TESTAMENT, *II Timothy, IV, 7*

We walk by faith, not by sight.
                    —NEW TESTAMENT, *II Corinthians, V, 7*

The old faiths light their candles all about,
But burly Truth comes by and puts them out.
                    —LIZETTE W. REESE, *Truth*

One by one, like leaves from a tree,
All my faiths have forsaken me.
                    —SARA TEASDALE, *Leaves*

Strong Son of God, immortal Love,
    Whom we, that have not seen thy face,
    By faith, and faith alone, embrace,
Believing where we cannot prove.
            —TENNYSON, *In Memoriam*

FAITHFUL

I have been faithful to thee, Cynara! in my fashion.
      —ERNEST DOWSON, *Non Sum Qualis* . . .

So spake the seraph Abdiel, faithful found,
Among the faithless, faithful only he.
        —MILTON, *Paradise Lost, V*

FALL

We fall to rise, are baffled to fight better,
Sleep to wake.   —R. BROWNING, *Asolando*

He that is down needs fear no fall,
   He that is low, no pride.
      —BUNYAN, *The Pilgrim's Progress*

Fallen, fallen, fallen, fallen,
Fallen from his high estate,
And welt'ring in his blood. —DRYDEN, *Alexander's Feast*

How art thou fallen from heaven, O Lucifer, son of the
morning!   —OLD TESTAMENT, *Isaiah, XIV, 12*

How are the mighty fallen!
      —OLD TESTAMENT, *II Samuel, I, 19*

O, what a fall was there, my countrymen!
Then I, and you, and all of us fell down.
      —SHAKESPEARE, *Julius Caesar, III, 2*

FALSEHOOD

O what a goodly outside falsehood hath!
— SHAKESPEARE, *Merchant of Venice, I, 3*

FAME

I awoke one morning and found myself famous.
— BYRON, after the publication of *Childe Harold,* 1812

O Fame!—if I e'er took delight in thy praises,
'Twas less for the sake of thy high-sounding phrases,
Than to see the bright eyes of the dear one discover
She thought that I was not unworthy to love her.
— BYRON, *Stanzas Written on the Road . . .*

If a man can write a better book, preach a better sermon, or make a better mouse-trap, than his neighbor, though he builds his house in the woods, the world will make a beaten path to his door.   — EMERSON, Lectures during 1871

Fame is the spur that the clear spirit doth raise
(That last infirmity of noble mind)
To scorn delights, and live laborious days.
— MILTON, *Lycidas*

We toil for fame,
    We live on crusts,
We make a name,
    Then we are busts.
— L. H. ROBBINS, *Lines for the Hall of Fame Ceremony*

Fame is the perfume of heroic deeds.
— SOCRATES (Quoted by Plato)

Fame has also this great drawback, that if we pursue it we must direct our lives in such a way as to please the fancy of men, avoiding what they dislike and seeking what is pleasing to them.   — SPINOZA, *Tractate on the Intellect*

Laurel is green for a season, and love is sweet for a day;
But love grows bitter with treason, and laurel outlives
   not May.   —SWINBURNE, *Hymn to Proserpine*

What rage for fame attends both great and small!
Better be d——n'd than mentioned *not at all.*
                —JOHN WOLCOT, *To the Royal Academicians*

FAMILIARITY

Be thou familiar, but by no means vulgar.
                        —SHAKESPEARE, *Hamlet, I, 3*

Familiarity breeds contempt—and children.
                        —MARK TWAIN, *Unpublished Diaries*

FAMILY

He that hath wife and children hath given hostages to
fortune; for they are impediments to great enterprises,
either of virtue or mischief.
—FRANCIS BACON, *Essays: Of Marriage and Single Life*

All happy families resemble one another; every unhappy
family is unhappy in its own way.
                        —TOLSTOY, *Anna Karenina*

FANCY

Tell me where is fancy bred,
Or in the heart or in the head?
How begot, how nourished?
   Reply, reply.
It is engender'd in the eyes,
With gazing fed; and fancy dies
In the cradle where it lies.
                —SHAKESPEARE, *Merchant of Venice, III, 2*

Good-bye my Fancy!
Farewell dear mate, dear love!

I'm going away, I know not where,
Or to what fortune, or whether I may ever see you again,
So Good-bye my Fancy!
                    —WALT WHITMAN, *Good-bye My Fancy*

FAREWELL

Fare thee well! and if for ever,
Still for ever, fare thee well.
                    —BYRON, *Fare Thee Well*

For ever, brother, hail and farewell.
(*In perpetuum, frater, ave atque vale.*)
                    —CATULLUS, *Ode, CI*

Farewell the tranquil mind! farewell content!
Farewell the plumed troop and the big wars,
That make ambition virtue! O, farewell!
Farewell the neighing steed, and the shrill trump,
The spirit-stirring drum, the ear-piercing fife,
The royal banner and all quality,
Pride, pomp and circumstance of glorious war!
And, O you mortal engines, whose rude throats
The immortal Jove's dread clamours counterfeit,
Farewell! Othello's occupation's gone!
                    —SHAKESPEARE, *Othello, III, 3*

FARMER

Oft did the harvest to their sickle yield;
    Their furrow oft the stubborn glebe has broke;
How jocund did they drive their team a-field!
    How bow'd the woods beneath their sturdy stroke!
                    —GRAY, *Elegy Written in a Country Churchyard*

Slave of the wheel of labor, what to him
Are Plato and the swing of Pleiades.
                    —EDWIN MARKHAM, *The Man With the Hoe*

. . . whoever could make two ears of corn, or two blades
of grass, to grow upon a spot of ground where only one
grew before, would deserve better of mankind, and do
more essential service to his country, than the whole race of
politicians put together.

—SWIFT, *Gulliver: Voyage to Brobdingnag*

Give fools their gold, and knaves their power;
    Let fortune's bubbles rise and fall;
Who sows a field, or trains a flower,
    Or plants a tree, is more than all.

—WHITTIER, *A Song of Harvest*

FASHION

National Socialism does not harbor the slightest aggres-
sive intent towards any European nation.

—ADOLF HITLER, at Nazi Congress, 1935

Cure the evils of Democracy by the evils of Fascism!
Funny therapeutics! I've heard of their curing syphilis by
giving the patient malaria, but I've never heard of their
curing malaria by giving the patient syphilis.

—SINCLAIR LEWIS, *It Can't Happen Here*

We do not believe in programs, in plans, in saints or
apostles, above all, we do not believe in happiness, in
salvation, in the promised land.

—BENITO MUSSOLINI, *Fascism*

FASHION

The fashion of this world passeth away.

—NEW TESTAMENT, *I Corinthians, VII, 31*

The glass of fashion, and the mould of form,
The observed of all observers.

—SHAKESPEARE, *Hamlet, III, 1*

FATE

Here's a sigh to those who love me,
    And a smile to those who hate;
And, whatever sky's above me,
    Here's a heart for any fate.
                    —BYRON, *To Thomas Moore*

It matters not how strait the gate,
    How charged with punishments the scroll,
I am the master of my fate:
    I am the captain of my soul.
                    —W. E. HENLEY, *Invictus*

All are architects of Fate,
    Working in these walls of Time;
Some with massive deeds and great,
    Some with ornaments of rhyme.
                    —LONGFELLOW, *The Builders*

Let us, then, be up and doing,
    With a heart for any fate.
                    —LONGFELLOW, *A Psalm of Life*

It lies not in our power to love or hate,
For will in us is over-ruled by fate.
                    —MARLOWE, *Hero and Leander*

Oh busy weaver! Unseen weaver! pause! one word!
whither flows the fabric? What palace may it deck?
Wherefore all these ceaseless toilings? Speak, weaver! Stay
thy hand!   —MELVILLE, *Moby Dick*

The Moving Finger writes; and, having writ,
Moves on: nor all your Piety nor Wit
    Shall lure it back to cancel half a Line,
Nor all your Tears wash out a Word of it.
                    —OMAR KHAYYÁM, *Rubáiyát* (FitzGerald trans.)

Miniver Cheevy, born too late,
   Scratched his head and kept on thinking;
Miniver coughed, and called it fate,
   And kept on drinking.
                        —E. A. ROBINSON, *Miniver Cheevy*

FAULT

The greatest of faults, I should say, is to be conscious
of none.   —CARLYLE, *Heroes and Hero-Worship*

Jupiter has loaded us with two wallets: the one, filled
with our own faults, he has placed at our backs; the other,
heavy with the faults of others, he has hung before.
                        —PHAEDRUS, *Fables*, X

Be to her virtues very kind,
Be to her faults a little blind.
                        —PRIOR, *An English Padlock*

The fault, dear Brutus, is not in our stars,
But in ourselves, that we are underlings.
                        —SHAKESPEARE, *Julius Caesar*, I, 2

Faultily faultless, icily regular, splendidly null,
   Dead perfection, no more.   —TENNYSON, *Maud*

FEAR

The thing that numbs the heart is this:
   That men cannot devise
Some scheme of life to banish fear
   That lurks in most men's eyes.
                        —JAMES NORMAN HALL, *Fear*

The only thing we have to fear is fear itself.
—FRANKLIN D. ROOSEVELT, First Inaugural Address, 1933

It was fear that first made gods in the world.
(*Primus in orbe deos fecit timor.*)
                              —STATIUS, *Thebais, III*

FENCE

My apple trees will never get across
And eat the cones under his pines, I tell him.
He only says, "Good fences make good neighbors."
                              —ROBERT FROST, *Mending Wall*

FIGHT

I propose to fight it out on this line if it takes all summer.
                    —U. S. GRANT, to Gen. Halleck, May 11, 1864

I have not yet begun to fight.
                    —JOHN PAUL JONES, at sea battle, Sept., 1779

Servant of God, well done! Well hast thou fought
The better fight.   —MILTON, *Paradise Lost, VI*

There is such a thing as a man being too proud to fight.
                    —WOODROW WILSON, *Speech*, May 10, 1915

FISHING

Oh, the gallant fisher's life!
   It is the best of any;
'Tis full of pleasure, void of strife,
   And 'tis beloved by many.
                              —IZAAK WALTON, *The Compleat Angler*

FITTEST

This is the Law of the Yukon, that only the Strong shall
      thrive;
That surely the Weak shall perish, and only the fit
      survive.   —R. W. SERVICE, *The Law of the Yukon*

FLAG, AMERICAN

I pledge allegiance to the flag of the United States of America and to the Republic for which it stands. One Nation, indivisible, with Liberty and Justice for all.
—JAMES B. UPHAM AND F. M. BELLAMY,
Pledge to the Flag (1892)

Hats off!
Along the street there comes
A blare of bugles, a ruffle of drums,
A flash of color beneath the sky:
Hats off!
The flag is passing by.
—H. H. BENNETT, *The Flag Goes By*

Off with your hat as the flag goes by!
And let the heart have its say;
You're man enough for a tear in your eye
That you will not wipe away.
—H. C. BUNNER, *The Old Flag*

Here's to the red of it,
There's not a thread of it,
No, not a shred of it,
In all the spread of it,
From foot to head,
For heroes bled for it,
Faced steel and lead for it,
Precious blood shed for it,
Bathing in red.
—JOHN DALY, *A Toast to the Flag*

If any one attempts to haul down the American flag, shoot him on the spot.
—JOHN A. DIX (Sec. of Treas. 1861)

When freedom from her mountain height
Unfurled her standard to the air,

She tore the azure robe of night,
   And set the stars of glory there.
          —JOSEPH RODMAN DRAKE, *The American Flag*

What flower is this that greets the morn,
Its hues from Heaven so freshly born?
With burning star and flaming band
It kindles all the sunset land:
Oh tell us what its name may be,—
Is this the Flower of Liberty?
   It is the banner of the free,
   The starry Flower of Liberty.
          —O. W. HOLMES, *The Flower of Liberty*

And the star-spangled banner in triumph shall wave
O'er the land of the free and the home of the brave.
          —FRANCIS SCOTT KEY, *The Star-Spangled Banner*

"Yes, we'll rally round the flag, boys, we'll rally once
    again,
   Shouting the battle-cry of Freedom."
          —GEORGE F. ROOT, *The Battle-Cry of Freedom*

"Shoot, if you must, this old gray head,
But spare your country's flag," she said . . . .
"Who touches a hair of yon gray head
Dies like a dog! March on!" he said.
          —WHITTIER, *Barbara Frietchie*

FLATTERY

One catches more flies with a spoonful of honey than
with twenty casks of vinegar.
          —HENRI IV of France, Maxim

'Tis an old maxim in the schools,
That flattery's the food of fools;

Yet now and then your men of wit
Will condescend to take a bit.
>   —SWIFT, *Cadenus and Vanessa*

FLEA

So Nat'ralists observe, a Flea
Hath smaller Fleas that on him prey;
And these have smaller still to bite 'em,
And so proceed *ad infinitum.*
>   —SWIFT, *On Poetry: A Rhapsody*

FLESH

The world, the flesh, and the devil.
>   —BOOK OF COMMON PRAYER

The spirit indeed is willing, but the flesh is weak.
>   —NEW TESTAMENT, *Matthew, XXVI, 41*

O, that this too too solid flesh would melt,
Thaw and resolve itself into a dew.
>   —SHAKESPEARE, *Hamlet, I, 2*

The way of all flesh.
>   —JOHN WEBSTER, *Westward Ho! II, 2*
>   (*cf.* the title of Butler's novel, 1903)

FLIES

One of your *(the invader's)* men got out of hand one
night and he said the flies had conquered the flypaper, and
now the whole nation knows his words. They made a song
of it. The flies have conquered the flypaper.
>   —JOHN STEINBECK, *The Moon is Down*

FLOWERS

The south wind searches for the flowers whose fragrance
   late he bore,

And sighs to find them in the wood and by the stream
   no more.
        —WILLIAM C. BRYANT, *The Death of the Flowers*

Full many a flower is born to blush unseen,
And waste its sweetness on the desert air.
        —GRAY, *Elegy Written in a Country Churchyard*

Fair pledges of the fruitful tree
   Why do ye fall so fast?
   Your date is not so past
But you may stay yet there awhile
   To blush and gently smile
   And go at last.   —HERRICK, *To Blossoms*

'Tis but a little faded flower,
   But oh, how fondly dear!
'Twill bring me back one golden hour,
   Through many a weary year.
   —ELLEN C. HOWARTH, *'Tis But a Little Faded Flower*

I know a bank where the wild thyme blows,
Where oxslips and the nodding violet grows,
Quite over-canopied with luscious woodbine,
With sweet musk-roses and with eglantine.
   —SHAKESPEARE, *A Midsummer-Night's Dream, II, 1*

When daisies pied and violets blue
   And lady-smocks all silver-white
And cuckoo-buds of yellow hue
   Do paint the meadows with delight.
        —SHAKESPEARE, *Love's Labour's Lost, V, 2*

FLY

The fly sat upon the axle-tree of the chariot-wheel, and
said, What a dust do I raise!
        —FRANCIS BACON, *Essays* (quoted from Aesop)

The wanton boy that kills a fly
Shall feel the spider's enmity.
>> —BLAKE, *Auguries of Innocence*

Dead flies cause the ointment of the apothecary to send
forth a stinking savour.
>> —OLD TESTAMENT, *Ecclesiastes, X, 1*
>> (Hence, "A fly in the ointment.")

Busy, curious, thirsty fly,
Drink with me, and drink as I;
Freely welcome to my cup,
Couldst thou sip and sip it up.
Make the most of life you may;
Life is short and wears away.
>> —WILLIAM OLDYS, *On a Fly Drinking Out of a Cup of Ale*

Baby bye, here's a fly,
Let us watch him, you and I.
>> How he crawls up the walls
>> Yet he never falls.   —THEODORE TILTON, *Baby Bye*

FLYING

For I dipt into the future, far as human eye could see,
Saw the Vision of the world, and all the wonder that
>> would be.
Saw the heavens fill with commerce, argosies of magic
>> sails,
Pilots of the purple twilight, dropping down with costly
>> bales;
Heard the heavens fill with shouting, and there rain'd a
>> ghastly dew
From the nations' airy navies grappling in the central
>> blue.   —TENNYSON, *Locksley Hall*

FOG

The fog comes
on little cat feet.

It sits looking
over the harbor and city
on silent haunches
and then, moves on.   —CARL SANDBURG, *Fog*

FOOL

Let a fool be made serviceable according to his folly.
          —JOSEPH CONRAD, *Under Western Eyes*

But when we play the fool, how wide
The theatre expands! beside,
How long the audience sits before us!
How many prompters! what a chorus!   —LANDOR, *Plays*

Answer a fool according to his folly, lest he be wise in
his own conceit.   —OLD TESTAMENT, *Proverbs, XXVI, 5*

Then I saw that wisdom excelleth folly, as far as light
excelleth darkness. The wise man's eyes are in his head;
but the fool walketh in darkness.
          —OLD TESTAMENT, *Ecclesiastes, II, 13*

. . . fools rush in where angels fear to tread.
          —POPE, *Essay on Criticism, III*

What fools these mortals be!
  —SHAKESPEARE, *A Midsummer-Night's Dream, III, 2*

Earth bears no balsam for mistakes;
  Men crown the knave and scourge the tool
That did his will; but Thou, O God,
  Be merciful to me, a fool!
          —E. R. SILL, *The Fool's Prayer*

Hain't we got all the fools in town on our side? And
hain't that a big enough majority in any town?
          —MARK TWAIN, *Huckleberry Finn*

At thirty man suspects himself a fool;
Knows it at forty, and reforms his plan;
At fifty chides his infamous delay,
Pushes his prudent purpose to resolve;
In all the magnanimity of thought
Resolves; and re-resolves; then dies the same.
—EDWARD YOUNG, *Night Thoughts*

FOOL'S PARADISE

Into a Limbo large and broad, since call'd
The Paradise of Fools, to few unknown.
—MILTON, *Paradise Lost, III*

FOOT

My feet, they haul me Round the House,
    They Hoist me up the Stairs;
I only have to steer them, and
    They Ride me Everywheres.
—GELETT BURGESS, *My Feet*

A foot more light, a step more true,
Ne'er from the heath-flower dashed the dew;
E'en the slight harebell raised its head,
Elastic from her airy tread.   —SCOTT, *Lady of the Lake*

Her feet beneath her petticoat,
Like little mice, stole in and out,
  As if they feared the light.
—SUCKLING, *Ballad Upon a Wedding*

FORCE

Every body perseveres in its state of rest or of uniform
motion in a straight line, except in so far as it is compelled
to change that state by impressed forces.
—ISAAC NEWTON, *Principia* (First Law of Motion)

FOREIGN

By foreign hands thy dying eyes were closed,
By foreign hands thy decent limbs composed,
By foreign hands thy humble grave adorn'd,
By strangers honour'd, and by strangers mourn'd.
　　—POPE, *Elegy to the Memory of an Unfortunate Lady*

Foreigners are contemporary posterity.
　　—MADAME DE STAËL (quoted in Crocker's *Memoirs*)

Father, Mother and Me,
Sister and Auntie say
All the people like us are We,
And every one else is They.　　—KIPLING, *We and They*

FORGET

And the best and the worst of this is
　　That neither is most to blame,
If you've forgotten my kisses
　　And I've forgotten your name.
　　　　　　—SWINBURNE, *An Interlude*

FORGIVENESS

And throughout all Eternity
　　I forgive you, you forgive me.　　—BLAKE, *Broken Love*

Forgive us our trespasses, as we forgive those that tres-
pass against us.
　　　　　—BOOK OF COMMON PRAYER, *The Lord's Prayer*

Good to forgive;
　　Best to forget!
Living, we fret;
Dying, we live.
　　　　　　—R. BROWNING, *La Saisiaz:* Dedication

Nobuddy ever fergits where he buried a hatchet.
　　　　　—KIN HUBBARD, *Abe Martin's Broadcast*

Father, forgive them; for they know not what they do.
    —NEW TESTAMENT, *Luke, XXIII, 34*

Forgive us our debts, as we forgive our debtors.
    —NEW TESTAMENT, *Matthew, VI, 12*

FORTUNE

Fortune never seems so blind as to those upon whom she
has bestowed no favors.
    —LA ROCHEFOUCAULD, *Maxims,* 391

Dame Fortune is a fickle gipsy,
And always blind, and often tipsy;
Sometimes for years and years together,
She'll bless you with the sunniest weather,
Bestowing honour, pudding, pence,
You can't imagine why or whence;—
Then in a moment Presto, Pass!—
Your joys are withered like the grass.
    —W. M. PRAED, *The Legend of the Haunted Tree*

Let us sit and mock the good housewife fortune from
her wheel, that her gifts may henceforth be bestowed
equally.   —SHAKESPEARE, *As You Like It, I, 2*

Fortune favors the bold.
(*Audentis Fortuna juvat.*)   —VIRGIL, *Aeneid, X*

FOX

Like Aesop's fox, when he had lost his tail, would have
all his fellow foxes cut off theirs.
    —BURTON, *Anatomy of Melancholy*

The little foxes, that spoil the vines.
    —OLD TESTAMENT, *Song of Solomon*

FRANKLIN, BENJAMIN

I succeed him; no one could replace him.
—THOMAS JEFFERSON, on being made envoy to France

He snatched the thunderbolt from heaven, the sceptre from tyrants.
(Eripuit coelo fulmen, mox sceptra tyrannis.)
—A. R. J. TURGOT, Inscription for Houdon's bust, 1778

FREEDOM

My angel—his name is Freedom—
  Choose him to be your King;
He shall cut pathways east and west,
  And fend you with his wing.
                              —EMERSON, *Boston Hymn*

Aye, call it holy ground,
  The soil where first they trod!
They left unstained what there they found—
  Freedom to worship God.
—FELICIA D. HEMANS, *Landing of the Pilgrim Fathers*

Off with the fetters
That chafe and restrain!
Off with the chain!   —RICHARD HOVEY, *Vagabondia*

In the beauty of the lilies Christ was born across the sea,
With a glory in his bosom that transfigures you and me;
As he died to make men holy, let us die to make men
    free,
  While God is marching on.
    —JULIA WARD HOWE, *Battle Hymn of the Republic*

If I have freedom in my love,
  And in my soul am free,
Angels alone that soar above
  Enjoy such liberty.
                    —LOVELACE, *To Althea from Prison*

They can only set free men free . . .
And there is no need of that:
Free men set themselves free.
                    —JAMES OPPENHEIM, *The Slave*

  O Freedom! if to me belong
  Nor mighty Milton's gift divine
  Nor Marvell's wit and graceful song,
  Still with a love as deep and strong
As theirs, I lay, like them, my best gifts on thy shrine!
                    —WHITTIER, *Proem*

FRIEND

  Love is only chatter,
  Friends are all that matter.
                    —GELETT BURGESS, *Willy and the Lady*

Should auld acquaintance be forgot,
  And never brought to min'?
Should auld acquaintance be forgot,
  And days o' auld lang syne? —BURNS, *Auld Lang Syne*

I would not enter on my list of friends,
(Though grac'd with polish'd manners and fine sense
Yet wanting sensibility) the man
Who needlessly sets foot upon a worm.
                    —COWPER, *The Task*

Elysium is as far as to
The very nearest room,
If in that room a friend await
Felicity or doom.   —EMILY DICKINSON, *Poems, III*

He who has a thousand friends has not a friend to spare,
And he who has one enemy shall meet him everywhere.
—EMERSON, *Conduct of Life* (Emerson attributes this to
                    Omar Khayyám)

He gain'd from Heav'n ('twas all he wish'd) a friend.
—GRAY, *Elegy Written in a Country Churchyard*

Green be the turf above thee,
   Friend of my better days!
None knew thee but to love thee,
   Nor named thee but to praise.
   —FITZ-GREENE HALLECK, *On Joseph Rodman Drake*

Friend of my bosom, thou more than a brother,
Why wert thou not born in my father's dwelling?
   —CHARLES LAMB, *The Old Familiar Faces*

When I remember all
   The friends, so link'd together,
I've seen around me fall,
   Like leaves in wintry weather,
      I feel like one
      Who treads alone
Some banquet-hall deserted . . .
   —MOORE, *Oft in the Stilly Night*

Thou wert my guide, philosopher, and friend.
   —POPE, *Essay on Man, IV*

Those friends thou hast, and their adoption tried,
Grapple them to thy soul with hoops of steel.
   —SHAKESPEARE, *Hamlet, I, 3*

Against a foe I can myself defend,—
But Heaven protect me from a blundering friend!
   —D'ARCY W. THOMPSON, *Sales Attici*

As old wood is best to burn, old horse to ride, old books
to read, and old wine to drink, so are old friends always
most trusty to use.
   —LEONARD WRIGHT, *Display of Dutie* (1589)

FRIENDSHIP

Friendship, peculiar boon of Heav'n,
   The noble mind's delight and pride,
To men and angels only giv'n,
   To all the lower world denied.
                    —SAMUEL JOHNSON, *Friendship: An Ode*

Most friendship is feigning, most loving mere folly.
                    —SHAKESPEARE, *As You Like It, II, 7*

FRUITS

Ye shall know them by their fruits. Do men gather
grapes of thorns, or figs of thistles?
                    —NEW TESTAMENT, *Matthew, VII, 16*

FUN

I've taken my fun where I've found it;
   I've rogued an' I've ranged in my time;
I've 'ad my pickin' o' sweethearts,
   An' four o' the lot was prime.   —KIPLING, *The Ladies*

FURY

Beware the fury of a patient man.
                    —DRYDEN, *Absalom and Achitophel, I*

FUTURE

I never think of the future. It comes soon enough.
                    —ALBERT EINSTEIN, Interview, Dec., 1930

Heav'n from all creatures hides the Book of Fate,
All but the page prescribed. their present state:
From brutes what men, from men what spirits know;
Or who could suffer being here below?
                    —POPE, *Essay on Man*

For I dipt into the future, far as human eye could see,
Saw the Vision of the world and all the wonder that
would be.   —TENNYSON, *Locksley Hall*

GALILEAN

Thou hast conquered, O pale Galilean; the world has
grown grey from Thy breath;
We have drunken of things Lethean, and fed on the
fulness of death.   —SWINBURNE, *Hymn to Proserpine*

GAMBLING

In my schooldays, when I had lost one shaft,
I shot his fellow of the self-same flight
The self-same way, with more advised watch,
To find the other forth; and by advent'ring both
I oft found both.
            —SHAKESPEARE, *Merchant of Venice, I, 1*

There are two times in a man's life when he should not
speculate: when he can't afford it, and when he can.
            —MARK TWAIN, *Pudd'nhead Wilson's Calendar*

It is the child of avarice, the brother of iniquity, and the
father of mischief.
      —GEORGE WASHINGTON, Letter to Bushod Washington

And once or twice to throw the dice
   Is a gentlemanly game,
But he does not win who plays with Sin
   In the secret House of Shame.
            —OSCAR WILDE, *The Ballad of Reading Gaol*

GAME

The game is not worth the candle.
(*Le jeu ne vaut pas la chandelle.*)
                  —MONTAIGNE, *Essays, II*

For when the One Great Scorer comes to write against
　　your name,
He marks—not that you won or lost—but how you played
　　the game.　　　—GRANTLAND RICE, *Alumnus Football*

GARDEN

God Almighty first planted a garden. And, indeed, it is
the purest of human pleasures.

—FRANCIS BACON, *Essays: Of Gardens*

The kiss of the sun for pardon,
　　The song of the birds for mirth,
One is nearer God's Heart in a garden
　　Than anywhere else on earth.

—DOROTHY F. GURNEY, *God's Garden*

I walk down the garden paths,
And all the daffodils
Are blowing, and the bright blue squills.
I walk down the patterned garden paths
In my stiff brocaded gown.
With my powdered hair, and jewelled fan,
I too am a rare
Pattern. As I wander down
The garden paths.　　　—AMY LOWELL, *Patterns*

The best place to seek God is in a garden. You can dig
for Him there.

—BERNARD SHAW, *Adventures of the Black Girl . . .*

Come into the garden, Maud,
　　For the black bat, night, has flown.

—TENNYSON, *Maud, I*

That is well said, replied Candide, but we must cultivate
our garden.

(. . . *il faut cultiver notre jardin.*)　　—VOLTAIRE, *Candide*

GENIUS

Doing easily what others find difficult is talent; doing what is impossible *for talent* is genius.
—AMIEL, *Journal,* Dec. 17, 1856

The eagle never lost so much time as when he submitted to learn of the crow.   —BLAKE, *Proverbs of Hell*

Great wits are sure to madness near allied,
And thin partitions do their bounds divide.
—DRYDEN, *Absalom and Achitophel, I*

Genius is one per cent inspiration and ninety-nine per cent perspiration.
—THOMAS A. EDISON, Newspaper Interview, 1931

Gift, like genius, I often think means only an infinite capacity for taking pains.
—JANE E. HOPKINS, *Work Amongst Working Men*

Talk not of genius baffled. Genius is master of man.
Genius does what it must, and Talent does what it can.
—OWEN MEREDITH, *Last Words of a Sensitive
Second-rate Poet*

Genius, cried the commuter,
As he ran for the 8:13,
Consists of an infinite capacity
For catching trains.
—CHRISTOPHER MORLEY, *The Commuter*

When a true genius appears in the world, you may know him by this sign, that the dunces are all in a confederacy against him.   —SWIFT, *Thoughts on Various Subjects*

I have nothing to declare except my genius.
—OSCAR WILDE, To revenue officers in America, 1882

GENTLEMAN

> When Adam dolve and Eve span
> Who was then the gentleman?
> —JOHN BALL, During Wat Tyler's Rebellion, 1381

> "My father's trade!—why, blockhead, art thou mad?
> My father, sir, did never stoop so low;
> He was a Gentleman, I'd have you know."
>   "Excuse the liberty I take,"
>   Modestus said, with archness on his brow—
> "Pray, why did not your father make
>   A Gentleman of you?"
>   —SELLECK OSBORN, *The Modest Retort*

GEORGES, THE FOUR

> I sing the Georges Four,
> For Providence could stand no more.
> Some say that far the worst
> Of all the Four was George the First.
> But yet by some 'tis reckoned
> That worser still was George the Second.
> And what mortal ever heard
> Any good of George the Third?

> When George the Fourth from earth descended,
> Thank God the line of Georges ended.
> —LANDOR, *Epigram* (after hearing Thackeray's lectures
>   on the Georges)

GERMANY

> Wherever Germany extends her sway, she ruins culture.
>   —NIETZSCHE, *Ecce Homo*

> Germany, the diseased world's bathhouse.
>   —MARK TWAIN, *Autobiography, I*

Destroyed by German fury, rebuilt by American generosity.—WHITNEY WARREN, Inscription for Louvain library

GHOST

I am thy father's spirit,
Doom'd for a certain time to walk the night.
—SHAKESPEARE, *Hamlet, I, 5*

The time has been
That when the brains were out, the man would die,
And there an end; but now they rise again,
With twenty mortal murders on their crowns.
—SHAKESPEARE, *Macbeth, III, 4*

GIANT

There were giants in the earth in those days.
—OLD TESTAMENT, *Genesis, VI, 4*

GIRL

There was a little girl
Who had a little curl
    Right in the middle of her forehead,
And when she was good
She was very, very good,
    And when she was bad she was horrid.
—LONGFELLOW (quoted by E. W. Longfellow,
Random Memories)

Men seldom makes passes
At girls who wear glasses.
—DOROTHY PARKER, *News Item*

What are little girls made of . . . ?
Sugar and spice and all things nice,
And such are little girls made of.
—SOUTHEY, *What All the World Is Made Of*

GIVING

Not what we give, but what we share,
For the gift without the giver is bare.
—J. R. LOWELL, *Vision of Sir Launfal, II*

That is no true alms which the hand can hold;
He gives only the worthless gold
   Who gives from a sense of duty.
         —J. R. Lowell, *Vision of Sir Launfal, I*

Go and sell that thou hast, and give to the poor, and
thou shalt have treasure in heaven.
         —New Testament, *Matthew, XIX, 21*

God loveth a cheerful giver.
         —New Testament, *II Corinthians, IX, 7*

It is more blessed to give than to receive.
         —New Testament, *Acts, XX, 35*

Behold, I do not give lectures or a little charity,
When I give I give myself.
         —Walt Whitman, *Song of Myself*

GLADIATOR

I see before me the Gladiator lie:
He leans upon his hand—his manly brow
Consents to death, but conquers agony, . . .
         —Byron, *Childe Harold, IV*

GLORY

What Price Glory?
         —Maxwell Anderson and Laurence Stallings,
                      Title of play, 1924

Go where glory waits thee;
But, while fame elates thee,
   O, still remember me!
         —Thomas Moore, *Go Where Glory Waits Thee*

Sound, sound the clarion, fill the fife,
   To all the sensual world proclaim

One crowded hour of glorious life
  Is worth an age without a name.
  —T. O. MORDAUNT, *Verses Written During the War,*
                                        1756-1763

The nearest way to glory is to strive to be what you wish
to be thought to be.   —SOCRATES (quoted by Cicero)

So Passes away the glory of the world.
(*Sic transit gloria mundi.*)
  —THOMAS à KEMPIS, *De Imitatione Christi* (phrase used
                            when a new Pope is installed)

GOD

Nearer, my God, to Thee,
  Nearer to Thee!
E'en though it be a cross
  That raiseth me. —SARAH F. ADAMS, *Nearer to Thee*

A picket frozen on duty—
  A mother starved for her brood—
Socrates drinking the hemlock,
  And Jesus on the rood;
And millions who humble and nameless,
  The strait hard pathway trod—
Some call it Consecration,
  And others call it God. —W. H. CARRUTH, *Evolution*

God moves in a mysterious way
  His wonders to perform;
He plants his footsteps in the sea
  And rides upon the storm.
                    —COWPER, *Light Shining out of Darkness*

Father expected a good deal of God. He didn't actually
accuse God of inefficiency, but when he prayed his tone

was loud and angry, like that of a dissatisfied guest in a
carelessly managed hotel.

—CLARENCE DAY, *God and My Father*

God is incorporeal, divine, supreme, infinite Mind, Spirit,
Soul, Principle, Life, Truth, Love.

—MARY BAKER EDDY, *Science and Health*

"Isn't God upon the ocean
    Just the same as on the land?"

JAMES T. FIELDS, *Ballad of the Tempest*

God is not a cosmic bell-boy for whom we can press a
button to get things.   —HARRY EMERSON FOSDICK, *Prayer*

Holy, Holy, Holy, Lord God Almighty!
    Early in the morning our song shall rise to Thee;
Holy, Holy, Holy, Merciful and Mighty!
    God in Three Persons, blessed Trinity!

—REGINALD HEBER, *Holy, Holy, Holy*

To the greater glory of God.
(*Ad majorem Dei gloriam.*)

—MOTTO of the Society of Jesus

Praise God from whom all Blessings flow;
Praise Him all creatures here below;
Praise Him above, ye Heavenly Host;
Praise Father, Son, and Holy Ghost.

—THOMAS KEN, *Morning and Evening Hymn* (1709)

An' you've gut to git up airly
    Ef you want to take in God.

—J. R. LOWELL, *The Biglow Papers*

A mighty fortress is our God,
    A bulwark never failing.

(*Ein feste Burg ist unser Gott*
  Ein gute Wehr und Waffen.)
                    —MARTIN LUTHER, *Ein feste Burg*

Abide with me: fast falls the even-tide;
The darkness deepens: Lord with me abide:
When other helpers fail, and comforts flee,
Help of the helpless, O abide with me!
                    —HENRY F. LYTE, *Abide With Me*

There is no god but God.
(*La illah illa allah.*)   —MAHOMET, *Koran, III*

    God doth not need
Either man's work or his own gifts; who best
Bear his mild yoke, they serve him best; his state
Is kingly. Thousands at his bidding speed
And post o'er land and ocean without rest;
They also serve who only stand and wait.
                    —MILTON, *On His Blindness*

    What in me is dark,
Illumine; what is low, raise and support;
That to the height of this great argument
I may assert Eternal Providence,
And justify the ways of God to men.
                    —MILTON, *Paradise Lost, I*

God is love; and he that dwelleth in love dwelleth in
God, and God in him.   —NEW TESTAMENT, *I John, IV, 16*

God is no respecter of persons.
                    —NEW TESTAMENT, *Acts, X, 34*

If God is for us, who can be against us?
                    —NEW TESTAMENT, *Romans, VIII, 31*

Our Father which art in heaven.
(Pater noster, qui est in coelis.)
—NEW TESTAMENT, *Matthew, VI, 9*

Canst thou by searching find out God?
—OLD TESTAMENT, *Job, XI, 7*

God is our refuge and strength, a very present help in trouble.   —OLD TESTAMENT, *Psalms, XLVII*

He maketh me to lie down in green pastures: he leadeth me beside the still waters. He restoreth my soul: he leadeth me in the path of righteousness for his name's sake.
—OLD TESTAMENT, *Psalms, XXIII*

Let us hear the conclusion of the whole matter: Fear God, and keep his commandments: for this is the whole duty of man.   —OLD TESTAMENT, *Ecclesiastes, XII, 13*

Though he slay me, yet will I trust him.
—OLD TESTAMENT, *Job, XIII, 5*

Suppose I had found a watch upon the ground. . . . The mechanism being observed, . . . the watch must have a maker; . . .   —WILLIAM PALEY, *Natural Theology*

God is truth and light his shadow.
—PLATO, *The Republic*

Thou Great First Cause, least understood,
    Who all my sense confin'd
To know but this, that thou art good,
    And that myself am blind.   —POPE, *Universal Prayer*

Man proposes, but God disposes.
(Homo proponit, sed Deus disponit.)
—THOMAS à KEMPIS, *De Imitatione Christi, I*

If God did not exist, it would be necessary to invent him.
—VOLTAIRE, Epistle to the author of *Livres des trois
Imposteurs*

O God, our help in ages past,
   Our hope for years to come,
Our shelter from the stormy blast,
   And our eternal home.
—ISAAC WATTS, *The Psalms of David*

Yet, in the maddening maze of things,
   And tossed by storm and flood,
To one fixed trust my spirit clings;
   I know that God is good.
—WHITTIER, *The Eternal Goodness*

... trailing clouds of glory do we come
From God, who is our home.
—WORDSWORTH, *Intimations of Immortality*

GOLD

Gold begets in brethren hate;
Gold in families debate;
Gold does friendship separate;
Gold does civil wars create.
—ABRAHAM COWLEY, *Anacreontics: Gold*

Every door is barred with gold, and opens but to golden
   keys.   —TENNYSON, *Locksley Hall*

O love of gold! thou meanest of amours!
—EDWARD YOUNG, *Night Thoughts*

GOLD, CROSS OF

I shall not help crucify mankind upon a cross of gold. I
shall not aid in pressing down upon the brow of labor this
crown of thorns.

—WILLIAM J. BRYAN, Speech, 1894 and 1896

GOLDEN RULE

Therefore all things whatsoever ye would that men should do unto you, do ye even so unto them.
—NEW TESTAMENT, *Matthew, VII, 12*

The golden rule is that there is no golden rule.
—BERNARD SHAW, *Maxims for Revolutionists*

Do unto the other feller the way he'd like to do unto you, an' do it fust. —E. N. WESTCOTT, *David Harum*

GOOD

Prove all things; hold fast that which is good.
—NEW TESTAMENT, *I Thessalonians, V, 21*

'Tis only noble to be good.
—TENNYSON, *Lady Clara Vere de Vere*

Be good and you will be lonesome.
—MARK TWAIN, *Following the Equator*

GOOD AND BAD

Here's to you, as good as you are,
And here's to me, as bad as I am;
But as good as you are, and as bad as I am,
I am as good as you are, as bad as I am.
—ANON., Old Scotch toast

There is no Good, there is no Bad; these be the whims of mortal will:
That works me weal that I call "good," what harms and hurts me I hold as "ill."
—SIR RICHARD BURTON, *The Kasidah*

Abhor that which is evil; cleave to that which is good.
—NEW TESTAMENT, *Romans, XII, 9*

Woe unto them that call evil good, and good evil; that put darkness for light, and light for darkness; and put bitter for sweet, and sweet for bitter!

—OLD TESTAMENT, *Isaiah, V, 20*

There is some soul of goodness in things evil,
Would men observingly distil it out.

—SHAKESPEARE, *Henry V, IV, 1*

O, yet we trust that somehow good
    Will be the final goal of ill,
    To pangs of nature, sins of will,
Defects of doubt, and taints of blood.

—TENNYSON, *In Memoriam*

Roaming in thought over the Universe, I saw the little
    that is Good steadily hastening towards immortality,
And the vast all that is call'd Evil I saw hastening to
    merge itself and become lost and dead.

—WALT WHITMAN, *Roaming in Thought*

GOODNESS

The man of upright life and free from sin needs no Moorish bow, nor dart, nor quiver bearing poison and death.

(Integer vitae scelerisque purus
Non eget Mauris jaculis neque arcu
Nec venenatis gravida sagittis,
*   fusce, pharetra.)*   —HORACE, *Odes, I, 22*

It is not growing like a tree
In bulk, doth make man better be;
Or standing long an oak, three hundred year,
To fall a log at last, dry, bald, and sere;
                —BEN JONSON, *Pindaric Ode to . . .*

Be good, sweet maid, and let who can be clever;
    Do noble things, not dream them all day long;

And so make life, and death, and that vast forever,
One grand sweet song.
—CHARLES KINGSLEY, *A Farewell*

Do all the good you can,
By all the means you can,
In all the ways you can,
In all the places you can,
At all the times vou can,
To all the people you can,
As long as ever you can.

—JOHN WESLEY, *His Rule*

GOVERNMENT

The whole of government consists in the art of being honest.   —THOMAS JEFFERSON, *Works, VI, 186*

Government of the people, by the people, for the people.
—ABRAHAM LINCOLN, Gettysburg Address

No man is good enough to govern another man without that other's consent.
—ABRAHAM LINCOLN, Lincoln-Douglas debate

Every country has the government it deserves.
—JOSEPH DE MAISTRE, Letter, Aug., 1811

Government, even in its best state, is but a necessary evil; in its worst state, an intolerable one.
—THOMAS PAINE, *Common Sense*

GRACE

An outward and visible sign of an inward and spiritual grace.   —BOOK OF COMMON PRAYER, *Catechism*

There, but for the grace of God, goes John Bradford.
—JOHN BRADFORD, On seeing a criminal led to execution

GRAMMAR

>For all your rhetorician's rules
>Teach nothing but to name his tools.
>
>—BUTLER, *Hudibras*, *I*

>Any fool can make a rule
>And every fool will mind it.
>
>—THOREAU, *Journal*, Feb. 3, 1860

GRAPES

>The fathers have eaten sour grapes, and the children's teeth are set on edge.
>
>—OLD TESTAMENT, *Ezekiel*, *XVIII*, *2*

GRASS

>I am tired of four walls and a ceiling;
>I have need of the grass.
>
>—RICHARD HOVEY, *Along the Trail: Spring*

>Pile the bodies high at Austerlitz and Waterloo.
>Shovel them under and let me work—
>I am the grass: I cover all.   —CARL SANDBURG, *Grass*

GRATITUDE

>Gratitude is the memory of the heart.
>
>—J. B. MASSIEU, Letter to the Abbé Sicard

>Two kinds of gratitude: the sudden kind
>We feel for what we take, the larger kind
>We feel for what we give.
>
>—E. A. ROBINSON, *Captain Craig*

>Gratitude is a lively sense of future favors.
>
>—SIR ROBERT WALPOLE (modified from La Rochefoucauld)

GRAVE

The boast of heraldry, the pomp of pow'r,
  And all that beauty, all that wealth e'er gave,
Awaits alike th' inevitable hour.
  The paths of glory lead but to the grave.
        —GRAY, *Elegy Written in a Country Churchyard*

Our hearts, though stout and brave,
  Still like muffled drums are beating
Funeral marches to the grave.
                —LONGFELLOW, *A Psalm of Life*

The grave's a fine and private place,
But none, I think, do there embrace.
        —ANDREW MARVELL, *To His Coy Mistress*

For rain it hath a friendly sound
To one who's six feet underground;
And scarce the friendly voice or face:
A grave is such a quiet place.
        —EDNA ST. VINCENT MILLAY, *Renascence*

Man goeth to his long home.
              —OLD TESTAMENT, *Ecclesiastes, XII, 5*

There are three things that are never satisfied, yea, four
things say not, It is enough: The grave; and the barren
womb; the earth that is not filled with water; and the fire
that saith not, It is enough.
                —OLD TESTAMENT, *Proverbs, XXX, 15*

There the wicked cease from troubling, and there the
weary be at rest.   —OLD TESTAMENT, *Job, III, 17*

GRAVEYARD

Beneath those rugged elms, that yew-tree's shade,
  Where heaves the turf in many a mouldering heap,

Each in his narrow cell for ever laid,
> The rude forefathers of the hamlet sleep.
>> —GRAY, *Elegy Written in a Country Churchyard*

GREATNESS

How dreary to be somebody!
How public, like a frog
To tell your name the livelong day
To an admiring bog!   —EMILY DICKINSON, *Poems, I*

The heights by great men reached and kept
> Were not attained by sudden flight,
But they, while their companions slept,
> Were toiling upward in the night.
>> —LONGFELLOW, *The Ladder of St. Augustine*

That man is great, and he alone,
Who serves a greatness not his own,
> For neither praise nor pelf:
Content to know and be unknown:
> Whole in himself. —OWEN MEREDITH, *A Great Man*

The great are only great because we are on our knees.
Let us rise!   —P. J. PROUDHON, *Revolutions of Paris: Motto*

But be not afraid of greatness: some are born great, some
achieve greatness and some have greatness thrust upon 'em.
>> —SHAKESPEARE, *Twelfth Night, II, 5*

Why, man, he doth bestride the narrow world
Like a Colossus, and we petty men
Walk under his huge legs and peep about
To find ourselves dishonourable graves.
>> —SHAKESPEARE, *Julius Caesar, I, 2*

Ah vanity of vanities!
> How wayward the decrees of fate are,

How very weak the very wise,
   How very small the very great are!
               —THACKERAY, *Vanitas Vanitatum*

GREECE

The isles of Greece, the isles of Greece!
   Where burning Sappho loved and sung,
Where grew the arts of war and peace,
   Where Delos rose, and Phoebus sprung!
Eternal summer gilds them yet,
But all, except their sun is set.   —BYRON, *Don Juan, III*

The mountains look on Marathon—
   And Marathon looks on the sea;
And musing there an hour alone,
   I dream'd that Greece might still be free.
               —BYRON, *Don Juan, III*

Achilles' wrath, to Greece the direful spring,
Of woes unnumber'd, heav'nly Goddess, sing!
          —HOMER, *Iliad, I, 1* (Pope trans.)

On desperate seas long wont to roam,
   Thy hyacinth hair, thy classic face,
Thy Naiad airs, have brought me home
   To the glory that was Greece
   And the grandeur that was Rome.   —POE, *To Helen*

GREEKS

I fear the Greeks, even when bringing gifts.
(*Timeo Danaos et dona ferentis.*)   —VIRGIL, *Aeneid, II*

GRENADIER, BRITISH

Some talk of Alexander, and some of Hercules;
Of Hector and Lysander, and such great names as these;

But of all the world's brave heroes there's none that can
compare
With a tow, row, row, row, row, row, for the British
Grenadier.   —ANON., *The British Grenadier*

Who comes here?
    A Grenadier.
What does he want?
    A pot of beer.   —DICKENS, *Our Mutual Friend*

GRIEF

No blessed leisure for love or hope
But only time for grief.
                              —THOMAS HOOD, *The Song of the Shirt*

I sometimes hold it half a sin
    To put in words the grief I feel;
    For words like Nature half reveal
And half conceal the Soul within.
                              —TENNYSON, *In Memoriam*

GUEST

For I, who hold sage Homer's rule the best,
Welcome the coming, speed the parting guest.
                              —POPE, *Satires, II*

"GUNGA DIN"

Though I've belted you and flayed you,
By the livin' Gawd that made you,
You're a better man than I am, Gunga Din.
                              —KIPLING, *Gunga Din*

HABIT

Habit with him was all the test of truth;
"It must be right: I've done it from my youth."
                              —GEORGE CRABBE, *The Borough*

Habit is the enormous fly-wheel of society, its most precious conservative agent.
—WILLIAM JAMES, Psychology, I

HAIR

My hair is gray, but not with years,
  Nor grew it white
  In a single night,
As men's have grown with sudden fears.
—BYRON, The Prisoner of Chillon

Babies haven't any hair;
Old men's heads are just as bare;—
Between the cradle and the grave
Lies a haircut and a shave.
—SAMUEL HOFFENSTEIN, Songs of Faith
in the Year after Next

Not ten yoke of oxen
Have the power to draw us
Like a woman's hair.
—LONGFELLOW, The Saga of King Olaf

HANDS

Pale hands I loved beside the Shalimar,
Where are you now? Who lies beneath your spell?
—LAURENCE HOPE, Kashmiri Song

His hand will be against every man, and every man's hand against him. —OLD TESTAMENT, Genesis, XVI, 12

The voice is Jacob's voice, but the hands are the hands of Esau. —OLD TESTAMENT, Genesis, XXVII, 22

All the perfumes of Arabia will not sweeten this little hand.
—SHAKESPEARE, Macbeth, V, 1

See how she leans her cheek upon her hand!
O, that I were a glove upon that hand,
That I might touch that cheek!
                    —SHAKESPEARE, *Romeo and Juliet, II, 2*

Will all great Neptune's ocean wash this blood
Clean from my hand? No, this my hand will rather
The multitudinous seas incarnadine,
Making the green one red.
                    —SHAKESPEARE, *Macbeth, II, 2*

HANGING

We must all hang together, else we shall all hang separately.
            —BENJAMIN FRANKLIN, To the others, at the signing
                    of the Declaration of Independence

And naked to the hangman's noose
    The morning clocks will ring
A neck God made for other use
    Than strangling in a string.
                    —A. E. HOUSMAN, *A Shropshire Lad*

For they're hangin' Danny Deever, you can hear the
    Dead March play,
The regiment's in 'ollow square—they're hangin' him to-
    day;
They've taken of his buttons off an' cut his stripes away,
    An' they're hangin' Danny Deever in the mornin'.
                    —KIPLING, *Danny Deever*

HAPPINESS

That action is best which procures the greatest happiness
for the greatest numbers.
—FRANCIS HUTCHESON, *An Inquiry into . . . Beauty and
                                        Virtue*

Happiness is the only good, reason the only torch, justice the only worship, humanity the only religion, and love the only priest.—R. G. INGERSOLL, *A Tribute to Eben Ingersoll*

Glad that I live am I;
That the sky is blue;
Glad for the country lanes,
And the fall of dew.
            —LIZETTE W. REESE, *A Little Song of Life*

O, how bitter a thing it is to look into happiness through another man's eyes! —SHAKESPEARE, *As You Like It*, V, 2

You have no more right to consume happiness without producing it than to consume wealth without producing it.
            —BERNARD SHAW, *Candida*, I

Ye seek for happiness—alas, the day!
Ye find it not in luxury nor in gold,
Nor in the fame, nor in the envied sway
For which, O willing slaves to Custom old,
Severe taskmistress! ye your hearts have sold.
            —SHELLEY, *The Revolt of Islam*, XI

HAPPY

Oh, make us happy and you make us good.
            —R. BROWNING, *The Ring and the Book*, IV

Now the heart is so full that a drop overfills it,
We are happy now because God wills it.
            —J. R. LOWELL, *The Vision of Sir Launfal*, Prelude

HARMONY

From harmony, from heavenly harmony
    This universal Frame began:
    From harmony to harmony

Through all the compass of the notes it ran,
The diapason closing full in Man.
                    —DRYDEN, *A Song for St. Cecelia's Day*

HARP

The harp that once through Tara's halls
    The soul of music shed,
Now hangs as mute on Tara's walls
    As if that soul were fled.
                    —THOMAS MOORE, *The Harp That Once . . .*

We hanged our harps upon the willows.
                    —OLD TESTAMENT, *Psalms, CXXXVII, 2*

HARVARD

Fair Harvard! Thy sons to thy jubilee throng,
    And with blessings surrender thee o'er,
By these festival rites, from the age that is passed,
    To the age that is waiting before.
                    —SAMUEL GILMAN, *Ode, Harvard Bicentennial*, 1836

HARVEST

. . . reaping where thou hast not sown, and gathering
where thou hast not strewed.
                    —NEW TESTAMENT, *Matthew, XXV, 24*

HASTE

Make haste slowly.
(*Festina lente.*) —EMPEROR AUGUSTUS (Suetonius' *Lives*)

HAT

As with my hat upon my head
    I walk'd along the Strand,
I there did meet another man
    With his hat in his hand.
                    —SAMUEL JOHNSON, A parody of Perry's
                    Hermit of Walkworth

HATE

Hating people is like burning down your own house to get rid of a rat.
—HARRY EMERSON FOSDICK, *The Wages of Hate*

For him who fain would teach the world
    The world holds hate in fee—
For Socrates, the hemlock cup;
    For Christ, Gethsemane.   —DON MARQUIS, *Wages*

Hated by fools, and fools to hate,
Be that my motto and my fate.   —SWIFT, *To Dr. Delany*

HEAD

And still they gaz'd, and still the wonder grew
That one small head could carry all he knew.
—GOLDSMITH, *The Deserted Village*

HEALTH

Every day, in every way, I am getting better and better.
—ÉMILE COUÉ, Formula of autosuggestion

Health is not a condition of matter, but of Mind; nor can the material senses bear reliable testimony on the subject of health.   —MARY BAKER EDDY, *Science and Health*

Early to bed and early to rise,
Makes a man healthy, wealthy and wise.
—FRANKLIN, *Poor Richard's Almanac* for 1758

O health! health! the blessing of the rich! the riches of the poor! who can buy thee at too dear a rate, since there is no enjoying this world without thee?
—BEN JONSON, *Volpone, II, 1*

The preservation of health is a duty. Few seem conscious that there is such a thing as physical morality.
—HERBERT SPENCER, *Education*

HEART

Maid of Athens, ere we part,
    Give, oh, give me back my heart!
Or, since that has left my breast,
    Keep it now, and take the rest! —BYRON, *Maid of Athens*

In the desert I saw a creature, naked, bestial,
Who, squatting upon the ground, Held his heart in his
    hand
And ate of it. I said, "Is it good, friend?"
"It is bitter—bitter," he answered; "But I like it
Because it is bitter, And because it is my heart."
                              —STEPHEN CRANE, *The Heart*

The heart of the fool is in his mouth, but the mouth of
the wise man is in his heart.
            —FRANKLIN, *Poor Richard's Almanac* for 1733

Bid me to live, and I will live
    Thy Protestant to be:
Or bid me love, and I will give
    A loving heart to thee.

A heart as soft, a heart as kind,
    A heart as sound and free
As in the whole world thou canst find,
    That heart I'll give to thee.
            —HERRICK, *To Anthea Who May Command Him
                                          Anything*

O hearts that break and give no sign
Save whitening lips and fading tresses.
                    —O. W. HOLMES, *The Voiceless*

When I was one-and-twenty
    I heard a wise man say:

"Give crowns and pounds and guineas
  But not your heart away."
                    —A. E. Housman, *A Shropshire Lad*

The head is always the dupe of the heart.
                    —La Rochefoucauld, *Maxims*, 102

No truer word, save God's, was ever spoken,
Than that the largest heart is soonest broken.
                    —Landor, *Epigrams*

Where your treasure is there will your heart be also.
                    —New Testament, *Luke, XII*, 34

He that is of merry heart hath a continual feast.
                    —Old Testament, *Proverbs, XV*, 15

The heart is deceitful above all things, and desperately
wicked.   —Old Testament, *Jeremiah, XVII*, 9

The heart has its reasons which reason does not know.
                    —Pascal, *Pensées, IV*

Ward has no heart, they say; but I deny it;—
He has a heart, and gets his speeches by it.
                    —Samuel Rogers, *On J. W. Ward*

My heart is like a singing bird
  Whose nest is in a water'd shoot;
My heart is like an apple-tree
  Whose boughs are bent with thick-set fruit;
My heart is like a rainbow shell
  That paddles in a halcyon sea;
My heart is gladder than all these,
  Because my love is come to me.
                    —Christina Rossetti, *A Birthday*

What stronger breastplate than a heart untainted!
—SHAKESPEARE, *Henry VI, II, III, 2*

I prithee send me back my heart,
    Since I cannot have thine:
For if from thine thou wilt not part,
    Why then shouldst thou have mine?
—SIR JOHN SUCKLING, *Song*

Kind hearts are more than coronets,
And simple faith than Norman blood.
—TENNYSON, *Lady Clara Vere de Vere*

HEAVEN

There is no Heaven, there is no Hell; these be the dreams
    of baby minds;

Tools of the wily Fetisheer, to fright the fools his cun-
    ning blinds.—SIR RICHARD BURTON, *The Kasidah, VIII*

One sweetly solemn thought
    Comes to me o'er and o'er;
I am nearer home to-day
    Than I ever have been before.
—PHOEBE CARY, *Nearer Home*

I never spoke with God,
Nor visited in heaven;
Yet certain am I of the spot
As if the chart were given.
—EMILY DICKINSON, *Poems, IV*

We are as near to heaven by sea as by land.
—SIR HUMPHREY GILBERT, Before his death at sea, 1583

Heaven is not reached by a single bound
    But we build the ladder by which we rise.
—J. G. HOLLAND, *Gradatim*

It was a childish ignorance,
  But now 'tis little joy,
To know I'm farther off from heaven
  Than when I was a boy.
              —THOMAS HOOD, *I Remember, I Remember*

For a cap and bells our loves we pay,
  Bubbles we buy with a whole soul's tasking:
'Tis heaven alone that is given away,
  'Tis only God may be had for the asking.
            —J. R. LOWELL, *The Vision of Sir Launfal*, Prelude

Not only around our infancy
Doth heaven with all its splendors lie;
Daily, with souls that cringe and plot,
We Sinais climb and know it not.
            —J. R. LOWELL, *The Vision of Sir Launfal*, Prelude

And I saw a new heaven and a new earth: for the first
heaven and the first earth were passed away; and there was
no more sea.   —NEW TESTAMENT, *Revelation, XXI, 1*

In my father's house are many mansions.
                    —NEW TESTAMENT, *John XIV, 2*

Lay up for yourselves treasures in heaven, where neither
moth nor rust doth corrupt and where thieves do not break
through nor steal.   —NEW TESTAMENT, *Matthew, VI, 20*

. . . strait is the gate and narrow is the way which leadeth unto life, and few there be that find it.
                  —NEW TESTAMENT, *Matthew, VII, 14*

The blessed damosel leaned out
  From the gold bar of Heaven.
                    —D. G. ROSSETTI, *The Blessed Damosel*

O world invisible, we view thee:
  O world intangible, we touch thee,
O world unknowable, we know thee,
  Inapprehensible, we clutch thee!
      —FRANCIS THOMPSON, *In No Strange Land*

There is a land of pure delight,
  Where saints immortal reign;
Infinite day excludes the night,
  And pleasures banish pain.
      —ISAAC WATTS, *There Is a Land*

HECUBA

What's Hecuba to him, or he to Hecuba?
      —SHAKESPEARE, *Hamlet, II, 2*

HELEN OF TROY

I hope there is a resurrection day
For bodies, as the ancient prophets say,
When Helen's naked limbs again will gleam
Regathered from the dust of death's long dream.
      —HARRY KEMP, *Resurrection*

Was this the face that launch'd a thousand ships,
And burnt the topless towers of Ilium?
Sweet Helen, make me immortal with a kiss.
      —MARLOWE, *Doctor Faustus*

HELL

Satan the envious said with a sigh:
Christians know more about their hell than I.
      —ALFRED KREYMBORG, *Envious Satan*

Here we may reign secure; and in my choice
To reign is worth ambition, though in Hell:
Better to reign in Hell, than serve in Heav'n.
      —MILTON, *Paradise Lost, I*

Which way I fly is Hell; myself am Hell;
And in the lowest depth a lower deep
Still threat'ning to devour me opens wide,
To which the Hell I suffer seems a Heav'n.
—MILTON, *Paradise Lost, IV*

Wide is the gate and broad is the way that leadeth to
destruction, and many there be which go in thereat:
—NEW TESTAMENT, *Matthew, VII, 13*

The descent to hell is easy.
(*Facilis descensus Averno.*)   —VIRGIL, *Aeneid, VI*

That's the greatest torture souls feel in hell:
In hell, that they must live and cannot die.
—JOHN WEBSTER, *Duchess of Malfi, IV, 1*

HELP

I'm learnin' one thing good. Learnin' it all a time, ever'
day. If you're in trouble, or hurt or need—go to the poor
people. They're the only ones that'll help—the only ones.
—JOHN STEINBECK, *The Grapes of Wrath*

HEN

A hen is only an egg's way of making another egg.
—SAMUEL BUTLER, *Life and Habit*

HERO

No man is a hero to his valet.
—MADAME DE CORNUEL (attributed to her
in Mlle Aissé's *Lettres*)

Many heroes lived before Agamemnon.
(*Vixere fortes ante Agamemnona multi.*)
—HORACE, *Odes, IV, 9*

In the world's broad field of battle,
In the bivouac of Life,

Be not like dumb, driven cattle!
  Be a hero in the strife!
                    —LONGFELLOW, *A Psalm of Life*

See the conquering hero comes!
Sound the trumpets, beat the drums!
            —DR. T. MOREL, in libretto for Handel's *Joshua*

Give honour to our heroes fall'n, how ill
Soe'er the cause that bade them forth to die.
                    —WILLIAM WATSON, *The English Dead*

HERO-WORSHIP

Hero-worship is strongest where there is least regard for human freedom.   —HERBERT SPENCER, *Social Statistics, IV*

HIGHBROW

A highbrow is a person educated beyond his intelligence.
                    —BRANDER MATTHEWS, *Epigrams*

HILL

The hills are going somewhere;
They have been on the way a long time.
They are like camels in a line
But they move more slowly.   —HILDA CONKLING, *Hills*

And I would love you all the day,
Every night would kiss and play,
If with me you'd fondly stray
Over the hills and far away.
                    —JOHN GAY, *The Beggars' Opera, I*

HISTORY

History is bunk.   —HENRY FORD

What is history but a fable agreed upon?
                    —NAPOLEON BONAPARTE, *Sayings*

The history of the world is the record of a man in quest
of his daily bread and butter.
>—H. W. VAN LOON, *The Story of Mankind*

HOME

Name me no names for my disease
With uninforming breath;
I tell you I am none of these,
But homesick unto death.
>—WITTER BYNNER, *The Patient to the Doctors*

'Tis sweet to hear the watch-dog's honest bark
  Bay deep-mouth'd welcome as we draw near home;
'Tis sweet to know there is an eye will mark
  Our coming, and look brighter when we come.
>—BYRON, *Don Juan, I*

Home is the place where, when you have to go there,
They have to take you in.
>—ROBERT FROST, *The Death of the Hired Man*

For them no more the blazing hearth shall burn,
  Or busy housewife ply her evening care;
Nor children run to lisp their sire's return,
  Or climb his knees the envied kiss to share.
>—GRAY, *Elegy Written in a Country Churchyard*

It takes a heap o' livin' in a house t' make it home
A heap o' sun an' shadder, an' ye sometimes have t' roam
Afore ye really 'preciate the things ye lef' behind,
An' hunger fer 'em somehow, with 'em allus on yer mind.
>—E. A. GUEST, *Home*

Oh, it was pitiful!
Near a whole city full
  Home she had none.
>—THOMAS HOOD, *The Bridge of Sighs*

The foxes have their holes, and the birds of the air have
their nests; but the Son of man hath not where to lay his
head.   —NEW TESTAMENT, *Matthew, VIII, 20*

'Mid pleasures and palaces though we may roam,
Be it ever so humble, there's no place like home.
                    —JOHN HOWARD PAYNE, *Home Sweet Home*

Happy the man, whose wish and care
    A few paternal acres bound,
Content to breathe his native air
    In his own ground.   —POPE, *Ode on Solitude*

Type of the wise, who soar, but never roam—
True to the kindred points of Heaven and Home.
                    —WORDSWORTH, *To a Skylark*

HOMER

Seven cities warred for Homer, being dead,
Who, living, had no roof to shroud his head.
                    —THOMAS HEYWOOD, *On Homer's Birthplace*

I, too, am indignant when the worthy Homer nods, but
in a long work it is allowable to snatch a little sleep.
                    —HORACE, *Ars Poetica*

Much have I travelled in the realms of gold,
And many goodly states and kingdoms seen;
Round many western islands have I been
Which bards in fealty to Apollo hold.
Oft of one wide expanse had I been told
That deep-browed Homer ruled as his demesne:
                    —KEATS, *On First Looking into Chapman's Homer*

There's a blind man here with a brow
As big and white as a cloud.
And all we fiddlers, from highest to lowest,

Writers of music and tellers of stories,
Sit at his feet,
And hear him sing of the fall of Troy.
                    —E. L. MASTERS, *Spoon River Anthology*

HONESTY

A prince can mak a belted knight,
    A marquis, duke, an' a' that;
But an honest man's aboon his might,
    Guid faith, he maunna fa' that! —BURNS, *For a' That*

An honest man's the noblest work of God.
                    —POPE, *Essay on Man, IV*

HONOR

When honour's lost, 'tis a relief to die;
Death's but a sure retreat from infamy.
                    —SAMUEL GARTH, *The Dispensary*

I could not love thee, Dear, so much
    Lov'd I not honour more.
                    —LOVELACE, *To Lucasta, Going to the Wars*

Honour and shame from no condition rise;
Act well your part: there all the honour lies.
                    —POPE, *An Essay on Man, IV*

By heaven, methinks it were an easy leap
To pluck bright honour from the pale-faced moon,
Or dive into the bottom of the deep,
Where fathom-line could never touch the ground,
And pluck up drowned honour by the locks.
                    —SHAKESPEARE, *Henry IV, II, 3*

Well, honour is the subject of my story.
I cannot tell what you and other men
Think of this life; but, for my single self,

I had as lief not be as live to be
In awe of such a thing as I myself.
                    —SHAKESPEARE, *Julius Caesar, I, 2*

When faith is lost, when honor dies,
    The man is dead!   —WHITTIER, *Ichabod*

HOPE

Still nursing the unconquerable hope,
    Still clutching the inviolable shade.
                    —MATTHEW ARNOLD, *The Scholar-Gipsy*

The heart bowed down by weight of woe
    To weakest hope will cling.
                    —A. BUNN, Song from *The Bohemian Girl*

Abandon hope, all ye who enter here.
(*Lasciate ogni speranza, voi ch'entrate.*)
                    —DANTE, *Inferno, II*

While there is life there's hope (he cried),
Then why such haste?—so groan'd and died.
                    —JOHN GAY, *The Sick Man and the Angel*

Hope springs eternal in the human breast:
Man never is, but always to be blest.
                    —POPE, *Essay on Man, I*

We did not dare to breath a prayer
    Or give our anguish scope!
Something was dead in each of us,
    And what was dead was Hope.
                    —OSCAR WILDE, *The Ballad of Reading Gaol*

HORSE

A horse misused upon the road
Calls to Heaven for human blood.
                    —BLAKE, *Auguries of Innocence*

God forbid that I should go to any heaven in which there
are no horses.
　—R. B. CUNNINGHAME-GRAHAM, *Letter to T. Roosevelt,*
1917

My beautiful, my beautiful that standest meekly by,
With thy proudly-arched and glossy neck, and dark and
　　fiery eye!
Fret not to roam the desert now, with all thy winged
　　speed:
I may not mount on thee again!—thou'rt sold, my Arab
　　steed!
　　　　　—CAROLINE E. S. NORTON, *The Arab's Farewell
　　　　　　　　　　　　　　　　　　to His Steed*

A horse! a horse! my kingdom for a horse!
　　　　　　　　—SHAKESPEARE, *Richard III, V, 4*

HOSPITALITY

I was a stranger, and ye took me in.
　　　　　　　—NEW TESTAMENT, *Matthew, XXV, 35*

HOURS

Lost, yesterday, somewhere between Sunrise and Sunset,
two golden hours, each set with sixty diamond minutes.
No reward is offered for they are gone forever.
　　　　　　—HORACE MANN, *Lost, Two Golden Hours*

Hours are golden links, God's token,
　　Reaching heaven; but, one by one,
Take them, lest the chain be broken
　　Ere the pilgrimage be done.
　　　　　　—ADELAIDE ANN PROCTOR, *One by One*

HOUSE

The house of every one is to him his castle and fortress,
as well for his defence against injury and violence, as for
his repose.　—SIR EDWARD COKE, *Semayne's Case* (1605)

HUMANITY

I am a man, and nothing human can be of indifference
to me.
(Homo sum; humani nil a me alienum puto.)
—TERENCE, *The Self-Torturer*

But hearing oftentimes
The still, sad music of humanity.
—WORDSWORTH, *Tintern Abbey*

HUMBLE

. . . 'umble we are, 'umble we have been, 'umble we shall
ever be.   —DICKENS, *David Copperfield*

HUMILITY

Whosoever shall smite thee on thy right cheek, turn to
him the other also.   —NEW TESTAMENT, *Matthew, V, 39*

HUNGER

The fields were fruitful, and starving men moved on
the roads. The granaries were full and the children of the
poor grew up rachitic, and the pustules of pellagra swelled
on their side. The great companies did not know that the
line between hunger and anger is a thin line.
—JOHN STEINBECK, *The Grapes of Wrath*

The best sauce for food is hunger.
—SOCRATES (quoted by Cicero)

HUNTING

D'ye ken John Peel with his coat so gay?
D'ye ken John Peel at the break of the day?
D'ye ken John Peel when he's far, far away,
With his hounds and his horn in the morning?
—ANON., *John Peel*

Detested sport,
That owes its pleasures to another's pain.
—COWPER, *The Task, III*

Wild animals never kill for sport. Man is the only one to whom the torture and death of his fellow creatures is amusing in itself. —J. A. FROUDE, *Oceana*

When a man wants to murder a tiger he calls it sport; when a tiger wants to murder him he calls it ferocity.
—BERNARD SHAW, *Maxims for Revolutionists*

HUSBAND

Ah, gentle dames! it gars me greet,
To think how mony counsels sweet,
How mony lengthened, sage advices,
The husband frae the wife despises!
—BURNS, *Tam O' Shanter*

There is only one real tragedy in a woman's life. The fact that the past is always her lover, and her future invariably her husband.
—OSCAR WILDE, *An Ideal Husband, III*

HYPOCRISY

He blam'd and protested, but join'd in the plan;
He shared in the plunder, but pitied the man.
—COWPER, *Pity for Poor Africans*

No man is a hypocrite in his pleasures.
—S. JOHNSON (Boswell, *Life* for the year 1783)

They set the sign of the cross over their outer doors, and sacrifice to their gut and their groin in their inner closets.
—BEN JONSON, *Explorata*

Hypocrisy is the homage which vice pays to virtue.
—LA ROCHEFOUCAULD, *Maxims, 218*

Thou hypocrite, first cast out the beam out of thine own eye; and then shalt thou see clearly to cast out the mote out of thy brother's eye.
—NEW TESTAMENT, *Matthew, VII, 5*

Woe unto you, scribes and Pharisees, hypocrites! for ye make clean the outside of the cup and of the platter, but within they are full of extortion and excess.
— NEW TESTAMENT, *Matthew, XXIII, 25*

With one hand he put
A penny in the urn of poverty,
And with the other took a shilling out.
— ROBERT POLLOK, *The Course of Time*

The devil can cite Scripture for his purpose.
An evil soul, producing holy witness,
Is like a villain with a smiling cheek,
A goodly apple rotten at the heart:
O, what a goodly outside falsehood hath!
— SHAKESPEARE, *Merchant of Venice, I, 3*

To beguile the time,
Look like the time; ...
. . . look like the innocent flower,
But be the serpent under't.
— SHAKESPEARE, *Macbeth, I, 5*

IDEALIST

Ah, would but one might lay his lance in rest,
And charge in earnest—were it but a mill.
— AUSTIN DOBSON, *Don Quixote*

An idealist is a person who helps other people to be prosperous. — HENRY FORD, on the witness stand, 1919

IDLENESS

As idle as a painted ship
Upon a painted ocean.
— S. T. COLERIDGE, *The Ancient Mariner*

He slept beneath the moon,
He basked beneath the sun;

He lived a life of going-to-do,
   And died with nothing done.
            —J. ALBERY, *Epitaph Written for Himself*

Wretched estate of men by fortune blessed,
That being ever idle never rest.
            —G. CHAPMAN, *The Tears of Peace*

God loves an idle rainbow,
No less than labouring seas.
            —RALPH HODGSON, *A Wood Song*

Kiddies and grown ups too-oo-oo,
If we haven't enough to do-oo-oo,
   We get the hump,
   Cameelious hump,
The hump that is black and blue.
            —KIPLING, *Just-So Stories*

Were it not better done, as others use,
To sport with Amaryllis in the shade,
Or with the tangles of Neaera's hair?
            —MILTON, *Lycidas*

Go to the ant, thou sluggard; consider her ways, and be
wise.   —OLD TESTAMENT, *Proverbs, VI, 6*

Their only labour was to kill time;
And labour dire it is, and weary woe.
            —THOMSON, *The Castle of Indolence*

'Tis the voice of the sluggard, I heard him complain,
"You have waked me too soon, I must slumber again";
As the door on its hinges, so he on his bed,
Turns his sides, and his shoulders, and his heavy head.
            —ISAAC WATTS, *The Sluggard*

I loaf and invite my soul,
I lean and loaf at my ease observing a spear of summer
grass. —WALT WHITMAN, *Song of Myself*

IDOLS

Four species of idols beset the human mind; idols of the
tribe; idols of the den; idols of the market; and idols of
the theatre. —FRANCIS BACON, *Novum Organum*

IGNORANCE

To be ignorant of one's ignorance is the malady of the
ignorant. —A. B. ALCOTT, *Table Talk*

I honestly believe it iz better tew know nothing than
tew know what aint so.
—JOSH BILLINGS, *Encyclopedia of Proverbial Philosophy*

Where ignorance is bliss,
'Tis folly to be wise.
—GRAY, *On a Distant Prospect of Eton College*

Ignorance is degrading only when found in company
with riches.
—SCHOPENHAUER, *Essays: On Books and Reading*

IMAGINATION

Were it not for imagination, Sir, a man would be as
happy in the arms of a chambermaid as of a Duchess.
—S. JOHNSON, (Boswell's *Life,* Vol. III)

The lunatic, the lover, and the poet
Are of imagination all compact:
—SHAKESPEARE, *A Midsummer-Night's Dream, V, 1*

IMITATION

Imitation is the sincerest of flattery.
—C. C. COLTON, *Lacon*

And the man who plants cabbages imitates too!
                    —Austin Dobson, *Ballade of Imitation*

Imitation is suicide.   —Emerson, *Essays: Self-Reliance*

IMMORTALITY

It must be so,—Plato, thou reason'st well!—
Else whence this pleasing hope, this fond desire,
This longing after immortality?   —Addison, *Cato, V, 1*

There is surely a piece of Divinity in us, something that
was before the elements, and owes no homage to the sun.
                    —Sir Thomas Browne, *Religio Medici, II*

Fool! All that is, at all,
    Lasts ever past recall;
Earth changes, but thy soul and God stand sure;
    What entered into thee,
    That was, is, and shall be:
Time's wheel runs back or stops; Potter and clay endure.
                    —R. Browning, *Rabbi Ben Ezra*

Suns may rise and set; we, when our short day has
closed, must sleep on during one perpetual night.
(Soles occidere et redire possunt; . . .) —Catullus, *Ode V*

Is there beyond the silent night
    An endless day?
Is death a door that leads to light?
    We cannot say.
                    —R. G. Ingersoll, *Declaration of the Free*

Dust thou art, to dust returnest,
    Was not spoken of the soul.
                    —Longfellow, *A Psalm of Life*

Beyond this vale of tears
    There is a life above,

Unmeasured by the flight of years;
   And all that life is love.
     —JAMES MONTGOMERY, *The Issues of Life and Death*

Our Saviour, Jesus Christ, who hath abolished death,
and hath brought life and immortality to light through the
gospel.   —NEW TESTAMENT, *II Timothy, I, 10*

If a man die, shall he live again?
     —OLD TESTAMENT, *Job XIV, 14*

Or ever the silver cord be loosed or the golden bowl be
broken, or the pitcher be broken at the fountain, or the
wheel broken at the cistern. Then shall the dust return to
the earth as it was; and the spirit shall return unto God
who gave it.   —OLD TESTAMENT, *Ecclesiastes, XII, 6, 7*

This life is but the passage of a day,
This life is but a pang and all is over;
But in the life to come which fades not away
Every love shall abide and every lover.
     —CHRISTINA ROSSETTI, *Saints and Angels*

To desire immortality is to desire the eternal perpetua-
tion of a great mistake.
     —SCHOPENHAUER, *The World as Will and Idea, II*

I do not set my life at a pin's fee;
And, for my soul, what can it do to that,
Being a thing immortal as itself?
     —SHAKESPEARE, *Hamlet, I, 4*

For tho' from out our bourne of Time and Place
   The flood may bear me far,
I hope to see my Pilot face to face
   When I have crost the bar.
     —TENNYSON, *Crossing the Bar*

This little life is all we must endure,
The grave's most holy peace is ever sure,
　　We fall asleep and never wake again;
Nothing is of us but the mouldering flesh
Whose elements dissolve and merge afresh
　　In earth, air, water, plants, and other men.
—JAMES THOMSON ("B.V."), *The City of Dreadful Night*

I swear I think now that everything without exception
　　has an eternal soul!
The trees have, rooted in the ground! the weeds of the
　　sea have! the animals!
　　　　　　—WALT WHITMAN, *To Think of Time*

Happy he whose inward ear
Angel comfortings can hear,
　　O'er the rabble's laughter;
And while Hatred's fagots burn,
Glimpses through the smoke discern
　　Of the good hereafter.　—WHITTIER, *Barclay of Ury*

IMPERIALISM

So that Lancashire merchants whenever they like
Can water the beer of a man in Klondike,
Or poison the beer of a man in Bombay;
And that is the meaning of Empire Day.
　　　　　—G. K. CHESTERTON, *Songs of Education*

Take up the White Man's burden—
　　Send forth the best ye breed—
Go, bind your sons to exile
　　To serve your captives' need;
To wait in heavy harness
　　On fluttered folk and wild—
Your new-caught, sullen peoples,
　　Half-devil and half-child.
　　　　　　—KIPLING, *The White Man's Burden*

In every part of the world the good desire of men for peace and decency is undermined by the dynamite of jingoism. And it needs only one spark, set off anywhere by one egomaniac, to send it all up in one final fatal explosion.
—ROBERT E. SHERWOOD, *Idiot's Delight*

INDECISION

No man, having put his hand to the plow, and looking back, is fit for the Kingdom of God.
—NEW TESTAMENT, *Luke, IX, 62*

INDEPENDENCE

If you want to get rich, you son of a bitch,
    I'll tell you what to do:
Never sit down with a tear or a frown,
    And paddle your own canoe.
—ANON. (*c.* 1880) (The expression *"Paddle your own canoe"* is used by Capt. Marryat in his *Settlers in Canada*, 1840)

So live that you can look any man in the eye and tell him to go to hell.   —ANON. (*c.* 1900)

The strongest man in the world is he who stands most alone.   —IBSEN, *An Enemy of the People*, V

He travels the fastest who travels alone.
—KIPLING, *The Winners*

I would rather sit on a pumpkin and have it all to myself than be crowded on a velvet cushion.
—THOREAU, *Walden*

How happy is he born and taught,
    That serveth not another's will;
Whose armour is his honest thought,
    And simple truth his utmost skill.
—SIR HENRY WOTTON, *The Character of a Happy Life*

INDEPENDENCE DAY

When in the course of human events, it becomes necessary for one people to dissolve the political bands which
have connected them with another, and to assume among
the powers of the earth the separate and equal station to
which the laws of nature and of nature's God entitle them,
a decent respect for the opinion of mankind requires that
they should declare the causes which impel them to the separation. —THOMAS JEFFERSON, *Declaration of Independence*

Sink or swim, live or die, survive or perish, I give my
heart and hand to this vote.
—DANIEL WEBSTER (Speech supposed to have been made
by John Adams)

INDIAN

Lo, the poor Indian! whose untutor'd mind
Sees God in clouds or hears him in the wind.
—POPE, *Essay on Man, I*

The only good Indian is a dead Indian.
—GEN. P. H. SHERIDAN, remark, reported, 1869

INDICTMENT

I do not know a method of drawing up an indictment
against a whole nation.
—EDMUND BURKE, *Conciliation with America*

INFANT

At first the infant,
Mewling and puking in the nurse's arms.
—SHAKESPEARE, *As You Like It, II, 7*

But what am I?
An infant crying in the night:
An infant crying for the light,
And with no language but a cry.
—TENNYSON, *In Memoriam, LIV*

INFERIORITY

The feeling of inferiority rules the mental life and can be clearly recognized in the sense of incompleteness and unfulfillment, and in the uninterrupted struggle both of individuals and of humanity. —ALFRED ADLER, *Social Interest*

INFINITY

To see a world in a grain of sand,
    And a heaven in a wild flower,
To hold infinity in the palm of your hand,
    And eternity in an hour.
                        —BLAKE, *Auguries of Innocence*

INFLUENCE

O may I join the choir invisible
Of those immortal dead who live again
In minds made better by their presence:
    —GEORGE ELIOT, *O May I Join the Choir Invisible*

Canst thou bind the sweet influence of the Pleiades, or loose the bands of Orion?
                —OLD TESTAMENT, *Job*, XXXVIII, 31

INGRATITUDE

Blow, blow, thou winter wind,
Thou art not so unkind
    As man's ingratitude:
Thy tooth is not so keen,
Because thou art not seen,
    Although thy breath be rude.
                —SHAKESPEARE, *As You Like It*, II, 7

Freeze, freeze, thou bitter sky,
Thou dost not bite so nigh
    As benefits forgot.
                —SHAKESPEARE, *As You Like It*, II, 7

Et tu Brute? Then fall, Caesar!
>   —SHAKESPEARE, *Julius Caesar, III, 1*

This was the most unkindest cut of all;
For when the noble Caesar saw him stab,
Ingratitude, more strong than traitors' arms,
Quite vanquish'd him; then burst his mighty heart.
>   —SHAKESPEARE, *Julius Caesar, III, 2*

How sharper than a serpent's tooth it is
To have a thankless child!
>   —SHAKESPEARE, *King Lear, I, 4*

INJURY

On adamant our wrongs we all engrave,
But write our benefits upon the wave.
>   —WILLIAM KING, *The Art of Love*

It is a principle of human nature to hate those whom you
have injured.   —TACITUS, *Agricola*

INJUSTICE

To do injustice is more disgraceful than to suffer it.
>   —PLATO, *Gorgias*

The seed ye sow, another reaps;
The wealth ye find, another keeps;
The robe ye weave, another wears;
The arms ye forge, another bears.
>   —SHELLEY, *Song to the Men of England*

INN

Souls of Poets dead and gone,
What Elysium have ye known,
Happy field or mossy cavern,
Choicer than the Mermaid Tavern?
>   —KEATS, *Lines on the Mermaid Tavern*

INSPIRATION

Gie me ae spark o' Nature's fire
That's a' the learning I desire;
Then, tho' I trudge thro' dub an' mire
    At pleugh or cart,
My muse, tho' hamely in attire,
    May touch the heart.   —Burns, *Epistle to J. Lapraik*

INTELLECTUALS

We are the hollow men
We are the stuffed men
Leaning together
Headpiece filled with straw. Alas!
Our dried voices, when
We whisper together
Are quiet and meaningless
As wind in dry grass
Or rats' feet over broken glass
In our dry cellar.   —T. S. Eliot, *The Hollow Men*

INTOLERANCE

And when religious sects ran mad,
    He held, in spite of all his learning,
That if a man's belief is bad,
    It will not be improved by burning.
                    —W. M. Praed, *The Vicar*

INVENTION

God hath made man upright, but they have sought out
many inventions.   —Old Testament, *Ecclesiastes, VII, 29*

IRELAND

Oh, Paddy dear, an' did ye hear the news that's goin'
    round?
The shamrock is by law forbid to grow on Irish ground!
St. Patrick's day no more we'll keep, his colour can't be
    seen,

For there's a cruel law agin the wearin' o' the green!
　　　　　—ANON., *The Shan-van-Voght* (c. 1800)

There came to the beach a poor Exile of Erin—

　　·　·　·　·　·　·　·　·

Green be thy fields, sweetest isle of the ocean!
And thy harp-striking bards sing aloud with devotion,—
"Erin mavourneen—Erin go bragh!"
　　　　　—THOMAS CAMPBELL, *Exile of Erin*

There's a dear little plant that grows in our isle,
'Twas St. Patrick himself sure that set it:

　　·　·　·　·　·　·　·　·

The sweet little shamrock, the dear little shamrock,
The sweet little, green little, shamrock of Ireland!
—ANDREW CHERRY, *The Green Little Shamrock of Ireland*

And if ever ye ride in Ireland,
　　The jest may yet be said,
There is the land of broken hearts,
　　And the land of broken heads.
　　　　　—G. K. CHESTERTON, *Ballad of the White Horse*

English, Scotchmen, Jews, do well in Ireland—Irishmen
never; even the patriot has to leave Ireland to get a hearing.
　　　　　—GEORGE MOORE, *Ave*

Nothing in Ireland lasts long except the miles.
　　　　　—GEORGE MOORE, *Ave*

And blest for ever is she who relied
Upon Erin's honour and Erin's pride.
　　　　　—THOMAS MOORE, *Rich and Rare*

　　The western isles
Of kerns and gallowglasses.
　　　　　—SHAKESPEARE, *Macbeth, I, 2*

If you want to interest the Irishman in Ireland, you've got to call the unfortunate island Kathleen ni Hoolihan and pretend she's a little old woman.

—BERNARD SHAW, *John Bull's Other Island*

Whether on the scaffold high
Or on the battle-field we die,
Oh, what matter, when for Erin dear we fall!

—T. D. SULLIVAN, *God Save Ireland*

Lovelier than thy seas are strong,
Glorious Ireland, sword and song
Gird and crown thee: none may wrong,
　　Save thy sons alone.   —SWINBURNE, *The Union*

IRISH

The Irish are the cry-babies of the Western world. Even the mildest quip will set them off into resolutions and protests.   —HEYWOOD BROUN, *The Piece That Got Me Fired*

ISLAND

O, it's a snug little island!
A right little, tight little island!

—THOMAS DIBDIN, *The Snug Little Island*

Many a green isle needs must be
In the deep wide sea of Misery,
Or the mariner, worn and wan,
Never thus could voyage on.

—SHELLEY, *Lines Written Among the Euganean Hills*

ISOLATION

. . . any mans *death* diminishes *me*, because I am involved in *Mankinde;* and therefore never send to know for whom the *bell* tolls; It tolls for *thee.*

—JOHN DONNE, *Devotions*

ITALY

Know'st thou the land where the lemon-trees bloom,
Where the gold orange glows in the deep thicket's
  gloom, . . .
(Kennst du das Land wo die Citronen blühn,
Im dunkeln Laub die Gold-Orangen glühn, . . .)
          —GOETHE, *Wilhelm Meister* (Carlyle trans.)

IVY

Oh, a dainty plant is the Ivy green,
That creepeth o'er ruins old!
          —DICKENS, *The Ivy Green* (in *Pickwick Papers*)

Yet once more, O ye laurels, and once more,
Ye myrtles brown, with ivy never sere,
I come to pluck your berries harsh and crude.
          —MILTON, *Lycidas* (opening lines)

JACK

Jack and Jill went up the hill
  To fetch a pail of water;
Jack fell down and broke his crown
  And Jill came tumbling after.
          —ANON., *Jack and Jill* (c. 1600)

Jack Sprat will eat no fat,
And Jill doth love no lean,
Yet betwixt them both,
They lick the dishes clean.
          —JOHN CLARKE, *Paraemiologia* (1639)

JEALOUSY

O, beware, my lord, of jealousy;
It is the green-eyed monster which doth mock
The meat it feeds on.   —SHAKESPEARE, *Othello, III, 3*

Trifles light as air
Are to the jealous confirmation strong
As proofs of holy writ.   —SHAKESPEARE, *Othello, III, 3*

I can endure my own despair,
    But not another's hope.   —WILLIAM WALSH, *Song*

JEFFERSON, THOMAS

A gentleman of thirty-two who could calculate an eclipse, survey an estate, tie an artery, plan an edifice, try a cause, break a horse, dance a minuet and play the violin.
                    —JAMES PARTON, *Life of Jefferson*

Here was buried Thomas Jefferson, author of the Declaration of American Independence, of the statute of Virginia for religious freedom, and father of the University of Virginia.   —JEFFERSON, Epitaph, written for himself

JEHOVAH

Tell them I am, Jehova said
To Moses; while earth heard in dread,
    And smitten to the heart
At once above, beneath, around,
All nature, without voice or sound,
    Replied, O Lord, Thou art.
                    —CHRISTOPHER SMART, *Song to David*

JERUSALEM

Jerusalem the golden, with milk and honey blest,
Beneath thy contemplation sink heart and voice oppressed.
—BERNARD OF CLUNY, *Hora Novissima* (J. M. Neale trans.)

If I forget thee, O Jerusalem, let my right hand forget her cunning.   —OLD TESTAMENT, *Psalms, CXXXVII, 5*

JEST

Haste thee Nymph, and bring with thee
Jest and joyful Jollity,
Quips and Cranks, and wanton Wiles,
Nods and Becks, and wreathèd Smiles.
—MILTON, *L'Allegro*

A jest's prosperity lies in the ear
Of him that hears it, never in the tongue
Of him that makes it.
—SHAKESPEARE, *Love's Labour's Lost*, V, 2

The right honourable gentleman is indebted to his memory for his jests and to his imagination for his facts.
—R. B. SHERIDAN, Speech, in reply to Mr. Dundas

JESTER

Alas, poor Yorick! I knew him, Horatio: a fellow of infinite jest, of most excellent fancy.
—SHAKESPEARE, *Hamlet*, V, 1

JESUS

How sweet the name of Jesus sounds
In a believer's ear!
It soothes his sorrows, heals his wounds,
And drives away his fears.
—JOHN NEWTON, *Olney Hymns*

Jesus, lover of my soul,
Let me to Thy bosom fly,
While the nearer waters roll,
While the tempest still is high!
—CHARLES WESLEY, *In Temptation*

JEW

A people still, whose common ties are gone;
Who, mixed with every race, are lost in none.
—GEORGE CRABBE, *The Borough*

Yes, I am a Jew, and when the ancestors of the right honourable gentleman were brutal savages in an unknown island, mine were priests in the temple of Solomon.
—B. DISRAELI, Reputed reply to Daniel O'Connell

If my theory of relativity is proven successful, Germany will claim me as a German and France will declare that I am a citizen of the world. Should my theory prove untrue, France will say that I am a German and Germany will declare that I am a Jew.
—ALBERT EINSTEIN, Address, at the Sorbonne

The Jews are among the aristocracy of every land; if a literature is called rich in the possession of a few classic tragedies, what shall we say to a national tragedy lasting for fifteen hundred years, in which the poets and the actors were also the heroes.   —GEORGE ELIOT, *Daniel Deronda*

Who gave the patient Christ? I say
Who gave your Christian creed? Yea, yea,
Who gave your very God to you?
Your Jew! Your Jew! Your hated Jew!
　　　—from *To Russia.*
　　　　　　Cincinnatus Heine ("Joaquin") Miller

His cup is gall, his meat is tears,
His passion lasts a thousand years.
　　　—EMMA LAZARUS, *Crowing of the Red Cock*

And Israel shall be a proverb and a by-word among all people.   —OLD TESTAMENT, *I Kings, IX, 7*

When Israel, of the Lord belov'd,
　　Out of the land of bondage came,
Her fathers' God before her mov'd,
　　An awful guide in smoke and flame. —SCOTT, *Ivanhoe*

Still have I borne it with a patient shrug,
For sufferance is the badge of all our tribe:

You call me misbeliever, cut-throat dog,
And spit upon my Jewish gaberdine.
                    —SHAKESPEARE, *Merchant of Venice, I, 3*

Hath not a Jew eyes? hath not a Jew hands, organs
. . . fed with the same food, hurt with the same weapons.
. . . If you prick us, do we not bleed? if you tickle us do we
not laugh? if you poison us, do we not die? and if you
wrong us, shall we not revenge?
                    —SHAKESPEARE, *Merchant of Venice, III, 1*

A race prone to superstition, opposed to religion.
                    —TACITUS, *Annals, V*

JEWEL

She hangs upon the cheek of night
Like a rich jewel in an Ethiope's ear.
                    —SHAKESPEARE, *Romeo and Juliet, I, 5*

JOHNSON, SAMUEL

If you were to make little fishes talk, they would talk
like whales.   —OLIVER GOLDSMITH, to Dr. Johnson, 1773

Here lies poor Johnson; reader have a care;
Tread lightly, lest you rouse a sleeping bear.
Religious, moral, generous, and humane
He was; but self-sufficient, rude, and vain;
Ill-bred, and overbearing in dispute,
A scholar and a Christian and a brute.
                    —SOAME JENYNS, *Epitaph on Samuel Johnson*

JONSON, BEN

Ah Ben!
Say how, or when
Shall we thy guests
Meet at those Lyric Feasts,

Made at the Sun,
The Dog, the Triple Tun?
> —HERRICK, *An Ode for Ben Jonson*

O rare Ben Jonson!
> —SIR JOHN YOUNG, Epitaph in Westminster Abbey

JOWETT, BENJAMIN

My name is Benjamin Jowett,
  I'm Master of Balliol College;
Whatever is knowledge I know it,
  And what I don't know isn't knowledge.
> —ANON., *Epigram* (c. 1870)

JOY

There's not a joy the world can give like that it takes
  away.   —BYRON, *Stanzas for Music*

All human joys are swift of wing,
  For heaven doth so allot it,
That when you get an easy thing,
  You find you haven't got it.
> —EUGENE FIELD, *Ways of Life*

Joy comes, grief goes, we know not how.
> —J. R. LOWELL, *The Vision of Sir Launfal*

Hence, vain deluding Joys,
The brood of Folly, without father bred.
> —MILTON, *Il Penseroso*

At Earth's great market where Joy is trafficked in,
Buy while thy purse yet swells with golden Youth.
> —ALAN SEEGER, *Ode to Antares*

I have drunken deep of joy,
And I will taste no other wine to-night.
> —SHELLEY, *The Cenci, I, 3*

I found more joy in sorrow
Than you could find in joy.
—SARA TEASDALE, *The Answer*

But we are pressed by heavy laws;
And often, glad no more,
We wear a face of joy, because
We have been glad of yore.
—WORDSWORTH, *The Fountain*

JUDAS

And while he yet spake, lo, Judas, one of the twelve, came . . . and forthwith he came to Jesus, and said, Hail! Master; and kissed him.
—NEW TESTAMENT, *Matthew, XXVI, 47, 49*

JUDGE

Judges ought to be more learned than witty, more reverend than plausible, and more advised than confident. Above all things, integrity is their portion and proper virtue. —BACON, *Essays: Of Judicature*

Ordained of God to be the judge of quick and dead.
—NEW TESTAMENT, *Acts, X, 42*

A Daniel come to judgment! yea a Daniel!
O, wise young judge, how I do honour thee!

. . . .

An upright judge, a learned judge!
—SHAKESPEARE, *Merchant of Venice, IV, 1*

And then the justice
In fair round belly with good capon lined.
—SHAKESPEARE, *As You Like It, III, 7*

JUDGMENT

There is so much good in the worst of us,
And so much bad in the best of us,

That it hardly becomes any of us
To talk about the rest of us.
                    —ANON., *Good and Bad* (c. 1900)

Judge not, that ye be not judged.
                    —NEW TESTAMENT, *Matthew, VII, 1*

Why beholdest thou the mote that is in thy brother's
eye, but considerest not the beam that is in thy own eye?
                    —NEW TESTAMENT, *Matthew, VII, 3*

Thou art weighed in the balance, and art found wanting.
                    —OLD TESTAMENT, *Daniel, V, 27*

'Tis with our judgements as our watches, none
Go just alike, yet each believes his own.
                    —POPE, *Essay on Criticism, 1*

O judgement! thou art fled to brutish beasts,
And men have lost their reason!
                    —SHAKESPEARE, *Julius Caesar, III, 2*

JUDGMENT DAY

Day of wrath, that day of burning,
Seer and Sibyl speak concerning,
All the world to ashes turning.
(*Dies irae, dies illa!*
Solvet saeclum in favilla,
Teste David cum Sybilla.)
                    —TOMASSO DI CELANO, *Dies Irae*

God will not look you over for medals, degrees or di-
plomas, but for scars.   —ELBERT HUBBARD, *Epigrams*

The deeds we do, the words we say,
    Into still air they seem to fleet,
        We count them ever past;

But they shall last,—
In the dread judgment they
   And we shall meet.
                    —JOHN KEBLE, *The Effect of Example*

Flee from the wrath to come.
                    —NEW TESTAMENT, *Matthew, III, 7*

JUNE

And what is so rare as a day in June?
   Then, if ever, come perfect days;
Then heaven tries earth if it be in tune,
   And over it softly her warm ear lays.
                    —J. R. LOWELL, *The Vision of Sir Launfal, I*

JURY

And hungry judges soon the sentence sign,
And wretches hang that jurymen may dine.
                    —POPE, *The Rape of the Lock, III*

JUSTICE

Fear not, then, thou child infirm,
There's no god dare wrong a worm.
                    —EMERSON, *Essays: Compensation* (Motto)

Justice is a machine that, when someone has given it a
starting push, rolls on of itself.
                    —GALSWORTHY, *Justice, II*

Live and let live is the rule of common justice.
                    —SIR ROGER L'ESTRANGE, *Fables of Aesop, 127*

Let justice be done, though the heavens fall.
(*Fiat justitia et ruant coeli.*)
                    —LORD MANSFIELD, In *Rex vs. Wilkes*

The memory of the just is blessed; but the name of the wicked shall rot.   —OLD TESTAMENT, *Proverbs, X, 7*

Thrice is he arm'd that hath his quarrel just,
And he but naked, though lock'd up in steel,
Whose conscience with injustice is corrupted.
                    —SHAKESPEARE, *Henry VI, II, III, 2*

Only the actions of the just
Smell sweet and blossom in their dust.
            —JAMES SHIRLEY, *Contention of Ajax and Ulysses*

. . . I might have live out my life, talking on street corners to scorning men. I might have die unmarked, unknown, a failure. Now we are not a failure . . . Our words—our lives—our pains—nothing! The taking of our lives—lives of a good shoemaker and a poor fishpeddler—all! The last moment belongs to us—that agony is our triumph.
    —BARTOLOMEO VANZETTI, Letter to his son, April, 1927

The administration of justice is the firmest pillar of government. —GEORGE WASHINGTON, Letter to Randolph, 1789

KEATS, JOHN

It is a better and wiser thing to be a starved apothecary than a starved poet; so back to the shop, Mr. John, back to "plasters, pills, and ointment boxes."
            —J. G. LOCKHART, Review of *Endymion* in
                    Blackwood's Magazine

He has outsoared the shadow of our night;
Envy and calumny, and hate and pain,
And that unrest which men miscall delight,
Can touch him not and torture not again.
—SHELLEY, *Adonais* (The first line was inscribed by Theodore Roosevelt over the grave of his son Quentin.)

"Here lies one whose name was writ in water."
                    —Epitaph on tombstone of Keats in Rome

KICK

When late I attempted your pity to move,
    Why seemed you so deaf to my prayers?
Perhaps it was right to dissemble your love,
    But—why should you kick me downstairs?
                    —Attributed to DR. SAMUEL JOHNSON

KIN

A little more than kin and less than kind.
                    —SHAKESPEARE, *Hamlet, I, 2*

KINDNESS

'Twas a thief said the last kind word to Christ:
Christ took the kindness, and forgave the theft.
                    —R. BROWNING, *The Ring and the Book, VI*

Have you had a kindness shown?
    Pass it on;
'Twas not given for thee alone,
    Pass it on;
Let it travel down the years,
Let it wipe another's tears,
Till in Heaven the deed appears—
    Pass it on.   —HENRY BURTON, *Pass It On*

Little drops of water, little grains of sand,
Make the mighty ocean and the pleasant land.

            .   .   .   .

Little deeds of kindness, little words of love,
Help to make earth happy like the heaven above.
                    —JULIA A. F. CARNEY, *Little Things*

If I can stop one heart from breaking,
    I shall not live in vain;
If I can ease one life the aching,
    Or cool one pain,

Or help one fainting robin
    Unto his nest again,
    I shall not live in vain.   —EMILY DICKINSON, *Poems, I*

Let me be a little kinder,
Let me be a little blinder
To the faults of those around me.
                                —EDGAR A. GUEST, *A Creed*

                    Yet do I fear thy nature;
It is too full o' the milk of human kindness
To catch the nearest way.
                        —SHAKESPEARE, *Macbeth, I, 5*

KING

There was a king of Yvetot,
    Of whom renown hath little said,
Who let all thoughts of glory go,
    And dawdled half his days in bed.
(*Il était un roi d'Yvetot,*
    Peu connu dans l'histoire;
Se levant tard, se couchant tôt,
    Dormant fort bien sans gloire.)
        —BÉRANGER, *Le Roi d'Yvetot* (Thackeray trans.)

That the king can do no wrong is a necessary and
fundamental principle of the English constitution.
                        —BLACKSTONE, *Commentaries, III*

Kings will be tyrants from policy, when subjects are
rebels from principle.
—EDMUND BURKE, *Reflections on the Revolution in France*

God bless the King, I mean the faith's defender,
God bless (no harm in blessing) the Pretender,
But who pretender is, or who is king,
God bless us all—that's quite another thing.
    —JOHN BYROM, *Extempore to an Officer in the Army*

God said, "I am tired of kings,
 I suffer them no more;
Up to my ear the morning brings
 The outrage of the poor." —EMERSON, *Boston Hymn*

There was a king of Thule,
 Was faithful till the grave,
To whom his mistress dying,
 A golden goblet gave.
(*Es war ein Konig in Tule
 Gar treu bis an das Grab,
Dem sterbend seine Buhle
 Einen gold'nen Becher gab.*)
 —GOETHE, *Faust* (Bayard Taylor trans.)

Ruin seize thee, ruthless king!
Confusion on thy banners wait;
Tho' fam'd by Conquest's crimson wing,
They mock the air with idle state.
 —THOMAS GRAY, *The Bard*

There is no king who has not had a slave among his
ancestors, and no slave who has not had a king among his.
 —HELEN KELLER, *Story of My Life*

For therein stands the office of a king,
His honour, virtue, merit, and chief praise,
That for the public all this weight he bears.
 —MILTON, *Paradise Regained, II*

The right divine of kings to govern wrong.
 —POPE, *The Dunciad, IV*

A king of shreds and patches.
 —SHAKESPEARE, *Hamlet, III, 4*

Ay, every inch a king. —SHAKESPEARE, *King Lear, IV, 6*

Not all the water in the rough rude sea
Can wash the balm from an anointed king.
—SHAKESPEARE, *Richard II, III, 2*

There's such a divinity doth hedge a king,
That treason can but peep to what it would.
—SHAKESPEARE, *Hamlet, IV, 5*

The King is dead. Long live the King!
(*Le Roi est mort. Vive le Roi!*)
—French form of proclamation of a new king

KISS

The moth's kiss first!
Kiss me as if you made believe
You were not sure, this eve,
How my face, your flower, had pursed
Its petals up.   —R. BROWNING, *In a Gondola*

Rose kissed me today.
  Will she kiss me tomorrow?
Let it be as it may,
Rose kissed me today.   —AUSTIN DOBSON, *A Kiss*

The anatomical juxtaposition of two orbicularis oris
muscles in a state of contraction.
—DR. HENRY GIBBONS, *Definition of a Kiss*

Jenny kissed me when we met,
  Jumping from the chair she sat in;
Time, you thief, who love to get
  Sweets into your list, put that in!
Say I'm weary, say I'm sad,
  Say that health and wealth have missed me:
Say I'm growing old, but add
  Jenny kissed me.   —LEIGH HUNT, *Jenny Kissed Me*

Leave a kiss but in the cup,
And I'll not look for wine.   —BEN JONSON, *To Celia*

Sweet Helen, make me immortal with a kiss!
Her lips suck forth my soul: see, where it flies!
            —CHRISTOPHER MARLOWE, *Doctor Faustus*

A kiss, when all is said, what is it?
            . . . a rosy dot
Placed on the "i" in loving; 'tis a secret
Told to the mouth instead of to the ear.
            —EDMOND ROSTAND, *Cyrano de Bergerac*, III

Give me kisses! Nay, 'tis true
I am just as rich as you;
And for every kiss I owe,
I can pay you back, you know.
    Kiss me, then,
Every moment—and again!
            —J. G. SAXE, *To Lesbia* (after Catullus)

Dear as remembered kisses after death,
And sweet as those by hopeless fancy feign'd
On lips that are for others.
            —TENNYSON, *The Princess*, IV

KISSING

Gin a body meet a body
    Comin' thro' the rye,
Gin a body kiss a body,
    Need a body cry?   —BURNS, *Comin' Thro' the Rye*

Oh, fie, Miss, you must not kiss and tell.
            —CONGREVE, *Love for Love*, II, 10

A little time for laughter,
    A little time to sing,

A little time to kiss and cling,
And no more kissing after.   —P. B. MARSTON, *After*

Yet whoop, Jack! Kiss Gillian the quicker,
Till she bloom like a rose, and a fig for the vicar!
                    —SCOTT, *The Lady of the Lake*, VI

Take, O take those lips away,
    That so sweetly were forsworn;
And those eyes. the break of day,
    Lights that do mislead the morn:
But my kisses bring again. bring again;
Seals of love, but seal'd in vain, seal'd in vain.
        —SHAKESPEARE, *Measure for Measure*, IV, 1

See the mountains kiss high Heaven,
    And the waves clasp one another;
No sister-flower would be forgiven
    If it disdained its brother;
And the sunlight clasps the earth,
    And the moonbeams kiss the sea:
What is all this sweet work worth,
    If thou kiss not me?   —SHELLEY, *Love's Philosophy*

KNAVE

A knave; a rascal; an eater of broken meats; a base,
proud, shallow, beggarly, three-suited, hundred-pound,
filthy, worsted-stocking knave; . . . .
                —SHAKESPEARE, *King Lear*, II, 2

'Gainst knaves and thieves men shut their gate.
            —SHAKESPEARE, *Twelfth Night*, IV, 1

KNEE

The human knee is a joint and not an entertainment.
        —PERCY HAMMOND (quoted by Mark Sullivan in
                            Our Times, III)

KNIGHT

He was a very parfit gentle knight.
—CHAUCER, *Canterbury Tales*, Prologue

A gentle knight was pricking on the plaine.
—SPENSER, *The Faerie Queene* (first line)

KNIGHT OF THE RED CROSS

And on his breast a bloody cross he bore,
The dear remembrance of his dying Lord,
For whose sweet sake that glorious badge he wore.
—SPENSER, *The Faerie Queene*, I

KNOWLEDGE

Knowledge is power.   —HOBBES, *Leviathan*

There are four sorts of men:
He who knows not and knows not he knows not: he is a
fool—shun him;
He who knows not and knows he knows not: he is simple
—teach him.
He who knows and knows not he knows: he is asleep—
wake him;
He who knows and knows he knows: he is wise—follow
him.   —LADY BURTON, In *Life of Sir Richard Burton*
(quoted as an Arabian proverb)

Knowledge is the only instrument of production that is
not subject to diminishing returns.
—J. M. CLARK, *Journal of Political Economy*, Oct., 1927

I have studied now Philosophy
And Jurisprudence, Medicine
And even, alas, Theology
From end to end with labor keen;
And here, poor fool, with all my lore
I stand no wiser than before.
—GOETHE, *Faust*, I (B. Taylor trans.)

But knowledge to their eyes her ample page,
Rich with the spoils of time, did ne'er unroll.
                —GRAY, *Elegy Written in a Country Churchyard*

All I know is what I read in the papers.   —WILL ROGERS

I know nothing except the fact of my ignorance.
                —SOCRATES (quoted in Diogenes Laertius)

Knowledge comes, but wisdom lingers.
                —TENNYSON, *Locksley Hall*

To know that we know what we know, and that we do
not know what we do not know, that is true knowledge.
                —THOREAU, *Walden* (quoting Confucius)

LABOR

To labor is to pray.
(*Laborare est orare.*) —Motto of the Benedictine monks

Labor: one of the processes by which A acquires property for B.   —AMBROSE BIERCE, *The Devil's Dictionary*

But the young, young children, O my brothers,
    They are weeping bitterly!
They are weeping in the playtime of the others,
    In the country of the free.
                —E. B. BROWNING, *The Cry of the Children*

We labour soon, we labour late,
    To feed the titled knave, man;
And a' the comfort we're to get
    Is that ayont the grave, man.
                —BURNS, *The Tree of Liberty*

For as labour cannot produce without the use of land,
the denial of the equal right to the use of land is necessarily
the denial of the right of labour to its own product.
                —HENRY GEORGE, *Progress and Poverty, VII*

If fifty men did all the work,
    And gave the price to five,
And let those five make all the rules—
You'd say the fifty men were fools,
    Unfit to be alive.
                —CHARLOTTE P. S. GILMAN, *Five and Fifty*

Toil is the lot of all, and bitter woe
The fate of many. —HOMER, *Iliad, XXI* (Bryant trans.)

With fingers weary and worn,
    With eyelids heavy and red,
A woman sat in unwomanly rags,
    Plying her needle and thread.

        .   .   .   .   .   .

O men with sisters dear,
    O men with mothers and wives,
It is not linen you're wearing out,
    But human creatures' lives!
                —THOMAS HOOD, *Song of the Shirt*

I hold that if the Almighty had ever made a set of men
that should do all the eating and none of the work, He
would have made them with mouths only and no hands;
and if He had ever made another class that He intended
should do all the work and no eating, He would have
made them with hands only and no mouths.
                —ABRAHAM LINCOLN, *Mud-sill Theory of Labor*

Toiling—rejoicing—sorrowing,
    Onward through life he goes;
Each morning sees some task begin,
    Each evening sees it close;
Something attempted, something done,
    Has earned a night's repose.
                —LONGFELLOW, *The Village Blacksmith*

Come unto me, all ye that labour and are heavy laden.
                    —NEW TESTAMENT, *Matthew, XI, 28*

What profit hath a man of all his labour which he taketh
under the sun?   —OLD TESTAMENT, *Ecclesiastes, I, 3*

Men of England, wherefore plough
For the lords who lay ye low?
Wherefore weave with toil and care
The rich robes your tyrants wear?
                    —SHELLEY, *Song: To the Men of England*

Labor conquers everything.
(*Labor omnia vincit.*)   —VIRGIL, *Georgics, I*

LABORER

Bowed by the weight of centuries he leans
Upon his hoe and gazes on the ground,
The emptiness of ages in his face,
And on his back the burden of the world.
                    —EDWIN MARKHAM, *The Man with the Hoe*

The labourer is worthy of his hire.
                    —NEW TESTAMENT, *Luke, X, 7*

LAMB

Little Lamb, who made thee?

. . . . . .

Little Lamb I'll tell thee:
He is callèd by thy name,
For He calls Himself a Lamb,
He is meek, and He is mild;
He became a little child.   —BLAKE, *Songs of Innocence*

Mary had a little lamb,
    Its fleece was white as snow,

And everywhere that Mary went
 The lamb was sure to go.
         —SARAH JOSEPHA HALE, *Mary's Lamb* (1830)

God tempers the wind to the shorn lamb.
         —STERNE, *A Sentimental Journey*

LARK

A skylark wounded on the wing
Doth make a cherub cease to sing.
         —BLAKE, *Auguries of Innocence*

To hear the lark begin his flight,
And singing, startle the dull night,
From his watch-tower in the skies,
Till the dappled Dawn doth rise.   —MILTON, *L'Allegro*

Hark, hark! the lark at heaven's gate sings,
And Phoebus 'gins arise.
         —SHAKESPEARE, *Cymbeline, II, 3*

Hail to thee, blithe Spirit!—
 Bird thou never wert!—
That from Heaven, or near it,
 Pourest thy full heart
In profuse strains of unpremeditated art.
         —SHELLEY, *To a Skylark*

Ethereal minstrel! pilgrim of the sky!
Dost thou despise the earth where cares abound?
         .   .   .   .
Type of the wise who soar but never roam:
True to the kindred points of Heaven and Home!
         —WORDSWORTH, *To a Skylark*

LAUGH

And if I laugh at any mortal thing,
'Tis that I may not weep.   —BYRON, *Don Juan, IV*

And the loud laugh that spoke the vacant mind.
—GOLDSMITH, *The Deserted Village*

He laughs best that laughs last.
—SIR J. VANBRUGH, *The Country House*, II, 5

Laugh and the world laughs with you,
  Weep and you weep alone,
For the sad old earth must borrow its mirth,
  But has trouble enough of its own.
—ELLA WHEELER WILCOX, *Solitude* (1883)

LAUGHTER

      On this hapless earth
There's small sincerity of mirth,
And laughter oft is but an art
To drown the outcry of the heart.
—HARTLEY COLERIDGE, *Address to Certain Gold-fishes*

As the crackling of thorns under a pot, so is the laughter
of the fool.   —OLD TESTAMENT, *Ecclesiastes*, VII, 6

Our sincerest laughter
With some pain is fraught.   —SHELLEY, *To a Skylark*

LAW

The law doth punish man or woman
That steals the goose from off the common,
But lets the greater felon loose,
That steals the common from the goose.
—ANON. (In 1764, when Enclosure Acts were passed)

Laws are dumb in the midst of arms.
(Silent enim leges inter arma.)   —CICERO, *Pro Milone*

The law, in its majestic equality, forbids the rich as well
as the poor to sleep under bridges, to beg in the streets,
and to steal bread.   —ANATOLE FRANCE, *Crainquebille*

The Law is the true embodiment
Of everything that's excellent.
It has no kind of fault or flaw,
And I, my Lords, embody the Law.
    —W. S. GILBERT, *Iolanthe: Lord Chancellor's Song*

Laws grind the poor, and rich men rule the law.
    —GOLDSMITH, *The Traveller*

I know no method to secure the repeal of bad or ob-
noxious laws so effective as their stringent execution.
    —U. S. GRANT, Inaugural Address, 1869

The laws of God, the laws of man,
He may keep that will and can;
Not I: let God and man decree
Laws for themselves and not for me.
    —A. E. HOUSMAN, *Last Poems*

The net of law is spread so wide,
No sinner from its sweep may hide.
Its meshes are so fine and strong,
They take in every child of wrong.
O wondrous web of mystery!
Big fish alone escape from thee!
    —J. J. ROCHE, *The Net of Law*

Ignorance of the law excuses no man: not that all men
know the law, but because 'tis an excuse every man will
plead, and no man can tell how to confute him.
    —JOHN SELDEN, *Table-Talk*

But in these nice sharp quillets of the law,
Good faith, I am no wiser than a daw.
    —SHAKESPEARE, *Henry VI, I, II, 4*

LAWYER

He saw a lawyer killing a viper
    On a dunghill hard by his own stable;
And the Devil smiled, for it put him in mind
    Of Cain and his brother Abel.
                    —S. T. COLERIDGE, *The Devil's Thoughts*

This house where once a lawyer dwelt
    Is now a smith's. Alas!
How rapidly the iron age
    Succeeds the age of brass!
                        —WILLIAM ERSKINE, *Epigram*

Necessity has no law; I know some attorneys of the same.
            —FRANKLIN, *Poor Richard's Almanac* for 1734

And whether you're an honest man or whether you're a
    thief
Depends on whose solicitor has given me my brief.
                    —W. S. GILBERT, *Utopia, Limited, I*

Woe unto you also, ye lawyers, for ye lade men with
burdens grievous to be borne, and ye yourselves touch not
the burdens with one of your fingers.
                    —NEW TESTAMENT, *Luke, XI, 46*

Why is there always a secret singing
When a lawyer cashes in?
Why does a hearse horse snicker
Hauling a lawyer away?
            —CARL SANDBURG, *The Lawyers Know Too Much*

A Lawyer art thou?—draw not nigh!
    Go carry to some fitter place
The keenness of that practised eye,
    The hardness of that sallow face.
                    —WORDSWORTH, *A Poet's Epitaph*

LEARNING

A little learning is a dangerous thing;
Drink deep, or taste not the Pierian spring.
—POPE, *Essay on Criticism, II*

LEISURE

Leisure with dignity.
(*Cum dignitate otium.*)   —CICERO, *Pro Publio Sestio*

A poor life this if, full of care,
We have no time to stand and stare.
—W. H. DAVIES, *Leisure*

LENDING

Very often he that his money lends
Loses both his gold and his friends.
—C. H. SPURGEON, *John Ploughman*

LETTER OF THE LAW

The letter killeth, but the spirit giveth life.
—NEW TESTAMENT, *II Corinthians, III, 6*

LEVIATHAN

Canst thou draw out leviathan with an hook?
—OLD TESTAMENT, *Job, XLI, 1*

LIAR

A liar needs a good memory.
—QUINTILIAN, *De institutione oratoria, IV*

I said in my haste, All men are liars.
—OLD TESTAMENT, *Psalms, CXVI, 11*

This is the punishment of a liar: He is not believed even
when he speaks the truth.
—BABYLONIAN TALMUD, *Sanhedrin*

LIBERAL AND CONSERVATIVE

I often think it's comical,
    How nature always does contrive
That every boy and every gal,
    That's born into the world alive,
Is either a little Liberal,
    Or else a little Conservative.
> —W. S. GILBERT, *Iolanthe, II*

LIBERTY

When Liberty is gone,
Life grows insipid and has lost its relish.
> —ADDISON, *Cato, II, 3*

The tree of liberty grows only when watered by the
blood of tyrants.   —BERTRAND BARÈRE, Speech, 1792

Eternal Spirit of the Chainless Mind!
    Brightest in dungeons, Liberty! thou art,
    For there thy habitation is the heart—
The heart which love of thee alone can bind.
> —BYRON, *The Prisoner of Chillon*

Is life so dear or peace so sweet as to be purchased at
the price of chains and slavery? Forbid it, Almighty God!
I know not what course others may take; but as for me,
give me liberty, or give me death!
> —PATRICK HENRY, Speech, March, 1775

What light is to the eyes—what air is to the lungs—what
love is to the heart, liberty is to the soul of man.
> —R. G. INGERSOLL, *Progress*

The God who gave us life, gave us liberty at the same
time.
> —THOMAS JEFFERSON, *Summary View of . . . Rights . . .*

"Make way for liberty!" he cried,
  Made way for liberty, and died.
> —JAMES MONTGOMERY, *The Patriot's Pass-Word*

Where the Spirit of the Lord is, there is liberty.
> —NEW TESTAMENT, *II Corinthians, III, 17*

Eternal vigilance is the price of liberty.
> —WENDELL PHILLIPS, *Public Opinion* (speech, 1852)

What in some is called liberty, in others is called licence.
> —QUINTILIAN, *De institutione oratoria, III*

We would rather die on our feet than live on our knees.
> —FRANKLIN D. ROOSEVELT, Address, 1939

Liberty, when it begins to take root, is a plant of rapid growth.   —GEORGE WASHINGTON, *Maxims of Washington*

LIBERTY, STATUE OF

Not like the brazen giant of Greek fame,
With conquering limbs astride from land to land;
Here at our sea-washed. sunset gates shall stand
A mighty woman with a torch, whose flame
Is the imprisoned lightning, and her name
Mother of exiles.   —EMMA LAZARUS, *The New Colossus*

LIBRARY

The true University of these days is a Collection of Books.   —CARLYLE, *Heroes and Hero-Worship, V*

Burn the libraries, for their value is in this one book. [i.e., the *Koran*].
> —CALIPH OMAR, At the capture of Alexandria

LIE

Ask me no questions, and I'll tell you no fibs.
> —GOLDSMITH, *She Stoops to Conquer, III, 1*

Figures won't lie, but liars will figure.
                    —GEN. C. H. GROSVENOR, Speech in
                                House of Representatives

Sin has many tools, but a lie is the handle which fits
them all.
    —O. W. HOLMES, *The Autocrat of the Breakfast-Table*

The Retort Courteous; . . . the Quip Modest; . . . the
Reply Churlish; . . . the Reproof Valiant; . . . the Counter-
check Quarrelsome; . . . the Lie with Circumstance; . . . the
Lie Direct   —SHAKESPEARE, *As You Like It*, V, 4

One of the striking differences between a cat and a lie
is that a cat has only nine lives.
                —MARK TWAIN, *Pudd'nhead Wilson's Calendar*

LIFE

Gosh! I feel like a real good cry!
    Life, he says, is a cheat, a fake.
Well, I agree with the grouchy guy—
    The best you get is an even break.
        —FRANKLIN P. ADAMS, *Ballade of Schopenhauer's
                                            Philosophy*

If life worth living? That depends on the liver.
                            —ANON. (*c.* 1855)

Let us live, then, and be glad,
While young life's before us;
After youthful pastime had,
After old age, hard and sad,
Earth will slumber o'er us.
(*Gaudeamus igitur juvenes dum sumus
Post jucundam juventutem,
Post molestam senectutem,
Nos habebit humus.*)
                —ANON., *Gaudeamus Igitur* (Symonds trans.)

And we are here as on a darkling plain
Swept with confused alarms of struggle and flight,
Where ignorant armies clash by night.
—MATTHEW ARNOLD, Dover Beach

Why should there be such turmoil and such strife,
To spin in length this feeble line of life?
—BACON, Translation of Psalm XC

Life! we've been long together
Through pleasant and through cloudy weather;
'Tis hard to part when friends are dear,—
Perhaps 't will cost a sigh, a tear;
Then steal away, give little warning,
    Choose thine own time;
    Say not "Good Night," but in some brighter clime
Bid me "Good-morning."   —ANNA L. BARBAULD, *Life*

I count life just a stuff
To try the soul's strength on.
—R. BROWNING, In a Balcony

I took one draught of life,
I'll tell you what I paid,
Precisely an existence—
The market-price, they said.
—EMILY DICKINSON, Further Poems

They are not long, the weeping and the laughter,
    Love and desire and hate:
I think they have no portion in us after
    We pass the gate.
—ERNEST DOWSON, Vitae Summa Brevis

When I consider Life, 'tis all a cheat.
Yet fool'd with hope, men favour the deceit;

Trust on, and think tomorrow will repay.
Tomorrow's falser than the former day;
                              —DRYDEN, *Aureng-Zebe, IV, 1*

Life ain't all beer and skittles, and more's the pity; but
what's the odds, so long as you're happy?
                              —GEORGE DU MAURIER, *Trilby*

A crust of bread and a corner to sleep in,
A minute to smile and an hour to weep in,
A pint of joy to a peck of trouble,
And never a laugh but the moans come double;
    And that is life!   —PAUL LAURENCE DUNBAR, *Life*

Life is a jest, and all things show it;
I thought so once, but now I know it.
                              —JOHN GAY, *My Own Epitaph*

Far from the madding crowd's ignoble strife,
    Their sober wishes never learn'd to stray;
Along the cool, sequester'd vale of life
    They kept the noiseless tenor of their way.
        —GRAY, *Elegy Written in a Country Churchyard*

Life is made up of sobs, sniffles, and smiles, with sniffles
predominating.   —O. HENRY, *Gift of the Magi*

Like leaves on trees the race of man is found,
Now green in youth, now with'ring on the ground:
Another race the following spring supplies,
They fall successive and successive rise.
                              —HOMER, *Iliad, VI* (Pope trans.)

Happy the man, and happy he alone,
He who can call to-day his own:
He who, secure within, can say:
"To-morrow do thy worst, for I have liv'd to-day."
                              —HORACE, *Odes, III, 29* (Dryden trans.)

Welcome, O life! I go to encounter for the millionth time the reality of experience and to forge in the smithy of my soul the uncreated conscience of my race.

—JAMES JOYCE, *Portrait of the Artist as a Young Man*

The weariness, the fever, and the fret
Here, where men sit and hear each other groan.

—KEATS, *Ode to a Nightingale*

I have fought my fight, I have lived my life,
    I have drunk my share of wine;
From Trier to Coln there was never a knight
    Led a merrier life than mine.

—CHARLES KINGSLEY, *The Knight's Leap*

Life is real! Life is earnest!
And the grave is not its goal.

—LONGFELLOW, *A Psalm of Life*

Our ingress into the world
Was naked and bare;
Our progress through the world
Is trouble and care;
Our egress from the world
Will be nobody knows where:
But if we do well here
We shall do well there.

—LONGFELLOW, *Cobbler of Hagenau*

Tell me not in mournful numbers
    Life is 'but an empty dream!'—
For the soul is dead that slumbers,
    And things are not what they seem.

—LONGFELLOW, *A Psalm of Life*

Tomorrow will I live, the fool does say;
Today itself's too late; the wise lived yesterday.

—MARTIAL, *Epigrams,* (Cowley trans.)

Life can be bitter to the very bone
When one is poor, and woman, and alone.
> —JOHN MASEFIELD, *The Widow in the Bye Street*

Degenerate sons and daughters,
Life is too strong for you—
It takes life to love Life.
> —E. L. MASTERS, *Spoon River Anthology: Lucinda
> Matlock*

Life is vain; a little love, a little hate, and then—Good-
  day!
Life is short; a little hoping, a little dreaming, and then—
  Good-night!

(*La vie est vaine:*	*La vie est brève:*
Un peu d'amour,	*Un peu d'espoir,*
Un peu de haine . . .	*Un peu de rêve . . .*
Et puis—bon jour!	*Et puis—bon soir!*)

—LÉON DE MONTENAEKEN, *Peu de chose et presque trop*

For what is your life? It is even a vapour, that appeareth
for a little time, and then vanisheth away.
> —NEW TESTAMENT, *James, IV, 14*

As for man his days are as grass: as a flower of the field,
so he flourisheth.
The wind passeth over it, and it is gone; and the place
thereof shall know it no more.
> —OLD TESTAMENT, *Psalms, CIII, 15, 16*

Life is just one damned thing after another.
> —FRANK WARD O'MALLEY (authorship disputed)

Ah, make the most of what we yet may spend,
Before we too into the Dust descend;

Dust unto Dust, and under Dust to lie,
Sans Wine, sans Song, sans Singer, and—sans End!
   —OMAR KHAYYÁM, *Rubáiyát* (FitzGerald trans.)

Strange interlude! Yes, our lives are merely strange dark
interludes in the electrical display of God the Father!
   —EUGENE O'NEILL, *Strange Interlude*

A little pain, a little pleasure,
A little heaping up of treasure;
Then no more gazing upon the sun.
All things must end that have begun.
   —JOHN PAYNE, *Kyrelle*

Life is adventure in experience, and when you are no
longer greedy for the last drop of it, it means no more than
that you have set your face ... to the day when you shall
depart. ...
   —DONALD C. PEATTIE, *An Almanac for Moderns*

What trifling coil do we poor mortals keep;
Wake, eat and drink, evacuate and sleep.
   —PRIOR, *Human Life*

When I consider Life and its few years—
A wisp of fog betwixt us and the sun;
A call to battle, and the battle done
Ere the last echo dies within our ears;
A rose choked in the grass; an hour of fears;
The gusts that past a darkening shore do beat;
The burst of music down an unlistening street—
I wonder at the idleness of tears.
   —LIZETTE W. REESE, *Tears*

Our past is clean forgot,
Our present is and is not,

Our future's a sealed seedplot,
And what betwixt them are we?
        —D. G. ROSSETTI, *The Cloud Confines*

Life is not a spectacle or a feast; it is a predicament.
        —GEORGE SANTAYANA, *Articles and Essays*

Life's but a walking shadow, a poor player
That struts and frets his hour upon the stage
And then is heard no more: it is a tale
Told by an idiot, full of sound and fury,
Signifying nothing.   —SHAKESPEARE, *Macbeth, V, 5*

   We are such stuff
As dreams are made on and our little life
Is rounded with a sleep.
        —SHAKESPEARE, *The Tempest, IV, 1*

Life like a dome of many-coloured glass
Stains the white radiance of Eternity.
        —SHELLEY, *Adonais*

From too much love of living,
   From hope and fear set free,
We thank with brief thanksgiving
   Whatever gods there be,
That no life lives forever;
That dead men rise up never;
That even the weariest river
   Winds somewhere safe to sea.
        —SWINBURNE, *The Garden of Proserpine*

And the wild regrets and the bloody sweats
   None knew so well as I:
For he who lives more lives than one
   More deaths than one must die.
        —OSCAR WILDE, *Ballad of Reading Gaol*

My life is like the autumn leaf
    That trembles in the moon's pale ray;
Its hold is frail—its date is brief,
    Restless,—and soon to pass away.
                —RICHARD HENRY WILDE, *My Life*

LIGHT

Hail holy light, offspring of Heav'n firstborn!
                —MILTON, *Paradise Lost, III*

And the light shineth in darkness; and the darkness comprehended it not.   —NEW TESTAMENT, *John, I, 5*

I am the light of the world.
            —NEW TESTAMENT, *John, VIII, 12*

Walk while ye have the light, lest darkness come upon
you.   —NEW TESTAMENT, *John XII, 35*

Lead, Kindly Light, amid the encircling gloom,
Lead Thou me on!
      —JOHN HENRY NEWMAN, *Pillar of the Cloud*

And God said, Let there be light: and there was light.
        —OLD TESTAMENT, *Genesis, I, 3*

A lamp unto my feet, and a light unto my path.
      —OLD TESTAMENT, *Psalms, CXIX, 10*

The light that never was, on sea or land,
The consecration, and the Poet's dream.
        —WORDSWORTH, *Elegiac Stanzas . . .*

LIGHTNING

I saw the lightning's gleaming rod
Reach forth and write upon the sky
The awful autograph of God.
      —JOAQUIN MILLER, *The Ship in the Desert*

LILAC

Go down to Kew in lilac-time, in lilac-time, in lilac-time;
> Go down to Kew in lilac-time (it isn't far from London!)
And you shall wander hand in hand with love in summer's wonderland;
> Go down to Kew in lilac-time (it isn't far from London!)   —ALFRED NOYES, *The Barrel-Organ*

When lilacs last in the dooryard bloom'd,
And the great star early droop'd in the western sky in the night,
I mourn'd, and yet shall mourn with ever-returning spring.   —WALT WHITMAN, *When Lilacs Last in the Dooryard Bloom'd*

LILY

Consider the lilies of the field, how they grow; they toil not, neither do they spin: And yet I say unto you, That even Solomon in all his glory was not arrayed like one of these.   —NEW TESTAMENT, *Matthew, VI, 28*

LIMERICKS (FAMOUS)

1. A wonderful bird is the pelican;
   His mouth holds more than his bellican;
   > He takes in his beak,
   > Enough food for a week,
   But I'm damned if I see how the hellican.
   > > —ANON., *The Pelican*

2. There was a young fellow of Clyde
   Who went to a funeral and cried:
   > When they asked who was dead,
   > He stammered and said,
   "I don't know—I just came for the ride."
   > > —ANON., *The Young Fellow of Clyde*

3. There's a wonderful family called Stein—
   There's Gert, and there's Epp, and there's Ein;
     Gert's poems are bunk,
     Epp's statues are junk,
   And no one can understand Ein. —ANON., *The Steins*

4. There was an old man of Nantucket
   Who kept all his cash in a bucket;
     But his daughter, named Nan,
     Ran away with a man—
   And as for the bucket, Nantucket.
                          —ANON. (in the *Princeton Tiger*)

5. As a beauty I'm not a great star,
   There are others more handsome by far;
     But my face I don't mind it
     Because I'm behind it—
   'Tis the folks out in front that I jar.
                          —A. EUWER, *Limeratomy*

6. There was a small boy of Quebec
   Who was buried in snow to the neck;
     When they said, "Are you friz?"
     He replied, "Yes, I is—
   But we don't call this cold in Quebec."
                          —KIPLING, *The Boy of Quebec*

7. There was an Old Man with a beard,
   Who said, "It is just as I feared!
     Two Owls and a Hen,
     Four Larks and a Wren,
   Have all built their nests in my beard!"
                          —EDWARD LEAR, *Nonsense Verses*

8. A canner, exceedingly canny,
   One morning remarked to his granny,

"A canner can can
Anything that he can,
But a canner can't can a can, can he?"
—CAROLYN WELLS, *The Canner*

9. A Tutor who tooted the flute
Tried to teach two young tooters to toot.
Said the two to the Tutor,
"Is it harder to toot, or
To tutor two tooters to toot?"
—CAROLYN WELLS, *The Tutor*

LINCOLN, ABRAHAM

Lincoln, six feet one in his stocking feet,
The lank man, knotty and tough as a hickory rail,
Whose hands were always too big for white-kid gloves,
Whose wit was a coonskin sack of dry, tall tales,
Whose weathered face was homely as a plowed field.
—STEPHEN VINCENT BENÉT, *John Brown's Body*

Oh, slow to smite and swift to spare,
Gentle, and merciful and just!
Who, in the fear of God, didst bear
The sword of power, a nation's trust!
—WILLIAM C. BRYANT, *Abraham Lincoln*

His heart was as great as the world, but there was no
room in it to hold the memory of a wrong.
—EMERSON, *Letters and Social Aims: Greatness*

We are coming, Father Abraham, three hundred thousand more.
—J. S. GIBBONS, *We Are Coming, Father Abraham* (1862)

I was a dog at Gettysburg. I trotted near the train
And nosed among the officers who kicked me to my pain.
A man came by . . . I could not see. I howled. The light
was dim,

But when I brushed against his legs, I liked the smell of
  him.   —MacKinlay Kantor, *Lincoln at Gettysburg*

A bronzed lank man! His suit of ancient black,
A famous high top-hat and plain worn shawl
Made him the quaint great figure that men love,
The prairie-lawyer, master of us all.
—Vachel Lindsay, *Abraham Lincoln Walks at Midnight*

The kindly-earnest, brave, foreseeing man,
Sagacious, patient, dreading praise, not blame,
New birth of our new soil, the first American.
                    —J. R. Lowell, *Commemoration Ode*

Here was a man to hold against the world,
A man to match the mountains and the sea.
          . . . .
The color of the ground was in him, the red earth,
The smack and tang of elemental things:
The rectitude and patience of the cliff,
The goodwill of the rain that loves the leaves,
          . . . .
The pity of the snow that hides all scars.
    —Edwin Markham, *Lincoln, The Man of the People*

I am Ann Rutledge who sleeps beneath these weeds.
Beloved of Abraham Lincoln,
Wedded to him, not through union,
But through separation.
Bloom forever, O Republic,
From the dust of my bosom.
                    —E. L. Masters, *Spoon River Anthology*

Our big, gaunt, homely brother—
Our huge Atlantic coast-storm in a shawl,
Our cyclone in a smile—our President.
                    —James Oppenheim, *The Lincoln-Child*

When Abraham Lincoln was shoveled into the tombs,
  he forgot the copperheads and the assassins . . . in
  the dust, in the cool tombs.
                —CARL SANDBURG, *Cool Tombs*

Now he belongs to the ages.
            —EDWIN M. STANTON, At the death of Lincoln,
                            April 15, 1865

No Caesar he whom we lament,
A man without a precedent,
Sent, it would seem, to do
His work, and perish, too.

One of the people! born to be
Their curious epitome;
To share, yet rise above
Their shifting hate and love.
            —R. H. STODDARD, *Abraham Lincoln*

O Captain! my Captain! our fearful trip is done,
The ship has weathered every rack, the prize we sought
    is won,
The port is near, the bells I hear, the people all exulting,
While follow eyes the steady keel, the vessel grim and
    daring;

  But O heart! heart! heart!
    O the bleeding drops of red,
      Where on the deck my Captain lies,
        Fallen cold and dead.
          —WALT WHITMAN, *O Captain! My Captain!*

LIPS

Lips, however rosy, must be fed.
            —A. B. CHEALES, *Proverbial Folk-Lore*

Cherry-ripe, Ripe, Ripe, I cry,
Full and fair ones; come and buy:
If so be, you ask me where
They doe grow, I answer, There,
Where my Julia's lips do smile;
There's the Land, or Cherry Ile.

—HERRICK, *Cherry-Ripe*

And steal immortal blessing from her lips,
Who, even in pure and vestal modesty,
Still blush, as thinking their own kisses sin.

—SHAKESPEARE, *Romeo and Juliet, III, 2*

. . . the lips that touch liquor must never touch mine.

—GEORGE W. YOUNG, *Lips That Touch Liquor* (*c.* 1870)

LITERATURE

There is first the literature of *knowledge,* and secondly, the literature of *power.* The function of the first is—to teach; the function of the second is—to move.

—DE QUINCEY, *Essays on the Poets: Pope*

Great literature is simply language charged with meaning to the utmost possible degree.

—EZRA POUND, *How to Read*

Literature always anticipates life. It does not copy it, but moulds it to its purpose.

—OSCAR WILDE, *The Decay of Lying*

Literature is the orchestration of platitudes.

—THORNTON WILDER, *Literature*

LIVE

I live for those who love me, for those who know me true;
For the heaven that smiles above me, and awaits my spirit too;

For the cause that lacks assistance, for the wrong that
   needs resistance,
For the future in the distance, and the good that I can
   do.   —G. L. BANKS, *My Aim*

So live, that when thy summons comes to join
The innumerable caravan, which moves
To that mysterious realm, where each shall take
His chamber in the silent halls of death,
Thou go not like the quarry-slave at night,
Scourged to his dungeon, . . .
                          —WILLIAM C. BRYANT, *Thanatopsis*

So may'st thou live, till like ripe fruit thou drop
Into thy mother's lap, or be with ease
Gathered, not harshly pluck'd, for death mature.
                          —MILTON, *Paradise Lost, II*

Plain living and high thinking are no more.
   —WORDSWORTH, *Poems . . . to National Independence*

LOGIC

He was in Logic, a great critic,
Profoundly skill'd in Analytic;
He could distinguish, and divide
A hair 'twixt south and south-west side.
                          —BUTLER, *Hudibras, I*

LONDON

Oh, London is a fine town,
   A very famous city,
Where all the streets are paved with gold,
   And all the maidens pretty.
               —G. COLMAN (the Younger), *The Heir-at-Law*

Here malice, rapine, accident conspire,
And now a rabble rages, now a fire;

Their ambush here relentless ruffians lay,
And here the fell attorney prowls for prey;
—SAMUEL JOHNSON, London

O gleaming lights of London,
   That gem of the city's crown;
What fortunes be within you,
   O Lights of London Town!
—G. R. SIMS, Lights of London

LORD

Mine eyes have seen the glory of the coming of the Lord;
He is trampling out the vintage where the grapes of
   wrath are stored;
He hath loosed the fateful lightning of his terrible swift
   sword;
   His truth is marching on.
—JULIA WARD HOWE, Battle Hymn of the Republic

Whom the Lord loveth he chasteneth.
—NEW TESTAMENT, Hebrews, XII, 6

Out of the depths have I cried unto thee, O Lord. Lord
hear my voice. ("*De profundis . . .*")
—OLD TESTAMENT, Psalms, CXXX, 1

The fear of the Lord is the beginning of wisdom.
—OLD TESTAMENT, Proverbs, I, 7

. . . The Lord gave and the Lord hath taken away;
blessed be the name of the Lord.
—OLD TESTAMENT, Job, I, 22

The Lord is my light and my salvation.
—OLD TESTAMENT, Psalms, XXVII

LOSE

All that's bright must fade,—
    The brightest still the fleetest;
All that's sweet was made
    But to be lost when sweetest.
        —THOMAS MOORE, *All That's Bright Must Fade*

The man who can fight to Heaven's own height
Is the man who can fight when he's losing.
        —R. W. SERVICE, *Carry On*

God, though this life is but a wraith,
    Although we know not what we use,
Although we grope with little faith,
    Give me the heart to fight—and lose.
        —LOUIS UNTERMEYER, *Prayer*

LOUSE

Ha! Wha're ye gaun, ye crowlin' ferlie!
Your impudence protects you sairly;

    . . . .

Oh, wad some Pow'r the giftie gi'e us
To see oursels as ithers see us!
        —BURNS, *To a Louse on a Lady's Bonnet*

Lady Montague told me, and in her own house,
"I do not care for you three skips of a louse."
I forgive her, for women, however well-bred,
Will still talk of that which runs most in their head.
        —HENRY FOX, *Impromptu Retort* . . .

LOVE

It is good to be merry and wise,
It is good to be honest and true;
'Tis well to be off with the old love
Before you go on with the new.
        —ANON. (modern version of an old song)

It's love, it's love that makes the world go round.
                —ANON. (used by W. S. Gilbert in *Iolanthe*)

Ask not of me, love, what is love?
Ask what is good of God above—
Ask of the great sun what is light—
Ask what is darkness of the night—

. . . .

Ask what is sweetness of thy kiss—
Ask of thyself what beauty is.   —P. J. BAILEY, *Festus*

For love is of sae mickle might,
That it all paines makis light.
                —JOHN BARBOUR, *The Bruce*

O Happy race of men, if love, which rules Heaven, rule
your minds.   —BOËTHIUS, *Consolations of Philosophy*

The night has a thousand eyes,
    And the day but one;
Yet the light of the bright world dies
    With the dying sun.

The mind has a thousand eyes,
    And the heart but one;
Yet the light of a whole life dies
    When love is done.   —F. W. BOURDILLON, *Light*

Flower o' the broom,
Take away love, and our earth is a tomb!

. . . .

Flower o' the clove,
All the Latin I construe is "amo," I love!
                —R. BROWNING, *Fra Lippo Lippi*

O lyric Love, half angel and half bird,
And all a wonder and a wild desire!
                —R. BROWNING, *The Ring and the Book, I*

Love is the business of the idle, but the idleness of the busy.   —BULWER-LYTTON, *Rienzi*

Had we never lov'd sae kindly,
Had we never lov'd sae blindly,
Never met, or never parted,
We had ne'er been broken-hearted!
                              —BURNS, *Ae Fond Kiss*

O, my luve is like a red, red rose
    That's newly sprung in June.
O, my luve is like the melodie
    That's sweetly play'd in tune.
                              —BURNS, *A Red, Red Rose*

The wisest man the warl' e'er saw,
He dearly lov'd the lasses, O.
                  —BURNS, *Green Grow the Rashes, O.*

To see her is to love her,
    And love but her forever;
For nature made her what she is,
    And ne'er made sic anither!
                  —BURNS, *O, Saw Ye Bonnie Lesley*

In her first passion woman loves her lover;
In all the others, all she loves is love.
                              —BYRON, *Don Juan, III*

Man's love is of man's life a thing apart,
'Tis woman's whole existence.   —BYRON, *Don Juan, I*

He that loves a rosy cheek,
    Or a coral lip admires,
Or from star-like eyes doth seek
    Fuel to maintain his fires,

As Old Time makes these decay,
  So his flames must waste away.
                    —THOMAS CAREW, *Disdain Returned*

Let us live, my Lesbia, and love, and value at a penny
all the talk of crabbed old men.
(*Vivamus, mea Lesbia, atque amemus, . . .*)
                    —CATULLUS, *Odes, V, 1*

For ever it was, and ever it shall befal
That Love is he that alle thing may bind.
                    —CHAUCER, *Troilus and Criseyde, I*

All thoughts, all passions, all delights,
  Whatever stirs this mortal frame,
Are but the ministers of Love,
  And feed his sacred flame. —S. T. COLERIDGE, *Love*

With all thy faults, I love thee still.
                    —COWPER, *The Task, II*

Oh, I'm in love with the janitor's boy,
  And the janitor's boy loves me;
He's going to hunt for a desert isle
  In our geography.
                    —NATHALIA CRANE, *The Janitor's Boy*

All for Love, or the World Well Lost.
                    —DRYDEN, Title of play on theme of
                        Antony and Cleopatra

Perhaps they were right in putting love into books, . . .
Perhaps it could not live anywhere else.
                    —WILLIAM FAULKNER, *Light in August*

There is a lady sweet and kind,
Was never face so pleased my mind;

I did but see her passing by,
And yet I love her till I die.
                —BARNABE GOOGE, *There Is a Lady* (1570)

He who for the first time loves,
Even vainly, is a God.
But the man who loves again,
And still vainly, is a fool.
                —HEINE, *Wer zum erstenmale liebt*

You say to me-wards your affection's strong;
Pray love me little, so you love me long.
                —HERRICK, *Love Me Little, Love Me Long*

Ah! a man's love is strong
    When fain he comes a-mating.
But a woman's love is long
    And grows when it is waiting.
                —LAURENCE HOUSMAN, *The Two Loves*

And, happy melodist, unwearied,
    For ever piping songs for ever new;
More happy love! more happy, happy love!
    For ever warm and still to be enjoy'd,
        For ever panting and for ever young.
                —KEATS, *Ode on a Grecian Urn*

No longer could I doubt him true—
    All other men may use deceit;
He always said my eyes were blue,
    And often swore my lips were sweet.
                —LANDOR, *Mother, I Cannot Mind My Wheel*

There are many people who would never have been in
love if they had never heard love spoken of.
                —LA ROCHEFOUCAULD, *Maxims*, 136

Come live with me and be my Love,
And we will all the pleasures prove
That hills and valleys, dale and field,
Or woods, or steepy mountains yield
  —MARLOWE, *The Passionate Shepherd to His Love*

Who ever lov'd, that lov'd not at first sight!
     —MARLOWE, *Hero and Leander, I*

Love is all in fire, and yet is ever freezing;
Love is much in winning, yet is more in leesing:
Love is ever sick, and yet is never dying;
Love is ever true, and yet is ever lying;
Love does doat in liking, and is mad in loathing;
Love indeed is anything, yet indeed is nothing.
    —THOMAS MIDDLETON, *Blurt, II, 2*

And if I loved you Wednesday,
 Well, what is that to you?
I do not love you Thursday—
 So much is true.
    —EDNA ST. VINCENT MILLAY, *Thursday*

There's nothing half so sweet in life
As love's young dream.
    —THOMAS MOORE, *Love's Young Dream*

Two souls with but a single thought,
Two hearts that beat as one.
—VON MÜNCH-BELLINGHAUSEN, *Ingomar the Barbarian*
      (Maria A. Lovell, trans.)

Thy love to me was wonderful, passing the love of
women.   —OLD TESTAMENT, *II Samuel, I, 26*

It was many and many a year ago,
 In a Kingdom by the sea,

That a maiden there lived whom you may know
  By the name of Annabel Lee;
And this maiden she lived with no other thought
  Than to love and be loved by me.

—POE, *Annabel Lee*

Thou wast all that to me, love,
  For which my soul did pine:
A green isle in the sea, love,
  A fountain and a shrine.

—POE, *To One in Paradise*

Though his suit was rejected,
He sadly reflected,
  That a lover forsaken
    A new love may get;
  But a neck that's once broken
    Can never be set.

—SCOTT, *Peveril of the Peak*

But love is blind, and lovers cannot see
The pretty follies that themselves commit.

—SHAKESPEARE, *Merchant of Venice, II, 6*

Doubt thou the stars are fire;
  Doubt that the sun doth move;
Doubt truth to be a liar;
  But never doubt I love.

—SHAKESPEARE, *Hamlet, II, 2*

Love is a smoke raised with the fume of sighs;
Being purged, a fire sparkling in lovers' eyes;
Being vex'd, a sea nourish'd with lovers' tears:
What is it else? a madness most discreet,
A choking gall and persevering sweet.

—SHAKESPEARE, *Romeo and Juliet, II, 1*

Men have died from time to time and worms have eaten them, but not for love.—SHAKESPEARE, *As You Like It, IV, 1*

Sigh no more, ladies, sigh no more,
　Men were deceivers ever,
One foot in sea and one on shore,
　To one thing constant never.
　　　　　　—SHAKESPEARE, *Much Ado About Nothing, II, 3*

When my love swears that she is made of truth,
I do believe her, though I know she lies.
　　　　　　　—SHAKESPEARE, *Sonnets, CXXXVIII*

The fountains mingle with the river,
　And the rivers with the ocean;
The winds of heaven mix for ever
　With a sweet emotion;
Nothing in the world is single;
　All things, by a law divine,
In one another's being mingle—
　Why not I with thine? —SHELLEY, *Love's Philosophy*

When the lamp is shattered
　The light in the dust lies dead—
When the cloud is scattered
　The rainbow's glory is shed.
When the lute is broken,
　Sweet notes are remembered not;
When the lips have spoken,
　Loved accents are soon forgot.
　　　　　　　—SHELLEY, *When the Lamp Is Shattered*

Across the gateway of my heart
I wrote "No Thoroughfare,"
But love came laughing by, and cried:
"I enter everywhere."
　　　　　　　—HERBERT SHIPMAN, *No Thoroughfare*

Out upon it! I have lov'd
   Three whole days together;
And am like to love three more,
   If it prove fair weather.
           —SUCKLING, *The Constant Lover*

If love were what the rose is,
And I were like the leaf,
Our lives would grow together
In sad or singing weather.   —SWINBURNE, *A Match*

I hold it true, whate'er befall;
   I feel it, when I sorrow most;
   'Tis better to have loved and lost
Than never to have loved at all.
           —TENNYSON, *In Memoriam, XXVII*

To say that you can love one person all your life is just
like saying that one candle will continue burning as long
as you live.   —TOLSTOY, *The Kreutzer Sonata*

Love conquers all; let us too yield to Love.
(*Omnia vincit Amor; et nos cedamus Amori.*)
           —VIRGIL, *Eclogues, X*

Oh, rank is good, and gold is fair,
   And high and low mate ill;
But love has never known a law
   Beyond its own sweet will!
           —WHITTIER, *Amy Wentworth*

Yet each man kills the thing he loves,
   By each let this be heard,
Some do it with a bitter look,
   Some with a flattering word,
The coward does it with a kiss,
   The brave man with a sword!
           —OSCAR WILDE, *Ballad of Reading Gaol*

I loved a lass, a fair one,
   As fair as e'er was seen;
She was indeed a rare one,
   Another Sheba queen;
But, fool as then I was,
   I thought she loved me too:
But now, alas! she's left me,
   Falero, lero, loo!
          —GEORGE WITHER, *The Lover's Resolution*

LOVE AND HATE

I hate and I love. Perhaps you ask why I do so. I do not know, but I feel it, and I am in torment.

(Odi et amo. Quare id faciam, fortasse requiris. Nescio; sed fieri sentio et excrucior.) —CATULLUS, *Odes, LXXXV*

LOVER

         And then the lover,
Sighing like furnace, with a woeful ballad
Made to his mistress' eyebrow.
          —SHAKESPEARE, *As You Like It, II, 7*

Why so pale and wan, fond lover?
   Prithee, why so pale?
Will, when looking well can't move her,
   Looking ill prevail?
   Prithee, why so pale?
          —SUCKLING, *Encouragements to a Lover*

LUCK

Little is the luck I've had,
   And oh, 'tis comfort small
To think that many another lad
   Has had no luck at all.
          —A. E. HOUSMAN, *Last Poems*

True luck consists not in holding the best of the cards at
  the table:
Luckiest he who knows just when to rise and go home.
                              —JOHN HAY, *Distichs*, XV

Good luck befriend thee, Son; for at thy birth
The fairy ladies danced upon the heath.
                              —MILTON, *At a Vacation Exercise*

LUTHER, MARTIN

Luther was guilty of two great crimes—he struck the
Pope in his crown, and the monks in their belly.
                              —ERASMUS, *Colloquies*

I can do no other.
(*Ich kann nicht anders.*)
                              —LUTHER, Speech, at Diet of Worms, 1521

MADNESS

Whom the gods destroy, they first make mad.
                              —EURIPIDES, Fragment

Have we eaten on the insane root
That takes the reason prisoner?
                              —SHAKESPEARE, *Macbeth*, I, 3

That he is mad, 'tis true: 'tis true 'tis pity;
And pity 'tis 'tis true.   —SHAKESPEARE, *Hamlet*, II, 2

Though this be madness, yet there is method in't.
                              —SHAKESPEARE, *Hamlet*, II, 2

MAID

The spinsters and the knitters in the sun
And the free maids that weave their thread with bones.
                              —SHAKESPEARE, *Twelfth Night*, II, 4

She dwelt among the untrodden ways
   Beside the springs of Dove,
A maid whom there were none to praise
   And very few to love.   —WORDSWORTH, *Lucy*

MAIDEN

Maidens' hearts are always soft:
Would that men's were truer!
       —WILLIAM C. BRYANT, *Song*

The rare and radiant maiden, whom the angels name
   Lenore—
Nameless here for evermore.   —POE, *The Raven*

MALICE

With malice toward none, with charity for all, with firm-
ness in the right, as God gives us to see the right.
      —LINCOLN, *Second Inaugural Address*

MAMMON

        Mammon led them on,
Mammon, the least erected Spirit that fell
From heav'n;   —MILTON, *Paradise Lost, I*

Ye cannot serve God and mammon.
      —NEW TESTAMENT, *Matthew, VI, 24*

MAN

Man is a noble animal, splendid in ashes, and pompous
in the grave, solemnizing nativities and deaths with equal
lustre, not omitting ceremonies of bravery, in the infamy of
his nature.   —SIR THOMAS BROWNE, *Hydriotaphia, V*

A man's a man for a' that.
      —BURNS, *For a' That and a' That*

Man's inhumanity to man
   Makes countless thousands mourn.
             —BURNS, *Man Was Made to Mourn*

A man said to the universe:
   "Sir, I exist!"
   "However," replied the universe,
   "The fact has not created in me
   A sense of obligation."
            —STEPHEN CRANE, *War Is Kind*, IV

I am seeking a man.
       —DIOGENES (with a lantern in broad daylight)

Men are but children of a larger growth.
            —DRYDEN, *All For Love*, IV, 1

Oh, wearisome condition of humanity!
Born under one law, to another bound,
Vainly begot and yet forbidden vanity.
        —FULKE GREVILLE, *Mustapha*, V, 4

Though every prospect pleases,
   And only man is vile.
   —REGINALD HEBER, *From Greenland's Icy Mountains*

For men on earth 'tis best never to be born at all; or
being born, to pass through the gates of Hades with all
speed.   —HOMER (?), *Contest of Homer and Hesiod*

Man, biologically considered, . . . is the most formidable
of all the beasts of prey, and, indeed, the only one that
preys systematically on its own species.
        —WILLIAM JAMES, *Memories and Studies*

O man, strange composite of heaven and earth!
   Majesty dwarf'd to baseness! fragrant flower

Running to poisonous seed! and seeming worth
    Cloaking corruption! . . .
        —JOHN HENRY NEWMAN, *The Dream of Gerontius*

Down with your pride of birth
    And your golden gods of trade!
A man is worth to his mother Earth,
    All that a man has made!
        —J. G. NEIHARDT, *Cry of the People*

Man is a rope connecting animal and superman—a rope over a precipice. . . . What is great in man is that he is a bridge and not a goal.
        —NIETZSCHE, *Thus Spake Zarathustra*

So God created man in his own image, in the image of God created he him.   —OLD TESTAMENT, *Genesis, I, 27*

Man that is born of woman is of few days, and full of trouble.   —OLD TESTAMENT, *Job, XIV, 1*

Thou hast made him a little lower than the angels.
        —OLD TESTAMENT, *Psalms, VIII, 5*

Man is a reed, the weakest in nature, but he is a thinking reed.   —PASCAL, *Pensées, VI*

Know then thyself, presume not God to scan;
The proper study of mankind is Man.
        —POPE, *Essay on Man, II*

Man is the measure of all things.
        —PYTHAGORAS (in Diogenes Laertius, *Pythagoras*)

    But man, proud man,
Drest in a little brief authority,
Most ignorant of what he's most assur'd,

His glassy essence, like an angry ape,
Plays such fantastic tricks before high heaven,
As make the angels weep.
                    —SHAKESPEARE, *Measure for Measure*, II, 2

His life was gentle, and the elements
So mix'd in him that Nature might stand up,
And say to all the world "This was a man!"
                    —SHAKESPEARE, *Julius Caesar*, V, 5

Before the beginning of years,
    There came to the making of man
Time, with a gift of tears;
    Grief, with a glass that ran.
                    —SWINBURNE, *Atalanta in Calydon*

He weaves, and is clothed with derision;
    Sows, and he shall not reap;
His life is a watch or a vision
    Between a sleep and a sleep.
                    —SWINBURNE, *Atalanta in Calydon*

Man is the only animal that blushes. Or needs to.
    —MARK TWAIN, *Pudd'nhead Wilson's New Calendar*

And much it grieved my heart to think
    What Man has made of Man.
                    —WORDSWORTH, *Lines Written in Early Spring*

MAN AND WOMAN

I'm not denyin' the women are foolish: God Almighty
made 'em to match the men. —GEORGE ELIOT, *Adam Bede*

Male and female created he them.
                    —OLD TESTAMENT, *Genesis, I*, 27

One man among a thousand have I found; but a woman among all those have I not found.
—OLD TESTAMENT, *Ecclesiastes, VII, 28*

"MANDALAY"

By the old Moulmein Pagoda, lookin' eastward to the
 sea,
There's a Burma girl a-settin', and I know she thinks of
 me;
. . . .

On the road to Mandalay,
Where the flyin'-fishes play
An' the dawn comes up like thunder outer
 China 'crost the Bay!   —KIPLING, *Mandalay*

MANKIND

Let observation with extensive view,
Survey mankind from China to Peru.
—SAMUEL JOHNSON, *Vanity of Human Wishes*

MANNERS

What times! what manners!
(*O tempora! O mores!*)
—CICERO, *First Oration against Catiline*

MARRIAGE

Needles and pins, needles and pins,
When a man marries his trouble begins.
—ANON., Nursery Rhyme

They stood before the altar and supplied
The fire themselves in which their fat was fried.
—AMBROSE BIERCE, *The Devil's Dictionary*

Things at home are crossways, and Betsy and I are out.
—WILL CARLETON, *Betsy and I Are Out*

With this ring I thee wed, with my body I thee worship, and with all my worldly goods I thee endow.

—BOOK OF COMMON PRAYER

To have and to hold from this day forward, for better, for worse, for richer, for poorer, in sickness, and in health, to love and to cherish, till death do us part.

—BOOK OF COMMON PRAYER

Where there's marriage without love, there will be love without marriage.

—FRANKLIN, *Poor Richard's Almanac* for 1734

Deceive not thyself by overexpecting happiness in the married estate. Remember the nightingales which sing only some months in the spring, but commonly are silent when they have hatched their eggs.

—THOMAS FULLER, *Of Marriage*

I'm Smith of Stoke, and sixty-odd,
    I've lived without a dame
From youth-time on; and would to God
    My dad had done the same.

—THOMAS HARDY, *Epitaph on a Pessimist*

Down to Gehenna or up to the Throne,
He travels the fastest who travels alone.

—KIPLING, *The Winners*

For the race is run by one and one and never by two and
    two.   —KIPLING, *Tomlinson*

Advice to those about to marry—Don't.

—HENRY MAYHEW, *Punch's Almanac*, 1845

A good marriage would be between a blind wife and a deaf husband.   —MONTAIGNE, *Essays, III*

Bone of my bones, and flesh of my flesh.
—OLD TESTAMENT, *Genesis, II, 23*

It is better to marry than to burn.
—NEW TESTAMENT, *I Corinthians, VII, 9*

What therefore God hath joined together, let not man put asunder. —NEW TESTAMENT, *Matthew, XIX, 6*

It is not good that man should be alone.
—OLD TESTAMENT, *Genesis, II, 18*

Therefore shall a man leave his father and his mother, and shall cleave unto his wife: and they shall be one flesh.
—OLD TESTAMENT, *Genesis, II, 24*

I asked of Echo 't other day
    (Whose words are few and often funny),
What to a novice she could say
    Of courtship, love, and matrimony.
Quoth Echo, plainly,—"Matter-o'-money."
—J. G. SAXE, *Echo*

A young man married is a man that's marr'd.
—SHAKESPEARE, *All's Well That Ends Well, II, 3*

The ancient saying is no heresy,
Hanging and wiving go by destiny.
—SHAKESPEARE, *Merchant of Venice, II, 9*

Some pray to marry the man they love,
    My prayer will somewhat vary:
I humbly pray to Heaven above
    That I love the man I marry.
—ROSE PASTOR STOKES, *My Prayer*

What they do in heaven we are ignorant of; but what

they do *not* we are told expressly, that they neither marry,
nor are given in marriage.
—SWIFT, *Thoughts on Various Subjects*

As the husband is, the wife is: thou art mated with a
clown,
And the grossness of his nature will have weight to drag
thee down.   —TENNYSON, *Locksley Hall*

Doänt thou marry for munny, but goä wheer munny is!
—TENNYSON, *Northern Farmer, New Style*

MARRIAGE, SECOND

He loves his bonds, who, when the first are broke,
Submits his neck unto a second yoke.
—HERRICK, *Hesperides, 42*

Alas! another instance of the triumph of hope over experience.   —JOHNSON (Boswell's *Life* for 1770)

"MARSEILLAISE"

Ye sons of freedom wake to glory . . .
(Allons, enfants de la patrie!
Le jour de gloire est arrivé!
Contre nous de la tyrannie
L'étendard sanglant est levé . . .)
—ROUGET DE LISLE, *La Marseillaise* (1792)

MASTER

No man can serve two masters.
—NEW TESTAMENT, *Matthew, VI, 24*

'Ban, 'Ban, Ca-Caliban
Has a new master: get a new man.
—SHAKESPEARE, *The Tempest, II, 2*

Hail, fellow, well met,
All dirty and wet:

Find out, if you can,
Who's master, who's man.
                    —SWIFT, *My Lady's Lamentation*

MAY

As it fell upon a day
In the merry month of May,
Sitting in a pleasant shade
Which a grove of myrtle made.
            —RICHARD BARNFIELD, *Address to a Nightingale*

You must wake and call me early, call me early, mother
    dear;
To-morrow 'ill be the happiest time of all the glad New-
    year;
Of all the glad New-year, mother, the maddest merriest
    day;
For I'm to be Queen o' the May, mother, I'm to be
    Queen o' the May.   —TENNYSON, *The May Queen*

MEDICINE

Like cures like.
(*Similia similibus curantur.*)
                —HAHNEMANN, Motto for homoeopathy

MEEK

Blessed are the meek: for they shall inherit the earth.
                    —NEW TESTAMENT, *Matthew, V, 5*

MEETING

We loved, sir—used to meet:
How sad and bad and mad it was—
But then, how it was sweet! —R. BROWNING, *Confessions*

Ships that pass in the night, and speak each other in
    passing,
Only a signal shows and a distant voice in the darkness;
            —LONGFELLOW, *Tales of a Wayside Inn: Elizabeth*

Journeys end in lovers meeting,
Every wise man's son doth know.
>   —SHAKESPEARE, *Twelfth Night, II, 3*

FIRST WITCH: When shall we three meet again,
>   In thunder, lightning or in rain?
SECOND WITCH: When the hurlyburly's done,
>   When the battle's lost and won.
>   —SHAKESPEARE, *Macbeth, I, 1*

MELANCHOLY

If there be a hell upon earth it is to be found in a melancholy man's heart.
>   —BURTON, *Anatomy of Melancholy,* "Democritus to the
>   Reader"

With eyes up-rais'd, as one inspir'd,
Pale melancholy sate retir'd;
>   —W. COLLINS, *The Passions*

There's not a string attun'd to mirth
But has its chord in melancholy.
>   —THOMAS HOOD, *Ode to Melancholy*

A feeling of sadness and longing
>   That is not akin to pain,
And resembles sorrow only
>   As the mist resembles the rain.
>   —LONGFELLOW, *The Day Is Done*

But hail, thou Goddess, sage and holy,
Hail, divinest melancholy,
Whose Saintly visage is too bright
To hit the Sense of human sight.
>   —MILTON, *Il Penseroso*

Hence, loathed Melancholy,
Of Cerberus and blackest Midnight born,

In Stygian cave forlorn,
'Mongst horrid shapes, and shrieks and sights unholy!
—MILTON, *L'Allegro*

MEMORY

When other lips and other hearts
  Their tales of woe shall tell,
In language whose excess imparts
  The power they feel so well,
There may, perhaps, in such a scene,
  Some recollection be
Of days that have as happy been,
  And you'll remember me.
—ALFRED BUNN, *The Bohemian Girl, III*

There is no greater sorrow than to recall, in misery, the
time when we were happy.
*(Nessun maggior dolore, Che ricordarsi del tempo felice
Nella miseria;)*   —DANTE, *Inferno, V*

I remember, I remember
The house where I was born,
The little window where the sun
Came peeping in at morn.
—THOMAS HOOD, *I Remember, I Remember*

'Tis but a little faded flower,
  But oh, how fondly dear!
'Twill bring me back one golden hour,
  Through many a weary year.
—ELLEN C. HOWARTH, *'Tis But a Little Faded Flower*

Long, long be my heart with such memories fill'd!
Like the vase in which roses have once been distill'd:
You may break, you may shatter the vase if you will,
But the scent of the roses will hang round it still.
—THOMAS MOORE, *Farewell! But Whenever . . .*

Oft, in the stilly night,
   Ere Slumber's chain has bound me,
Fond Memory brings the light
  Of other days around me.
               —THOMAS MOORE, *The Light of Other Days*

Better by far you should forget and smile,
Than that you should remember and be sad.
               —CHRISTINA ROSSETTI, *A Birthday*

When to the sessions of sweet silent thought
I summon up remembrance of things past,
I sigh the lack of many a thing I sought,
And with old woes new wail my dear time's waste.
               —SHAKESPEARE, *Sonnets, XXX*

Rose-leaves, when the rose is dead,
Are heaped for the beloved's bed;
And so thy thoughts, when thou art gone,
Love itself shall slumber on.
    —SHELLEY, *To —— (Music, When Soft Voices Die)*

          This is the truth the poet sings
That sorrow's crown of sorrow is remembering happier
things.   —TENNYSON, *Locksley Hall*

Out of the cradle endlessly rocking,
Out of the mocking-bird's throat, the musical shuttle . . .
A reminiscence sing.
           —WALT WHITMAN, *Out of the Cradle*

MERCY

Blessed are the merciful: for they shall obtain mercy.
          —NEW TESTAMENT, *Matthew, V, 7*

Teach me to feel another's woe,
   To hide the fault I see;

That mercy I to others show,
    That mercy show to me.   —POPE, *Universal Prayer*

The quality of mercy is not strain'd;
It droppeth as the gentle rain from heaven
Upon the place beneath: it is twice blest;
It blesseth him that gives and him that takes:
'Tis mightiest in the mightiest: it becomes
The throned monarch better than his crown;

. . . .

And earthly power doth then show likest God's
When mercy seasons justice.
                —SHAKESPEARE, *Merchant of Venice, IV, 1*

MERRIMENT

There was a jolly miller once,
    Lived on the river Dee;
He work'd and sung, from morn till night,
    No lark more blythe than he.
And this the burthen of his song,
    For ever us'd to be,
"I care for nobody, not I,
    If no one cares for me."
            —ISAAC BICKERSTAFFE, *Love in a Village, I, 5*

A merry heart maketh a cheerful countenance.
            —OLD TESTAMENT, *Proverbs, XV, 13*

Merrily, merrily, shall I live now
Under the blossom that hangs on the bough.
                —SHAKESPEARE, *The Tempest, V, 1*

For the good are always the merry,
Save by an evil chance,
And the merry love the fiddle,
And the merry love to dance.
                —W. B. YEATS, *The Fiddler of Dooney*

MIDNIGHT

I stood on the bridge at midnight,
  As the clocks were striking the hour,
And the moon rose o'er the city
  Behind the dark church-tower.
                    —LONGFELLOW, *The Bridge*

Once upon a midnight dreary, while I pondered, weak
  and weary, . . .   —POE, *The Raven*

'Tis now the very witching time of night,
When churchyards yawn and hell itself breathes but
Contagion to this world. —SHAKESPEARE, *Hamlet, III, 2*

MIGHT

Let us have faith that right makes might, and in that
faith let us to the end dare to do our duty as we understand it.   —LINCOLN, *Address*, Feb., 1860

I proclaim that might is right, justice the interest of the
stronger.   —PLATO, *The Republic, I*

MILL

And a proverb haunts my mind
  As a spell is cast,
"The mill cannot grind
  With the water that is past."
        —SARAH DOUDNEY, *The Lesson of the Water-Mill*

MILTON, JOHN

Three Poets, in three distant Ages born,
Greece, Italy, and England did adorn.
The first in loftiness of thought surpass'd,
The next in majesty, in both the last:
The force of nature could no farther go;
  To make the third she join'd the former two.
          —DRYDEN, *Lines under the Portrait of Milton*

O Mighty-Mouth'd inventor of harmonies,
O skill'd to sing of Time or Eternity,
God-gifted organ-voice of England,
Milton, a name to resound for ages.
—TENNYSON, *Milton*

Thy soul was like a Star, and dwelt apart;
Thou hadst a voice whose sound was like the sea:
Pure as the naked heavens, majestic, free,
So didst thou travel on life's common way,
In cheerful godliness; and yet thy heart
The lowliest duties on herself did lay.
—WORDSWORTH, *Sonnet: London, 1802*

MIND

My mind to me a Kingdom is;
  Such present joys therein I find,
That it excels all other bliss
  That earth affords or grows by kind:
Though much I want which most would have,
Yet still my mind forbids to crave.
—EDWARD DYER, *My Mind to Me a Kingdom Is*

God is Mind, and God is infinite; hence all is Mind.
—MARY BAKER EDDY, *Science and Health*

A sound mind in a sound body.
(*Mens sana in corpore sano.*)   —JUVENAL, *Satires, X*

What is mind? No matter. What is matter? Never mind.
—T. H. KEY (quoted by F. J. Furnivall)

Canst thou minister to a mind diseased,
Pluck from the memory a rooted sorrow,
Raze out the written troubles of the brain,
And with some sweet oblivious antidote

Cleanse the stuff'd bosom of that perilous matter
Which weighs upon the heart?
                    —SHAKESPEARE, *Macbeth*, V, 3

O what a noble mind is here o'erthrown!

. . . .

. . . that noble and most sovereign reason,
Like sweet bells jangled, out of tune and harsh.
                    —SHAKESPEARE, *Hamlet*, III, 1

The lightning-bug is brilliant, but he hasn't any mind;
He stumbles through existence with his head-light on
    behind.   —E. F. WARE, *The Lightning-Bug*

I have a single-track mind.
        —WOODROW WILSON, Speech, National Press Club

MINUTE

One by one the sands are flowing,
    One by one the moments fall;
Some are coming, some are going:
    Do not strive to grasp them all.
                    —ADELAIDE A. PROCTOR, *One by One*

MIRROR

I change, and so do women too;
But I reflect, which women never do.
                —ANON., *Written on a Looking-Glass*

Be sure to keep a mirror always nigh
    In some convenient, handy sort of place,
And now and then look squarely in thine eye,
    And with thyself keep ever face to face.
                    —JOHN K. BANGS, *Face to Face*

To hold as 'twere, the mirror up to nature.
                    —SHAKESPEARE, *Hamlet*, III, 2

MIRTH

> Come, thou Goddess fair and free,
> In Heaven yclept Euphrosyne,
> And by men, heart-easing Mirth. —MILTON, *L'Allegro*

MISCHIEF

> But when to mischief mortals bend their will,
> How soon they find fit instruments of ill!
> —POPE, *The Rape of the Lock, III*

MISERY

> Remembering mine affliction and my misery, the worm-
> wood and the gall.
> —OLD TESTAMENT, *Lamentations, III, 19*

> Misery acquaints a man with strange bed-fellows.
> —SHAKESPEARE, *The Tempest, II, 2*

> If misery loves company, misery has company enough.
> —THOREAU, *Journal*, Sept., 1851

> Preach to the storm, and reason with despair,
> But tell not Misery's son that life is fair.
> —H. K. WHITE, *Lines on Reading . . .*

MISFORTUNE

> When sorrows come, they come not single spies,
> But in battalions.   —SHAKESPEARE, *Hamlet, IV, 5*

MISSIONARY

> From Greenland's icy mountains,
>   From India's coral strand,
> Where Afric's sunny fountains
>   Roll down their golden sand;
> From many an ancient river,
>   From many a palmy plain,
> They call us to deliver
>   Their land from error's chain.
> —REGINALD HEBER, *Missionary Hymn*

If I were a Cassowary
   On the plains of Timbuctoo,
I would eat a missionary,
   Coat and bands and hymn-book too.
            —BISHOP S. WILBERFORCE, *Epigram*

MISTAKE

Earth bears no balsam for mistakes;
   Men crown the knave, and scourge the tool
That did his will: but thou, O Lord,
   Be merciful to me, a fool.
            —E. R. SILL, *The Fool's Prayer*

MISTRESS

Chaste to her husband, frank to all beside,
A teeming mistress, but a barren bride.
            —POPE, *Moral Essays, III*

Next to the pleasure of making a new mistress is that
of being rid of an old one.
            —WYCHERLEY, *The Country Wife, I*

MOB

The fickle mob.
(*Mobile . . . vulgus.*)   —CLAUDIAN, *Panegyricus . . .*

MODERATION

O grant me, Heaven, a middle state,
Neither too humble nor too great;
More than enough for nature's ends,
With something left to treat my friends.
            —DAVID MALLET, *Imitation of Horace*

MODESTY

I have done one braver thing
   Than all the Worthies did,
And yet a braver thence did spring,
   Which is, to keep that hid. —DONNE, *The Undertaking*

MONARCH

I am monarch of all I survey,
My right there is none to dispute;
From the center all round to the sea,
I am lord of the fowl and the brute.
—COWPER, *Verses Supposed to Be Written
by Alexander Selkirk*

MONEY

I cannot afford to waste my time making money.
—AGASSIZ (when offered a large sum for
a course of lectures)

If you want to know what God thinks of money, look at
the people he gives it to. —ANON. (New England saying)

Money is honey, my little sonny,
And a rich man's joke is always funny.
—T. E. BROWN, *The Doctor*

Annual income twenty pounds, annual expenditure
nineteen nineteen six, result happiness. Annual income
twenty pounds, annual expenditure twenty pounds ought
and six, result misery. —DICKENS, *David Copperfield*

Money is like an arm or a leg—use it or lose it.
—HENRY FORD, Interview, *N. Y. Times*, Nov. 8, 1931

Never ask of money spent
Where the spender thinks it went.
Nobody was ever meant
To remember or invent
What he did with every cent.
—ROBERT FROST, *The Hardship of Accounting*

Put not your trust in money, but put your money in trust.
—O. W. HOLMES, *The Autocrat of the Breakfast-Table*

Up and down the City Road, in and out the Eagle,
That's the way the money goes—pop goes the weasel!
        —W. R. MANDALE (?), *Pop Goes the Weasel*

For the love of money is the root of all evil.
                —NEW TESTAMENT, *I Timothy, VI, 10*

Not greedy of filthy lucre.
                —NEW TESTAMENT, *I Timothy, III, 3*

Get Place and Wealth, if possible with grace;
If not, by any means get Wealth and Place.
            —POPE, *Imitations of Horace: Epistles*

O, what a world of vile ill-favoured faults
Looks handsome in three hundred pounds a-year.
        —SHAKESPEARE, *The Merry Wives of Windsor, III, 4*

Who steals my purse steals trash.
                —SHAKESPEARE, *Othello, III, 3*

Let all the learned say what they can,
'Tis ready money makes the man.
            —WILLIAM SOMERVILLE, *Ready Money*

When it is a question of money, everybody is of the same
religion.   —VOLTAIRE (in conversation)

MONROE DOCTRINE

... We should consider any attempt on their [European
nations] part to extend their system to any portion of this
hemisphere, as dangerous to our peace and safety.
            —JAMES MONROE, Message to Congress, 1823

MONTHS

Thirty days hath September,
April, June, and November
All the rest have thirty-one,

Save February alone,
Which hath twenty-eight, in fine,
Till Leap-Year gives it twenty-nine.
—RICHARD GRAFTON (1570)

MONUMENT

I would much rather have men ask why I have no statue
than why I have one.
—MARCUS CATO (Plutarch, *Life of Cato*)

If you would see his monument, look around.
(Si monumentum requiris circumspice.)
—CHRISTOPHER WREN, Epitaph for his father, Sir C. Wren,
in St. Paul's

MOON

By the light of the moon,	*(Au clair de la lune,*
My friend Pierrot,	*Mon ami Pierrot,*
Lend me thy pen	*Prête moi ta plume,*
to write a word;	*Pour écrire un mot;*
My candle is out,	*Ma chandelle est morte,*
I've no more fire,	*Je n'ai plus de feu,*
Open your door to me,	*Ouvre moi ta porte,*
for the love of God.	*Pour l'amour de Dieu.)*

—ANON., (French song, quoted in Du Maurier's *Trilby*)

Late, late yestreen I saw the new moon,
Wi' the auld moon in hir arm.
—ANON., *Sir Patrick Spence*

The moon, like a flower,
In heaven's high bower
With silent delight
Sits and smiles on the night. —BLAKE, *Night*

The moving Moon went up the sky,
And no where did abide:

Softly she was going up,
    And a star or two beside.
                    —S. T. Coleridge, *The Ancient Mariner*

Queen and huntress, chaste and fair,
    Now the sun is laid to sleep,
Seated in thy silver chair
    State in wonted manner keep.
—Ben Jonson, *Hymn to Diana (Cynthia's Revels, V, 3)*

To behold the wandering Moon
Riding near her highest noon,
Like one that has been led astray
Through the heav'n's wide pathless way;
And oft, as if her head she bow'd,
Stooping through a fleecy cloud.
                            —Milton, *Il Penseroso*

The moon was a ghostly galleon tossed upon cloudy seas.
                    —Alfred Noyes, *The Highwayman*

O, swear not by the moon, the inconstant moon,
That monthly changes in her circled orb,
Lest that thy love prove likewise variable
                    —Shakespeare, *Romeo and Juliet, II, 2*

That orbèd maiden with white fire laden,
Whom mortals call the moon, . . .
                    —Shelley, *The Cloud*

You meaner beauties of the night,
    That poorly satisfy our eyes
More by your number than your light
    You common people of the skies,—
    What are you when the moon shall rise?
    —Sir Henry Wotton, *On His Mistress, the Queen of
                                    Bohemia*

MORALITY

Morality is a private and costly luxury.
      —HENRY ADAMS, *The Education of Henry Adams*

What we call "morals" is simply blind obedience to words of command.—HAVELOCK ELLIS, *The Dance of Life*

. . . What is moral is what you feel good after and what is immoral is what you feel bad after . . .
      —ERNEST HEMINGWAY, *Death in the Afternoon*

MORNING

Full many a glorious morning have I seen
Flatter the mountain-tops with sovereign eye.
      —SHAKESPEARE, *Sonnets, XXXIII*

See how the morning opes her golden gates,
And takes her farewell of the glorious sun!
      —SHAKESPEARE, *Henry VI, III, II, 1*

MORTALITY

All that's bright must fade,—
   The brightest still the fleetest;
All that's sweet was made
   But to be lost when sweetest.
      —THOMAS MOORE, *All That's Bright Must Fade*

All flesh is grass, and all the goodliness thereof is as the flower of the field.   —OLD TESTAMENT, *Isaiah, XL, 6*

   Consider
The lilies of the field whose bloom is brief:—
   We are as they;
   Like them we fade away
As doth a leaf.   —CHRISTINA ROSSETTI, *Consider*

   . . . who would fardels bear,
To grunt and sweat under a weary life,

But that the dread of something after death,
The undiscover'd country from whose bourn
No traveller returns, puzzles the will
And makes us rather bear those ills we have
Than fly to others that we know not of?
                              —SHAKESPEARE, *Hamlet, III, 1*

MOSES

By Nebo's lonely mountain,
    On this side Jordan's wave,
In a vale in the land of Moab,
    There lies a lonely grave; . . .
          —CECIL FRANCES ALEXANDER, *The Burial of Moses*

Now the man Moses was very meek, above all the men
which were upon the face of the earth.
                        —OLD TESTAMENT, *Numbers, XII, 3*

MOTHER

God could not be everywhere and therefore he made
mothers.   —ANON. (Jewish proverb)

The sweetest sounds to mortals given
Are heard in Mother, Home and Heaven.
                    —W. G. BROWN, *Mother, Home, Heaven*

My mother! when I learn'd that thou wast dead,
Say, wast thou conscious of the tears I shed?
Hover'd thy spirit o'er thy sorrowing son,
Wretch even then, life's journey just begun?
Perhaps thou gav'st me, though unseen, a kiss;
Perhaps a tear, if souls can weep in bliss—
Ah, that maternal smile! it answers—Yes.
          —COWPER, *On the Receipt of My Mother's Picture*

Where yet was ever found a mother,
Who'd give her booby for another?   —GAY, *Fables, 1*

What is home without a mother?
                    —ALICE HAWTHORNE, *What is home . . .*

If I were hanged on the highest hill,
    Mother o' mine, O mother o' mine!
I know whose love would follow me still,
    Mother o' mine, O mother o' mine!
    —KIPLING, *Mother o' Mine* (in *The Light That Failed*)

I pray that our Heavenly Father may assuage the anguish of your bereavement and leave you only the cherished memory of the loved and lost, and the solemn pride that must be yours to have laid so costly a sacrifice upon the altar of freedom.
                    —LINCOLN, Letter to Mrs. Bixby, 1864

Her children arise and call her blessed.
                    —OLD TESTAMENT, *Proverbs, XXXI, 28*

The angels . . . singing unto one another,
Can find among their burning terms of love,
None so devotional as that of "mother."
                    —POE, *To My Mother*

For the hand that rocks the cradle
    Is the hand that rules the world.
        —W. S. ROSS, *The Hand That Rocks the Cradle*

Who ran to help me when I fell,
And would some pretty story tell,
Or kiss the place to make it well?
    My Mother.   —ANN TAYLOR, *My Mother*

Mother is the name for God in the lips and hearts of little children.   —THACKERAY, *Vanity Fair*

MOUNTAIN

I am homesick for my mountains—
  My heroic mother hills—
And the longing that is on me
  No solace ever stills.
                    —BLISS CARMAN, *The Cry of the Hill-born*

Whoever shall say unto this mountain, be thou removed
and be thou cast into the sea; and shall not doubt in his
heart, but shall believe that those things which he saith
shall come to pass; he shall have what ever he saith.
                    —NEW TESTAMENT, *Mark, XI, 23*

The mountain groaned in pangs of birth:
Great expectation filled the earth;
  And lo! a mouse was born!
                    —PHAEDRUS, *Fables, IV* (anonymous metrical
                                          rendering)

MOURNING

Round, round the cypress bier
  Where she lies sleeping,
On every turf a tear,
  Let us go weeping!   —GEORGE DARLEY, *Dirge*

It is better to go to the house of mourning than to go to
the house of feasting.
                    —OLD TESTAMENT, *Ecclesiastes, VII, 2*

Soft is the note, and sad the lay,
  That mourns the lovely Rosabelle.
                    —SCOTT, *Lay of the Last Minstrel, VI*

MOUSE

Wee sleekit, cow'rin', tim'rous beastie,
Oh, what a panic's in thy breastie!—BURNS, *To a Mouse*

MOUSE-TRAP

If a man can write a better book, preach a better sermon, or make a better mouse-trap than his neighbor, though he builds his house in the woods, the world will make a beaten path to his door.—EMERSON, lecture in 1871

MOUTH

Mouth: In man the gateway to the soul; in woman, the outlet of the heart.   —BIERCE, *The Devil's Dictionary*

MUGWUMP

A mugwump is a fellow with his mug on one side of the fence and his wump on the other.
—HAROLD W. DODDS (quoted in Pollard's *A Connotary*)

MURDER

Thou shalt not kill; but needst not strive
Officiously to keep alive.
            —A. H. CLOUGH, *The Latest Decalogue*

Cut off even in the blossoms of my sin,
Unhousel'd, disappointed, unaneled,
No reckoning made, but sent to my account
With all my imperfections on my head.
            —SHAKESPEARE, *Hamlet, I, 5*

   The great King of Kings
Hath in the tables of his law commanded
That thou shalt do no murder.
            —SHAKESPEARE, *Richard III, 1, 4*

Yet each man kills the thing he loves.
            —OSCAR WILDE, *Ballad of Reading Gaol*

MUSE

Alas! what boots it with incessant care
To tend the homely, slighted shepherd's trade,

And strictly meditate the thankless Muse?
> —MILTON, *Lycidas*

MUSIC

Such sweet
Soft notes as yet musician's cunning
Never gave the enraptured air.
> —R. BROWNING, *The Pied Piper*

There's music in the sighing of a reed;
    There's music in the gushing of a rill;
There's music in all things, if men had ears:
Their earth is but an echo of the spheres.
> —BYRON, *Don Juan, XV*

O Music, sphere-descended maid,
Friend of pleasure, wisdom's aid.
> —WILLIAM COLLINS, *The Passions*

When Music, Heav'nly Maid, was young,
While yet in early Greece she sung,
The Passions oft, to hear her shell,
Throng'd around her magic cell.
> —WILLIAM COLLINS, *The Passions*

Music hath charms to soothe a savage breast,
To soften rocks, or bend a knotted oak.
> —CONGREVE, *The Mourning Bride, I, 1*

Heard melodies are sweet, but those unheard
    Are sweeter; therefore, ye soft pipes, play on;
Not to the sensual ear, but, more endear'd,
    Pipe to the spirit ditties of no tone.
> —KEATS, *Ode on a Grecian Urn*

In notes, with many a winding bout
Of linkèd sweetness, long drawn out.
> —MILTON, *L'Allegro*

There's a barrel-organ carolling across a golden street
    In the city as the sun sinks low;
And the music's not immortal; but the world has made it
    sweet
    And fulfilled it with the sunset's glow.
                            —ALFRED NOYES, *The Barrel-Organ*

When the morning stars sang together, and all the sons
of God shouted for joy.—OLD TESTAMENT, *Job, XXXVIII, 7*

We are the music-makers,
    And we are the dreamers of dreams,
Wandering by lone sea-breakers,
    And sitting by desolate streams.
                        —A. O'SHAUGHNESSY, *The Music-Makers*

Seated one day at the organ,
    I was weary and ill at ease,
And my fingers wandered idly
    Over the noisy keys.
I know not what I was playing,
    Or what I was dreaming then,
But I struck one chord of music
    Like the sound of a great Amen.
                        —ADELAIDE A. PROCTOR, *The Lost Chord*

If music be the food of love, play on;
Give me excess of it, that, surfeiting,
The appetite may sicken, and so die.
                        —SHAKESPEARE, *Twelfth Night, I, 1*

Orpheus with his lute made trees,
And the mountain tops that freeze,
    Bow themselves when he did sing:
To his music plants and flowers
Ever sprung; as sun and showers,
    There had made a lasting spring.
                        —SHAKESPEARE, *Henry VIII, III, 1*

The man that hath no music in himself,
Nor is not moved with concord of sweet sounds,
Is fit for treasons, stratagems and spoils.
                    —SHAKESPEARE, *Merchant of Venice*, V, 1

Music, when soft voices die,
Vibrates in the memory; —SHELLEY, *To* —— (1821)

Open my ears to music; let
    Me thrill with Spring's first flutes and drums—
But never let me dare forget
    The bitter ballads of the slums.
                            —LOUIS UNTERMEYER, *Prayer*

MYSELF

I celebrate myself, and sing myself,
And what I assume you shall assume,
For every atom belonging to me as good belongs to you.
                        —WALT WHITMAN, *Song of Myself*

NAME

I have fallen in love with American names,
The sharp names that never get fat,
The snakeskin-titles of mining-claims,
The plumed war-bonnet of Medicine Hat,
Tucson and Deadwood and Lost Mule Flat.
                —STEPHEN VINCENT BENÉT, *American Names*

He left a name, at which the world grew pale,
To point a moral or adorn a tale.
                    —JOHNSON, *The Vanity of Human Wishes*

My name is Legion: for we are many.
                        —NEW TESTAMENT, *Mark*, V, 9

What's in a name? That which we call a rose
By any other name would smell as sweet;
                    —SHAKESPEARE, *Romeo and Juliet*, II, 2

NATION

The first panacea for a mismanaged nation is inflation of the currency; the second is war. Both bring a temporary prosperity; both bring a permanent ruin. But both are the refuge of political and economic opportunists.
—ERNEST HEMINGWAY, *Notes on the Next War*

NATURE

Nature, to be commanded, must be obeyed.
—FRANCIS BACON, *Novum Organum*

To him who in the love of Nature holds
Communion with her visible forms, she speaks
A various language;
—WILLIAM C. BRYANT, *Thanatopsis*

There is a pleasure in the pathless woods,
There is rapture on the lonely shore,
There is society where none intrudes,
By the deep sea, and music in its roar;
I love not Man the less, but Nature more,
From these our interviews. —BYRON, *Childe Harold, IV*

I do not count the hours I spend
In wandering by the sea;
The forest is my loyal friend,
Like God it useth me. —EMERSON, *Waldeinsamkeit*

The meanest floweret of the vale,
The simplest note that swells the gale,
The common sun, the air, the skies,
To him are opening Paradise.
—GRAY, *On the Pleasures Arising from Vicissitude*

Nature does not proceed by leaps.
(*Natura non facit saltus.*)
—LINNAEUS, *Philosophia Botanica*

Over our manhood bend the skies;
   Against our fallen and traitor lives
The great winds utter prophesies;
   With our faint hearts the mountain strives;
Its arms outstretched, the druid wood
   Waits with its benedicite;
And to our age's drowsy blood
   Still shouts the inspiring sea.
                —J. R. LOWELL, *The Vision of Sir Launfal*

Wherefore did Nature pour her bounties forth
With such a full and unwithdrawing hand,
Covering the earth with odours, fruits, and flocks,
Thronging the seas with spawn innumerable,
But all to please, and sate the curious taste?
                —MILTON, *Comus*

The heavens declare the glory of God, and the firmament sheweth his handywork.
                —OLD TESTAMENT, *Psalms, XIX, 1*

All are but parts of one stupendous Whole,
Whose body Nature is, and God the soul;
                —POPE, *Essay on Man, I*

One touch of nature makes the whole world kin.
                —SHAKESPEARE, *Troilus and Cressida, III, 3*

. . . Nature is hitting back. Not with the old weapons—
floods, plagues, holocausts. We can neutralize them. She's
fighting back with strange instruments called neuroses.
She's deliberately inflicting mankind with the jitters. . . .
She's taking the world away from the intellectuals and
giving it back to the apes.
                —ROBERT E. SHERWOOD, *The Petrified Forest*

Are God and Nature then at strife,
   That Nature lends such evil dreams?

So careful of the type she seems,
So careless of the single life. —TENNYSON, *In Memoriam*

Talk not of temples, there is one
  Built without hands, to mankind given;
Its lamps are the meridian sun
  And all the stars of heaven,
Its walls are the cerulean sky,
  Its floor the earth so green and fair,
The dome its vast immensity,
  All Nature worships there.
             —DAVID VEDDER, *The Temple of Nature*

  Nature never did betray
The heart that loved her.
             —WORDSWORTH, *Tintern Abbey*

NAZARETH

Can there any good thing come out of Nazareth?
          —NEW TESTAMENT, *John, I, 46*

NEAT

Still to be neat, still to be drest,
As you were going to a feast;
Still to be powder'd, still perfumed:
Lady, it is to be presumed,
Though art's hid causes are not found,
All is not sweet, all is not sound.
             —BEN JONSON, *Epicoene*, Song, *I*

NECESSITY

Necessity is the mother of invention.
(Mater artium necessitas.)   —ANON. (Latin proverb)

Necessity knows no law.
(Necessitas non habet legem.)
          —ST. AUGUSTINE, *Solil. Animae ad Deum*

NEGRO

My mother bore me in the southern wild,
And I am black, but O my soul is white!

—BLAKE, *The Little Black Boy*

Not for myself I make this prayer,
    But for this race of mine
That stretches forth from shadowed places
    Dark hands for bread and wine.

—COUNTEE CULLEN, *Pagan Prayer*

She thinks that even up in heaven
    Her class lies late and snores,
While poor black cherubs rise at seven
    To do celestial chores.

—COUNTEE CULLEN, *Epitaph: A Lady I Know*

A bright bowl of brass is beautiful to the Lord.
Bright polished brass like the cymbals
Of King David's dancers
Like the wine cups of Solomon.
    Hey, boy!
A clean spittoon on the altar of the Lord.
A clean bright spittoon all newly polished,—
At least I can offer that.
    Com'mere, boy!

—LANGSTON HUGHES, *Brass Spittoons*

The night is beautiful
So the faces of my people.

The stars are beautiful
So the eyes of my people.

Beautiful also is the sun.
Beautiful also are the souls of my people.

—LANGSTON HUGHES, *My People*

In the right to eat the bread . . . which his own hand earns, he [the Negro] *is my equal and the equal of Judge Douglas, and the equal of every living man.*
—LINCOLN, Lincoln-Douglas Debates, Aug., 1858

Can the Ethiopian change his skin, or the leopard his spots?   —OLD TESTAMENT, *Jeremiah, XIII, 23*

. . . the negroes had been regarded as beings of an inferior order . . . so far inferior that they had no rights which a white man was bound to respect.
—CHIEF-JUSTICE R. B. TANEY,
In the Dred-Scott Decision, 1857

NEIGHBOR

In the field of world policy I would dedicate this nation to the policy of the good neighbor.
—FRANKLIN D. ROOSEVELT, First Inaugural Address

''NEVERMORE''

Take thy beak from out my heart and take thy form from off my door!
Quoth the Raven, "Nevermore!"   —POE, *The Raven*

NEW YORK

. . . little old Noisyville-on-the-Subway is good enough for me.   —O. HENRY, *The Gentle Grafter*

Vulgar of manner, overfed,
Overdressed and underbred;
. . . .
Crazed with avarice, lust and rum,
New York, thy name's Delirium.
—B. R. NEWTON, *Owed to New York* (1906)

City of hurried and sparkling waters! city of spires and
masts!
City nested in bays! my city!
—WALT WHITMAN, *When Lilacs Last in the
Dooryard Bloom'd*

A little strip of an island with a row of well-fed folks up and down the middle, and a lot of hungry folks on each side.   —HARRY LEON WILSON, *The Spenders*

NEWS

When a dog bites a man that is not news, but when a man bites a dog that is news.

—JOHN B. BOGART (usually attributed to C. A. Dana)

NEWTON, SIR ISAAC

I do not know what I may appear to the world, but to myself I seem to have been only like a boy playing on the seashore and diverting myself in now and then finding a smoothe pebble or a prettier shell than ordinary whilst the great ocean of truth lay all undiscovered before me.

—ISAAC NEWTON (quoted in Brewster's *Memoirs of Newton*)

Nature and Nature's laws lay hid in Night:
God said, Let Newton bel and all was Light.
            —POPE, *Epitaph for Sir Isaac Newton*

NIGHT

The day is done, and the darkness
    Falls from the wings of Night,
As a feather is wafted downward
    From an eagle in his flight.
            —LONGFELLOW, *The Day Is Done*

Come, civil night,
Thou sober-suited matron, all in black, ...
With thy black mantle.
            —SHAKESPEARE, *Romeo and Juliet, III, 2*

Come seeling night,
Scarf up the tender eye of pitiful day.

. . . Light thickens; and the crow
Makes wing to the rooky wood.

—SHAKESPEARE, *Macbeth, III, 2*

Mysterious Night! when our first parent knew
Thee from report divine, and heard thy name,
Did he not tremble for this lovely frame,
This glorious canopy of light and blue?

—J. BLANCO WHITE, *Sonnet: Night*

NIGHTINGALE

The nightingales are singing near
The Convent of the Sacred Heart
And sang within the bloody wood
When Agamemnon cried aloud.

—T. S. ELIOT, *Sweeney Among the Nightingales*

Thou wast not born for death, immortal Bird!
No hungry generations tread thee down;
The voice I hear this passing night was heard
In ancient days by emperor and clown:
Perhaps the self-same song that found a path
Through the sad heart of Ruth, when, sick for home
She stood in tears amid the alien corn;
The same that oft-times hath
Charm'd magic casements, opening on the foam
Of perilous seas, in faery lands forlorn.

—KEATS, *Ode to a Nightingale*

O nightingale, that on yon bloomy spray
Warblest at eve, when all the woods are still.

—MILTON, *Sonnet: To a Nightingale*

Sweet bird that shunn'st the noise of folly,
Most musical, most melancholy!
Thee, chauntress, oft, the woods among,
I woo, to hear thy even-song.   —MILTON, *Il Penseroso*

Last night the nightingale woke me,
Last night, when all was still.
It sang in the golden moonlight,
From out the woodland hill.
                    —C. Winther, *Sehnsucht* (T. Marzials trans.)

NOBILITY

Howe'er it be, it seems to me,
'Tis only noble to be good.
                    —Tennyson, *Lady Clara Vere de Vere*

There is
One great society alone on earth:
The noble Living and the noble Dead.
                    —Wordsworth, *The Prelude, XI*

NONSENSE

A little nonsense now and then
Is relished by the best of men.
                    —Anon. (old nursery rhyme)

NONSENSE VERSES, FAMOUS

1. If all the world were paper
    And all the sea were ink,
    And all the trees were bread and cheese,
    What should we do for drink?
                    —Anon., *Interrogation Cantilena* (1641)

2. Peter Piper picked a peck of pickled peppers,
    A peck of pickled peppers did Peter Piper pick;
    If Peter Piper picked a peck of pickled peppers,
    Where's the peck of pickled peppers that Peter
        Piper picked?   —Anon. (old nursery rhyme)

3. The conductor when he receives a fare,
    Must punch in the presence of the passenjare;
    A blue trip slip for an 8-cent fare,

A buff trip slip for a 6-cent fare,
A pink trip slip for a 3-cent fare,
All in the presence of the passenjare.
Punch, boys, punch, punch with care,
All in the presence of the passenjare.
                    —I. H. BROMLEY (*not* Mark Twain) 1875

4. The piper he piped on the hill-top high
       (*Butter and eggs and a pound of cheese*)
   Till the cow said, "I die," and the goose said,
       "Why?"
   And the dog said nothing, but searched for fleas.
                    —C. S. CALVERLEY, *Ballad of the Period*

5. He thought he saw an Elephant,
       That practised on a fife:
   He looked again, and found it was
       A letter from his wife.
   "At length I realise," he said,
       "The bitterness of Life!"
                    —LEWIS CARROLL, *The Gardener's Song*
                             (from *Sylvie and Bruno*)

6. 'Twas brillig and the slithy toves
       Did gyre and gimble in the wabe;
   All mimsy were the borogoves,
       And the mome raths outgrabe.
                    —LEWIS CARROLL, *Jabberwocky* (in *Through
                             the Looking Glass*)

7. Sally Satter, she was a young teacher who taught,
   And her friend, Charley Church, was a preacher
       who praught,
   Though his enemies called him a screecher who
       scraught.   —PHOEBE CARY, *The Lovers*

8. If the man who turnips cries,
   Cry not when his father dies,
   'Tis proof that he had rather
   Have a turnip than a father.
   —SAMUEL JOHNSON, Burlesque of Lope de Vega

9. The Owl and the Pussy-Cat went to sea
   In a beautiful pea-green boat
   . . . .
   They dined on mince with slices of quince,
   Which they ate with a runcible spoon,
   And hand in hand, on the edge of the sand,
   They danced by the light of the moon.
   —EDWARD LEAR, *The Owl and the Pussy-Cat*

10. The Pobble who has no toes
    Had once as many as we;
    When they said, "Some day you may lose them all,"
    He replied, "Fish fiddle-de-dee!"
    And his Aunt Jobiska made him drink
    Lavender water tinged with pink,
    For she said, "The World in general knows
    There's nothing so good for a Pobble's toes!"
    —EDWARD LEAR, *The Pobble Who Had No Toes*

11. Said Opie Read to E. P. Roe,
    "How do you like Gaboriau?"
    "I like him very much indeed,"
    Said E. P. Roe to Opie Read."
    —JULIAN STREET AND J. M. FLAGG, *Read and Roe*

12. One, whom we see not, is; and one, who is not, we
    see;
    Fiddle, we know, is diddle; and diddle, we take it,
    is dee.
    —SWINBURNE, *The Higher Pantheism in a Nutshell*

NOSE

Cleopatra's nose: had it been shorter, the whole aspect
of the world would have been altered.—PASCAL, *Pensées, II*

NOTHING

Nothing to do but work,
    Nothing to eat but food,
Nothing to wear but clothes
    To keep one from going nude.

Nothing to breathe but air,
    Quick as a flash 'tis gone;
Nothing to fall but off,
    Nowhere to stand but on.   —BEN KING, *The Pessimist*

NUDITY

And they were both naked, the man and his wife, and
were not ashamed.   —OLD TESTAMENT, *Genesis, II, 25*

We shift and bedeck and bedrape us,
    Thou art noble and nude and antique;
Libitina thy mother, Priapus
    Thy father, a Tuscan and Greek.
                                    —SWINBURNE, *Dolores*

NUN

If you become a nun, dear,
    A friar I will be;
In any cell you run, dear,
    Pray look behind for me.   —LEIGH HUNT, *The Nun*

OAK

A song to the oak, the brave old oak,
    Who hath ruled in the greenwood long;
          .   .   .   .
Then here's to the oak, the brave old oak,
    Who stands in his pride alone!

And still flourish he, a hale green tree,
    When a hundred years are gone!
                —H. F. CHORLEY, *The Brave Old Oak*

OATH

Let my right hand forget her cunning. . . . Let my
tongue cleave to the roof of my mouth.
                —OLD TESTAMENT, *Psalms, CXXXVII*

OBEDIENCE

Now these are the Laws of the Jungle, and many and
    mighty are they;
But the head and the hoof of the Law and the haunch
    and the hump is—Obey!—KIPLING, *First Jungle Book*

OBLIVION

The iniquity of oblivion blindly scattereth her poppy,
and deals with the memory of men without distinction to
merit of perpetuity. —SIR THOMAS BROWNE, *Hydriotaphia*

. . . a slow and silent stream,
Lethé, the River of Oblivion, rolls
Her wat'ry labyrinth, . . .   —MILTON, *Paradise Lost, II*

I met a traveller from an antique land
Who said: "Two vast and trunkless legs of stone
Stand in the desert. . . .
And on the pedestal these words appear:
'My name is Ozymandias, King of Kings:
Look on my works, ye Mighty, and despair!'
Nothing beside remains. . . .
                —SHELLEY, *Ozymandias of Egypt*

Once in Persia reigned a king
Who upon his signet ring
Graved a maxim true and wise,
    .   .   .   .   .   .

Solemn words, and these are they:
"Even this shall pass away."
—THEODORE TILTON, The King's Ring

OBSCURITY

Full many a gem of purest ray serene
    The dark unfathom'd caves of ocean bear:
Full many a flower is born to blush unseen,
    And waste its sweetness on the desert air.

. . . .

Some village Hampden, that with dauntless breast
    The little tyrant of his fields withstood;
Some mute, inglorious Milton here may rest,
    Some Cromwell guiltless of his country's blood.
—GRAY, Elegy Written in a Country Churchyard

Thus let me live, unseen, unknown,
    Thus, unlamented let me die;
Steal from the world, and not a stone
    Tell where I lie.   —POPE, Ode to Solitude

OBSERVATION

Let observation with extensive view,
Survey mankind from China to Peru;
Remark each anxious toil, each eager strife,
And watch the busy scenes of crowded life.
—JOHNSON, Vanity of Human Wishes

OCCUPATION

Absence of occupation is not rest,
A mind quite vacant is a mind distress'd.
—COWPER, Retirement

OCEAN

Roll on, thou deep and dark-blue ocean, roll!
—BYRON, Childe Harold, IV

OCTOBER

The skies they were ashen and sober;
  The leaves they were crispèd and sere—
  The leaves they were withering and sere;
It was night in the lonesome October
  Of my most immemorial year.   —POE, *Ulalume*

OFFENSE

O, my offense is rank, it smells to heaven.
                    —SHAKESPEARE, *Hamlet, III, 3*

Time to me this truth has taught
  ('Tis a treasure worth revealing),
More offend from want of thought
  Than from any want of feeling.
                    —CHARLES SWAIN, *Want of Thought*

OPINION

The man who never alters his opinion is like standing
water, and breeds reptiles of the mind.
                    —BLAKE, *Proverbs of Hell*

He that complies against his will,
Is of his own opinion still,
Which he may adhere to, yet disown,
For reasons to himself best known.
                    —BUTLER, *Hudibras, III*

Public opinion, a vulgar, impertinent, anonymous tyrant
who deliberately makes life unpleasant for anyone who is
not content to be the average man.
                    —DEAN W. R. INGE, *Outspoken Essays*

The pressure of public opinion is like the pressure of the
atmosphere; you can't see it—but, all the same, it is sixteen
pounds to the square inch.
                    —J. R. LOWELL, interview with Julian Hawthorne

Some praise at morning what they blame at night,
But always think the last opinion right.
                                    —POPE, *Essay on Criticism, II*

Opinion's but a fool, that makes us scan
The outward habit by the inward man.
                                    —SHAKESPEARE, *Pericles, II, 2*

So many men, so many minds.
(Quot homines tot sententiae.)—TERENCE, *Phormio, II, 4*

OPPORTUNITY

O, once in each man's life, at least,
    Good luck knocks at his door;
And wit to seize the witting guest
    Need never hunger more.   —L. J. BATES, *Good Luck*

With doubt and dismay you are smitten,
    You think there's no chance for you, son?
Why the best books haven't been written,
    The best race hasn't been run.
                                    —BERTON BRALEY, *Opportunity*

Man's extremity is God's opportunity.
                                    —JOHN FLAVEL, Pamphlet, *c.* 1680

Master of human destinies am I!
Fame, love, and fortune on my footsteps wait.
Cities and fields I walk; I penetrate
Deserts and seas remote, and passing by
Hovel and mart and palace, soon or late
I knock unbidden once at every gate. . . .
                                    —J. J. INGALLS, *Opportunity*

They do me wrong who say I come no more
    When once I knock and fail to find you in;

For every day I stand outside your door
   And bid you wake, and rise to fight and win.
                —WALTER MALONE, *Opportunity*

He that will not when he may,
He shall not when he will.
         —ROBERT MANNYNG, *Handlyng Synne* (1303)

There is a tide in the affairs of men,
Which, taken at the flood, leads on to fortune.
           —SHAKESPEARE, *Julius Caesar, IV, 3*

OPTIMISM

God's in his Heaven—
All's right with the world! —R. BROWNING, *Pippa Passes*

One who never turned his back but marched breast for-
    ward,
   Never doubted clouds would break,
Never dreamed, though right were worsted, wrong
    would triumph,
Held we fall to rise, are baffled to fight better,
   Sleep to wake.   —R. BROWNING, *Asolando,* Epilogue

             He who, from zone to zone,
Guides through the boundless sky thy certain flight,
In the long way that I must tread alone,
Will lead my steps aright.
        —WILLIAM C. BRYANT, *To a Waterfowl*

The place where optimism most flourishes is the lunatic
asylum.   —HAVELOCK ELLIS, *The Dance of Life*

A health unto the happy,
   A fig for him who frets!
It is not raining rain to me,
   It's raining violets.   —R. LOVEMAN, *April Rain*

There's a good time coming, boys!
A good time coming.
                    —CHARLES MACKAY, *The Good Time Coming*

Who brought me hither
Will bring me hence; no other guide I seek.
                    —MILTON, *Paradise Regained, I*

And spite of Pride, in erring Reason's spite,
One truth is clear, *Whatever is, is right.*
                    —POPE, *Essay on Man, I*

Behold, we know not anything;
  I can but trust that good shall fall
  At last—far off—at last, to all,
And every winter change to spring.
                    —TENNYSON, *In Memoriam, LIV*

All is for the best in the best of possible worlds.
(*Tout est pour le mieux dans le meilleur des mondes pos-
    sibles.*)   —VOLTAIRE, *Candide*

OPTIMIST AND PESSIMIST

I hate the Pollyanna pest
Who says that All is for the Best.
                    —FRANKLIN P. ADAMS, *Thoughts on the Cosmos*

The optimist proclaims that we live in the best of all
possible worlds; and the pessimist fears this is true.
                    —BRANCH CABELL, *The Silver Stallion*

Two men look out through the same bars:
One sees the mud, and one the stars.
                    —F. LANGBRIDGE, *A Cluster of Quiet Thoughts*

'Twixt optimist and pessimist
  The difference is droll:

The optimist sees the doughnut,
    The pessimist, the hole.
                —McL. WILSON, *Optimist and Pessimist*

ORATORY

All epoch-making revolutionary events have been produced not by the written but by the spoken word.
                —ADOLF HITLER, *Mein Kampf*

ORDER

Order is Heav'n's first law; and, this confest,
Some are and must be greater than the rest.
                —POPE, *Essay on Man, IV*

A place for everything and everything in its place.
                —SAMUEL SMILES, *Thrift*

ORIGINALITY

No bird has ever uttered note
That was not in some first bird's throat;
Since Eden's freshness and man's fall
No rose has been original.   —T. B. ALDRICH, *Originality*

Originality, I fear, is too often only undetected and fre-
quently unconscious plagiarism.
                —DEAN W. R. INGE, *Wit and Wisdom*, Preface

ORPHAN

He reminds me of the man who murdered both his
parents, and then, when sentence was about to be pronounced, pleaded for mercy on the grounds that he was an
orphan.
                —ABRAHAM LINCOLN (Gross, *Lincoln's Own Stories*)

OWL

From yonder ivy-mantled tower
The moping owl does to the moon complain.
                —GRAY, *Elegy Written in a Country Churchyard*

St. Agnes' Eve—ah, bitter chill it was!
The owl, for all his feathers, was a-cold.

—KEATS, *The Eve of St. Agnes*

A wise old owl sat on an oak,
The more he sat the less he spoke;
The less he spoke the more he heard;
Why aren't we like that wise old bird?

E. H. RICHARDS, *A Wise Old Owl*

The owl, ... the fatal bellman,
Which gives the stern'st good-night.

—SHAKESPEARE, *Macbeth, II, 2*

Then nightly sings the staring owl,
Tu-whit; tu-who, a merry note.

—SHAKESPEARE, *Love's Labour's Lost, V, 2*

Alone and warming his five wits,
The white owl in the belfry sits.

—TENNYSON, *Song: The Owl*

O X

Thou shalt not muzzle the mouth of the ox that treadeth
out the corn.   —NEW TESTAMENT, *I Corinthians, IX, 9*

As an ox goeth to the slaughter.

—OLD TESTAMENT, *Jeremiah, IX, 19*

It depends upon whose ox is gored.

—NOAH WEBSTER, *American Spelling Book*

OXFORD

Home of lost causes, and forsaken beliefs, and unpopular
names, and impossible loyalties!

—MATTHEW ARNOLD, *Essay in Criticism,* Preface

I saw the spires of Oxford
    As I was passing by,
The gray spires of Oxford
    Against a pearl-gray sky.
                —WINIFRED M. LETTS, *The Spires of Oxford*

The ancient seat of pedantry where they manufacture prigs as fast as butchers in Chicago handle hogs.
                —R. B. CUNNINGHAME-GRAHAM, *With the North-West Wind*

OYSTER

It is the sick oyster which possesses the pearl.
                —J. A. SHEDD, *Salt From My Attic*

Oysters must not be eaten in those months, which in pronouncing want the letter R.
                —WILLIAM VAUGHAN, *Directions for Health* (1600)

PAGAN

    Great God! I'd rather be
A Pagan suckled in a creed outworn;
So might I, standing on the pleasant lea,
Have glimpses that would make me less forlorn,
Have sight of Proteus rising from the sea,
Or hear old Triton blow his wreathèd horn.
                —WORDSWORTH, *Sonnet: The World Is Too Much With Us*

PAIN

For all the happiness mankind can gain
Is not in pleasure, but in rest from pain.
                —DRYDEN, *The Indian Emperor, IV, 1*

One fire burns out another's burning;
One pain is lessen'd by another's anguish.
                —SHAKESPEARE, *Romeo and Juliet, I, 2*

Nothing begins, and nothing ends,
   That is not paid with moan;
For we are born in other's pain,
   And perish in our own.   —FRANCIS THOMPSON, *Daisy*

PAINTING

Paint me as I am. If you leave out the scars and wrinkles,
I will not pay you a shilling.
   —OLIVER CROMWELL, remark to the painter, Peter Lely

A flattering painter who made it his care
To draw men as they ought to be, not as they are.
            —GOLDSMITH, on Reynolds, in *Retaliation*

I mix them with my brains, sir.
            —JOHN OPIE, in reply to the question,
            "What do you mix your paints with?"

PAN

And that dismal cry rose slowly
And sank slowly through the air,

   .   .   .   .

"Pan is dead!—Great Pan is dead—
   Pan, Pan is dead."
                  —E. B. BROWNING, *The Dead Pan*

PARADISE

Or were I in the wildest waste,
   Sae black and bare, sae black and bare,
The desert were a Paradise,
   If thou wert there, if thou wert there.
            —BURNS, *Oh! Wert Thou in the Cauld Blast*

For he on honey dew hath fed,
And drunk the milk of Paradise.
                  —S. T. COLERIDGE, *Kubla Khan*

O Paradise! O Paradise!
   Who doth not crave for rest?

Who would not seek the happy land
    Where they that love are blest?
                    —F. W. FABER, *Paradise*

Verily for the pious is a blissful abode
Gardens and vineyards
Damsels with swelling breasts of suitable age
And a brimming cup.   —MAHOMET, *Koran, LXXVIII*

If God hath made this world so fair,
    Where sin and death abound,
How beautiful, beyond compare,
    Will paradise be found!
        —JAMES MONTGOMERY, *The Earth is Full of God's
                                        Goodness*

A Book of Verses underneath the Bough,
A Jug of Wine, a Loaf of Bread—and Thou
    Beside me singing in the Wilderness—
Oh, Wilderness were Paradise enow!
        —OMAR KHAYYÁM, *Rubáiyát* (FitzGerald trans.)

The loves that meet in Paradise shall cast out fear,
And Paradise hath room for you and me and all.
        —CHRISTINA ROSSETTI, *Saints and Angels*

PARADISE LOST

Of Man's first disobedience, and the fruit
Of that forbidden tree whose mortal taste
Brought death into the world, and all our woe, . . .
        —MILTON, *Paradise Lost, I, 1*

The world was all before them, where to choose
Their place of rest, and Providence their guide.
They hand in hand, with wand'ring steps and slow,
Through Eden took their solitary way.
                    —MILTON, *Paradise Lost* (last lines)

PARDON

To understand is to pardon.
(*Comprendre c'est pardonnner.*)
—MADAME DE STAËL, a phrase from *Corinne*

PARENTS

Honour thy father and thy mother: that thy days may be long upon the land which the Lord thy God giveth thee.
—OLD TESTAMENT, *Exodus, XX, 12* (5th Commandment)

Children begin by loving their parents; as they grow older they judge them; sometimes they forgive them.
—OSCAR WILDE, *The Picture of Dorian Gray*

PARIS

Good Americans, when they die, go to Paris.
—T. G. APPLETON (quoted by Holmes in *The Autocrat of the Breakfast-Table*)

Paris is well worth a Mass.
(*Paris vaut bien une Messe.*)
—HENRI IV, referring to his conversion to Catholicism

PARTING

When we two parted
    In silence and tears,
Half broken-hearted
    To sever for years,
Pale grew thy cheek and cold
    Colder thy kiss. . . .
—BYRON, *When We Two Parted*

To meet, to know, to love—and then to part,
Is the sad tale of many a human heart.
—S. T. COLERIDGE, *Couplet Written in a Volume of Poems*

Kathleen Mavourneen, the grey dawn is breaking,
. . . .

Oh, hast thou forgotten how soon we must sever?
Oh, hast thou forgotten this day we must part?
It may be for years, and it may be forever!
Oh, why art thou silent, thou voice of my heart?
—LOUISA M. CRAWFORD, *Kathleen Mavourneen*

Since there's no help, come, let us kiss and part;
Nay, I have done, you get no more of me;
And I am glad, yea, glad with all my heart,
That thus so cleanly I myself can free.
—MICHAEL DRAYTON, *Idea*, Sonnet 61

Excuse me, then! you know my heart;
But dearest friends, alas! must part.
—JOHN GAY, *Fables*, I, 51

Nice while it lasted, an' now it is over—
Tear out your 'eart an' good-bye to your lover!
What's the use o' grievin', when the mother that bore you
(Mary, pity women!) knew it all before you?
—KIPLING, *Mary, Pity Women*

Good night, good night! parting is such sweet sorrow,
That I shall say good night till it be morrow.
—SHAKESPEARE, *Romeo and Juliet*, II, 2

PASSION

It is with our passions, as it is with fire and water, they
are good servants but bad masters.
—SIR ROGER L'ESTRANGE, *Aesop*, 38

On life's vast ocean diversely we sail,
Reason the card, but Passion is the gale.
—POPE, *Moral Essays*, I

Give me that man
That is not passion's slave, and I will wear him
In my heart's core, ay, in my heart of heart.
—SHAKESPEARE, *Hamlet, III, 2*

PAST

Not heaven itself upon the past has power.
—DRYDEN, *Imitations of Horace, III, 29*

Let the dead Past bury its dead.
—LONGFELLOW, *A Psalm of Life*

Nor deem the irrevocable Past
   As wholly wasted, wholly vain,
If, rising on its wrecks, at last
   To something nobler we attain.
—LONGFELLOW, *The Ladder of St. Augustine*

Those who cannot remember the past are condemned to
repeat it.   —SANTAYANA, *Life of Reason*

The dark backward and abysm of time.
—SHAKESPEARE, *The Tempest, 1, 2*

Man hath a weary pilgrimage
   As through the world he wends,
On every stage from youth to age,
   Still discontent attends;
With heaviness he casts his eye
   Upon the road before,
And still remembers with a sigh
   The days that are no more. —SOUTHEY, *Remembrance*

But the tender grace of a day that is dead
Will never come back to me.
—TENNYSON, *Break, Break, Break*

Old, unhappy, far-off things
And battles long ago.
                    —WORDSWORTH, *The Solitary Reaper*

PATIENCE

How far then, Catiline, will you abuse our patience?
(*Quo usque tandem abutere, Catilina, patientia nostra?*)
                    —CICERO, *First Catilinarian Oration*

Beware the fury of a patient man.
                    —DRYDEN, *Absalom and Achitophel*

Patience is the virtue of an ass,
That trots beneath his burthen, and is quiet.
                    —GEORGE GRANVILLE, *Heroic Love, I*

Ye have heard of the patience of Job.
                    —NEW TESTAMENT, *James, V, 2*

She sat like patience on a monument,
Smiling at grief.   —SHAKESPEARE, *Twelfth Night, II, 4*

Since you will buckle fortune on my back,
To bear her burthen, whether I will or no,
I must have patience to endure the load.
                    —SHAKESPEARE, *Richard III, III, 7*

That which in mean men we intitle patience
Is pale cold cowardice in noble breasts.
                    —SHAKESPEARE, *Richard II, 1, 2*

PATRICK, SAINT

Oh! St. Patrick was a gentleman
    Who came of decent people;
He built a church in Dublin town,
    And on it put a steeple.
                    —HENRY BENNETT, *Saint Patrick*

PATRIOTISM

No man can be a patriot on an empty stomach.
—W. C. BRANN, *The Iconoclast*

To make us love our country, our country ought to be lovely.
—EDMUND BURKE, *Reflections on the French Revolution*

He who loves not his country, can love nothing.
—BYRON, *The Two Foscari, III, 1*

The patriot's blood's the seed of Freedom's tree.
—THOMAS CAMPBELL, *To the Spanish Patriots*

Patriotism is not enough. I must have no hatred or bitterness towards anyone.
—EDITH CAVELL, to Rev. Mr. Gahan, on night before her execution in 1915

I am French, I am Chauvin.
(*J'suis Français, j'suis Chauvin.*)
—T. AND H. COGNIARD, *La Cocarde tricolore* (1831)

And they who for their country die
  Shall fill an honored grave,
For glory lights the soldier's tomb,
  And beauty weeps the brave.
—J. R. DRAKE, *To the Defenders of New Orleans*

How can a man be said to have a country when he has no right to a square inch of it.
—HENRY GEORGE, *Social Problems*

Strike—till the last armed foe expires;
Strike—for your altars and your fires;
Strike—for the green graves of your sires;
  God—and your native land.
—FITZ-GREENE HALLECK, *Marco Bozzaris*

It is sweet and glorious to die for one's country.
(*Dulce et decorum est pro patria mori.*)
—HORACE, *Odes, III, 2*

We don't want to fight,
    But, by Jingo, if we do,
We've got the ships, we've got the men,
    We've got the money too.
—G. W. HUNT, Music-hall song, 1878

Indeed I tremble for my country when I reflect that God
is just.   —THOMAS JEFFERSON, *Notes on Virginia*

Patriotism is the last refuge of a scoundrel.
—JOHNSON (Boswell's *Life* for the year 1775)

God gave all men all earth to love,
    But since our hearts are small,
Ordained for each one spot should prove
    Belovèd over all.   —KIPLING, *Sussex*

And thus we see on either hand
    We name our blessings whence they've sprung;
We call our country Father Land,
    We call our language Mother Tongue.
—SAMUEL LOVER, *Father Land and Mother Tongue*

And how can man die better
    Than facing fearful odds,
For the ashes of his fathers
    And the temples of his gods?   —MACAULAY, *Horatius*

Who dare to love their country and be poor.
—POPE, *On His Grotto at Twickenham*

For country, children, hearth, and home.
(*Pro patria, pro liberis, pro aris atque focis.*)
—SALLUST, *Catiline*

Breathes there a man with soul so dead,
Who never to himself hath said,
    This is my own, my native land?
Whose heart hath ne'er within him burn'd
As home his footsteps he hath turn'd
    From wandering on a foreign strand?
                            —SCOTT, *Lay of the Last Minstrel*, VI

One drop of blood drawn from thy country's bosom
Should grieve thee more than streams of foreign gore.
                            —SHAKESPEARE, *Henry VI*, I, III, 3

Who is here so vile that will not love his country?
                            —SHAKESPEARE, *Julius Caesar*, III, 2

Let our object be, our country, our whole country, and
nothing but our country.
    —DANIEL WEBSTER, Address at . . . Bunker Hill (1825)

PATRONAGE

Maecenas, sprung from royal stock, my bulwark and my
glory dearly cherished.
*(Maecenas atavis edite regibus,
O et praesidium et dulce decus meum.)*
                            —HORACE, *Odes*, I, 1

Is not a patron, my Lord, one who looks with unconcern
on a man struggling for life in the water, and, when he has
reached ground, encumbers him with help?
                —SAMUEL JOHNSON, Letter to Lord Chesterfield

Patron: Commonly a wretch who supports with inso-
lence, and is paid with flattery.
                            —JOHNSON, Definition in *Dictionary*

PEACE

I prefer the most unjust peace to the justest war that was
ever waged.   —CICERO, *Letters to Atticus*

In His will is our peace.
(*In la sua voluntade è nostra pace.*)
—DANTE, *Paradiso, III*

Peace with honor.   —B. DISRAELI, Speech, 1878

Let us have peace.   —U. S. GRANT, Letter, 1868

Peace at any price.
—LAMARTINE (as quoted by A. H. Clough)

Buried was the bloody hatchet;
Buried was the dreadful war-club;
Buried were all warlike weapons,
And the war-cry was forgotten.
There was peace among the nations.
—LONGFELLOW, *Hiawatha, XIII*

War in men's eyes shall be
A monster of iniquity
    In the good time coming.
Nations shall not quarrel then,
    To prove which is the stronger;
Nor slaughter men for glory's sake;—
    Wait a little longer.
—C. MACKAY, *The Good Time Coming*

In proportion as the antagonism between the classes vanishes, the hostility of one nation to another will come to an end.   —MARX AND ENGELS, *Communist Manifesto*

Peace hath her victories
No less renown'd than war.
—MILTON, *Sonnet: To the Lord Gen. Cromwell*

Blessed are the peace-makers.
—NEW TESTAMENT, *Matthew, V, 9*

Glory to God in the highest, and peace on earth, good will toward men. —NEW TESTAMENT, *Luke, II, 14*

The peace of God which passeth all understanding.
—NEW TESTAMENT, *Philippians, IV, 7*

How beautiful upon the mountains are the feet of him that bringeth good tidings, that publisheth peace.
—OLD TESTAMENT, *Isaiah, LII, 7*

Peace, peace; where there is no peace.
—OLD TESTAMENT, *Jeremiah, VI, 14*

The wolf also shall dwell with the lamb, and the leopard shall lie down with the kid.
—OLD TESTAMENT, *Isaiah, XI, 6*

They shall beat their swords into ploughshares, and their spears into pruning-hooks: nation shall not lift sword against nation, neither shall they learn war any more.
—OLD TESTAMENT, *Isaiah, II, 4*

Till the war-drum throbb'd no longer and the battle-flags were furl'd
In the Parliament of man, the Federation of the world.
—TENNYSON, *Locksley Hall*

Why do they prate of the blessings of peace? we have made them a curse, . . .
And lust of gain, in the spirit of Cain, is it better or worse
Than the heart of the citizen hissing in war. . . .
—TENNYSON, *Maud, I*

They have not wanted *Peace* at all; they have wanted to be spared war—as though the absence of war was the same as peace. —DOROTHY THOMPSON, *On the Record*

It must be a peace without victory.
—WOODROW WILSON, Address to Senate, Jan., 1917

God for His service needeth not proud work of human skill;
They please Him best who labour most in peace to do His will. —WORDSWORTH, *The Poet's Dream*

PEARL

. . . neither cast ye your pearls before swine, lest they trample them under their feet.
—NEW TESTAMENT, *Matthew, VII, 6*

One whose hand
Like the base Indian, threw a pearl away
Richer than all his tribe. —SHAKESPEARE, *Othello, V, 2*

PEASANTRY

But a bold peasantry, their country's pride,
When once destroy'd, can never be supplied.
—GOLDSMITH, *The Deserted Village*

PEDIGREE

The pedigree of honey
Does not concern the bee;
A clover, any time, to him
Is Aristocracy. —EMILY DICKINSON, *Poems, II*

PEN

A pen becomes a clarion.
—LONGFELLOW, *Monte Cassino*

Pens are most dangerous tools, more sharp by odds
Than swords, and cut more keen than whips or rods.
—JOHN TAYLOR, *News from Hell, Hull and Halifax*

PENGUIN

The penguin flies backwards because he doesn't care to see where he's going, but wants to see where he's been.
—FRED ALLEN, *The Backward View*

PENSION

Pension: An allowance made to anyone without an equivalent. In England it is generally understood to mean pay given to a state hireling for treason to his country.
—JOHNSON, Definition in his *Dictionary*

PEOPLE

The voice of the people is the voice of God.
(*Vox populi, vox dei.*)
—ALCUIN, Epistle to Charlemagne, *c.* 800

I hate the vulgar herd and hold it far.
(*Odi profanum vulgus et arceo.*)   —HORACE, *Odes, III*

The Lord prefers common-looking people. That is the reason He made so many of them.
—LINCOLN (quoted by J. Morgan, *Our Presidents*)

No doubt but ye are the people, and wisdom shall die with you.   —OLD TESTAMENT, *Job, XII, 2*

Who o'er the herd would wish to reign,
Fantastic, fickle, fierce, and vain?
Vain as the leaf upon the stream,
And fickle as the changeful dream;
Fantastic as a woman's mood,
And fierce as Frenzy's fever'd blood.
Thou many-headed monster thing,
O who would wish to be thy king?
—SCOTT, *The Lady of the Lake, V*

You got to have patience. Why Tom, us people will go
on livin' when all them people is gone. . . . Rich fellas
come up an' they die, an' their kids ain't no good an' they
die out. But we keep a-comin'.

—JOHN STEINBECK, *The Grapes of Wrath*

PERFECTION

Trifles make perfection, and perfection is no trifle.

—MICHELANGELO (quoted by C. C. Colton in *Lacon*)

Be ye therefore perfect even as your Father which is in
heaven is perfect.   —NEW TESTAMENT, *Matthew, V, 48*

PERFUME

Sabean odours from the spicy shore
Of Arabie the blest.   —MILTON, *Paradise Lost, IV*

And all your courtly civet-cats can vent
Perfume to you, to me is excrement.

—POPE, *Epilogue to the Satires*

All the perfumes of Arabia will not sweeten this little
hand.   —SHAKESPEARE, *Macbeth, V, 1*

PERSEVERANCE

'Tis a lesson you should heed:
　　Try, try, try again.
If at first you don't succeed,
　　Try, try, try again.

—W. E. HICKSON, *Try and Try Again*

"Brave admiral, say but one good word:
What shall we do when hope is gone?"
The words leapt like a leaping sword:
"Sail on! sail on! sail on! and on!"

—JOAQUIN MILLER, *Columbus*

'Taint no use to sit and whine
'Cause the fish ain't on your line;
Bait your hook an' keep on tryin',
   Keep a-goin'!   —FRANK L. STANTON, *Keep A-goin'*

PERSONALITY

I am the owner of the sphere,
Of the seven stars and the solar year,
Of Caesar's hand, and Plato's brain,
Of Lord Christ's heart, and Shakespeare's strain.
                —EMERSON, *Essays: History* (Motto)

There are three Johns: 1, the real John; known only to his Maker; 2, John's ideal John, never the real one, and often very unlike him; 3, Thomas's ideal John, never the real John, nor John's John, but often very unlike either.
   —O. W. HOLMES, *The Autocrat of the Breakfast-Table*

Personality is to man what perfume is to a flower.
   —CHARLES M. SCHWAB, *Ten Commandments of Success*

PHILANTHROPY

He who bestows his goods upon the poor,
Shall have as much again, and ten times more.
              —BUNYAN, *Pilgrim's Progress, II*

I expect to pass through this world but once. Any good therefore that I can do, or any kindness that I can show to any fellow creature let me do it now. Let me not defer or neglect it, for I shall not pass this way again.
        —STEPHEN GRELLET (also credited to others)

Abou Ben Adhem (may his tribe increase!)
    · · · · · · ·

   "I pray thee, then,
Write me as one that loves his fellow men."
    · · · · · · ·

And lo! Ben Adhem's name led all the rest.
—LEIGH HUNT, *Abou Ben Adhem*

Blessed is he that considereth the poor.
—OLD TESTAMENT, *Psalms, XLI, 1*

I was eyes to the blind, and feet was I to the lame.
—OLD TESTAMENT, *Job, XXIX, 15*

The milk of human kindness ran
In rich abundance in his breast,
It left thin grease stains on the tan
Of his asbestos vest. —PAUL TANAQUIL, *Philanthropist*

PHILOSOPHY

It's easy 'nough to titter w'en de stew is smokin' hot,
But hit's mighty ha'd to giggle w'en dey's nuffin' in de
pot. —PAUL LAURENCE DUNBAR, *Philosophy*

Philosophy is the highest music. —PLATO, *Phaedo*

It is a great advantage for a system of philosophy to be
substantially true. —SANTAYANA, *The Unknowable*

For there was never yet philosopher
That could endure the toothache patiently.
—SHAKESPEARE, *Much Ado About Nothing, V, 1*

There are more things in heaven and earth, Horatio,
Than are dreamt of in your philosophy.
—SHAKESPEARE, *Hamlet, I, 5*

PIANO

Five and thirty black slaves,
    Half-a-hundred white,
All their duty but to sing
    For their Queen's delight.
—WILLIAM WATSON, *The Key-Board*

PILGRIM FATHERS

The Pilgrims landed, worthy men,
  And, saved from wreck on raging seas,
They fell upon their knees, and then
  Upon the Aborigines.
    —ARTHUR GUITERMAN, *The Pilgrims' Thanksgiving*

Ay, call it holy ground,
  The soil where first they trod!
They left unstained what there they found—
  Freedom to worship God!
    FELICIA D. HEMANS, *The Landing of the Pilgrims*

They talk about their Pilgrim blood,
  Their birthright high and holy!
A mountain-stream that ends in mud
  Methinks is melancholy.
    —J. R. LOWELL, *Interview with Miles Standish*

PIONEER

Conquering, holding, daring, venturing as we go the
  unknown ways,
  Pioneers! O pioneers!
    —WALT WHITMAN, *Pioneers! O Pioneers!*

PIRATES

Fifteen men on the Dead Man's Chest—
  Yo-ho-ho, and a bottle of rum!
Drink and the devil had done for the rest—
  Yo-ho-ho, and a bottle of rum!
    —STEVENSON, *Treasure Island*

PITY

Careless their merits or their faults to scan,
His pity gave ere charity began.
    —GOLDSMITH, *The Deserted Village*

Taught by the Power that pities me,
    I learn to pity them.
        —GOLDSMITH, *Ballad* (in *Vicar of Wakefield*)

But yet the pity of it, Iago!
O Iago, the pity of it, Iago!
        —SHAKESPEARE, *Othello, IV, 1*

'Tis true 'tis pity; And pity 'tis 'tis true.
        —SHAKESPEARE, *Hamlet, II, 2*

O brother man! fold to thy heart thy brother.
Where pity dwells, the peace of God is there.
        —WHITTIER, *Worship*

PLAGIARISM

They steal my thunder!
        —JOHN DENNIS, at a performance of *Macbeth*

When 'Omer smote 'is bloomin' lyre,
    He'd 'eard men sing by land and sea;
An' what 'e thought 'e might require,
    'E went an' took—the same as me!
        —KIPLING, *Barrack-Room Ballads,* Introduction

Though old the thought and oft exprest,
'Tis his at last who says it best.
        —J. R. LOWELL, *For an Autograph*

Read my little fable:
    He that runs may read.
Most can raise the flowers now,
    For all have got the seed.   —TENNYSON, *The Flower*

PLEASURE

But pleasures are like poppies spread:
You seize the flow'r, its bloom is shed!

Or like the snow-fall in a river,
A moment white—then melts forever;
                              —BURNS, *Tam O' Shanter*

The rule of my life is to make business a pleasure, and
pleasure my business.   —AARON BURR, Letter to Pichon

Pleasure's a sin, and sometimes sin's a pleasure.
                              —BYRON, *Don Juan, I*

  Rich the treasure,
    Sweet the pleasure,—
Sweet is pleasure after pain.
                              —DRYDEN, *Alexander's Feast*

I built my soul a lordly pleasure-house,
    Wherein at ease for aye to dwell.
I said, "O Soul, make merry and carouse,
    Dear soul, for all is well."
                              —TENNYSON, *The Palace of Art*

All human race, from China to Peru,
Pleasure, howe'er disguis'd by art, pursue.
                              —T. WARTON, *Universal Love of Pleasure*

PLEDGE

We mutually pledge to each other our lives, our fortunes
and our sacred honor. . . .
                              —JEFFERSON, *Declaration of Independence*

I pledge allegiance to the flag of the United States of
America and to the Republic for which it stands. One nation indivisible, with liberty and justice for all.
                              —JAMES B. UPHAM AND FRANCIS BELLAMY,
                              Pledge to the Flag (1892)

POE, EDGAR ALLAN

There comes Poe, with his raven, like Barnaby Rudge,

Three fifths of him genius and two fifths sheer fudge.
—J. R. LOWELL, *A Fable for Critics*

POET

A poet is born, not made.
(*Poeta nascitur, non fit.*)   —ANON. (old Latin phrase)

"Give me a theme," the little poet cried,
    "And I will do my part;"
" 'Tis not a theme you need," the world replied;
    "You need a heart."
—R. W. GILDER, *Wanted, a Theme*

The irritable tribe of poets.
(*Genus irritabile vatum.*)   —HORACE, *Epistles, II*

Bards of Passion and of Mirth,
Ye have left your souls on earth!
Ye have souls in heaven too,
Double-lived in regions new.
—KEATS, *Ode to Beaumont and Fletcher*

Read from some humble poet,
    Whose songs gushed from his heart,
As showers from the clouds of summer,
    Or tears from the eyelids start.
—LONGFELLOW, *The Day Is Done*

The bards sublime,
Whose distant footsteps echo
Through the corridors of Time.
—LONGFELLOW, *The Day Is Done*

More safe I sing with mortal voice, unchang'd
To hoarse or mute, though fall'n on evil days,
On evil days though fall'n, and evil tongues.
—MILTON, *Paradise Lost, VII*

Dreamer of dreams, born out of my due time,
    Why should I strive to set the crooked straight?
        —WILLIAM MORRIS, *The Earthly Paradise: Apology*

Remember me a little then, I pray,
The idle singer of an empty day.
        —WILLIAM MORRIS, *The Earthly Paradise: Apology*

If I could dwell
Where Israfel
    Hath dwelt, and he where I,
He might not sing so wildly well
    A mortal melody,—
While a bolder note than this might swell
    From my lyre within the sky.   —POE, *Israfel*

As yet a child, nor yet a foal to fame,
I lisp'd in numbers, for the numbers came.
        —POPE, *Epistle to Dr. Arbuthnot*

Call it not vain:—they do not err
Who say that when the poet dies
Mute Nature mourns her worshipper,
And celebrates his obsequies.
        —SCOTT, *Lay of the Last Minstrel*, V

The poet's eye, in a fine frenzy rolling,
Doth glance from heaven to earth, from earth to heaven;
And as imagination bodies forth
The forms of things unknown, the poet's pen
Turns them to shapes, and gives to airy nothing
A local habitation and a name.
        —SHAKESPEARE, *A Midsummer Night's Dream*, V, 1

A poet is a nightingale who sits in darkness and sings to
cheer its own solitude with sweet sounds.
        —SHELLEY, *A Defence of Poetry*

I sound my barbaric yawp over the roofs of the world.
> —WALT WHITMAN, *Song of Myself*

POETRY

Some ladies now make pretty songs,
    And some make pretty nurses;
Some men are good for righting wrongs,
    And some for writing verses.
> —F. LOCKER-LAMPSON, *The Jester's Plea*

A poem should not mean
But be.
> —ARCHIBALD MACLEISH, *Ars Poetica*

Lap me in soft Lydian airs
Married to immortal verse.
> —MILTON, *L'Allegro*

I'll make thee glorious by my pen
And famous by my sword.
> —MARQUIS OF MONTROSE, *My Dear and Only Love*

My definition of pure poetry, something that the poet
creates outside of his own personality.
> —GEORGE MOORE, Introduction to
> *Anthology of Pure Poetry*

Among our literary scenes,
Saddest this sight to me.
The graves of little magazines
That died to make verse free.
> —KEITH PRESTON, *The Liberators*

When falls the soldier brave,
    Dead at the feet of wrong,
The poet sings and guards his grave
    With sentinels of song.
> —A. J. RYAN, *Sentinel Songs*

Not marble nor the gilded monuments
Of princes, shall outlive this powerful rhyme.

>—SHAKESPEARE, *Sonnets, LV*

O for a muse of fire, that would ascend
The brightest heaven of invention.

>—SHAKESPEARE, *Henry V, Prologue*

Then, rising with Aurora's light,
The Muse invok'd, sit down to write;
Blot out, correct, insert, refine,
Enlarge, diminish, interline.

>—SWIFT, *On Poetry*

Jewels five-words-long
That on the stretch'd finger of all Time
Sparkle for ever.

>—TENNYSON, *The Princess, II*

Poetry is the spontaneous overflow of powerful feelings:
it takes its origin from emotion recollected in tranquillity.

>—WORDSWORTH, *Lyrical Ballads*, Preface

POISON

What's one man's poison, signior,
Is another's meat or drink.

>—BEAUMONT AND FLETCHER, *Love's Cure, III, 2*

The gnat that sings his summer song
Poison gets from Slander's tongue,
The poison of the snake and newt
Is the seat of Envy's foot.
The poison of the honey-bee
Is the artist's jealousy.   —BLAKE, *Auguries of Innocence*

POLITICIAN

An honest politician is one who, when he is bought, will
stay bought.

>—SIMON CAMERON (Republican boss of Pennsylvania,
>c. 1860)

The only difference, after all their rout,
Is that the one is *in*, the other *out*.
　　　　　　　—CHARLES CHURCHILL, *The Conference*

Ez to my princerples, I glory
　　In hevin' nothin' o' the sort;
I ain't a whig, I ain't a Tory,
　　I'm jest a canderdate, in short.
　　　　　　　—J. R. LOWELL, *The Biglow Papers, II*

O ye who lead,
Take heed!
Blindness we may forgive, but baseness we will smite.
　　　　　　　—WILLIAM VAUGHN MOODY, *An Ode
　　　　　　　　　　in Time of Hesitation*

Here lies beneath this mossy stone
　　A politician who
Touched a live issue without gloves
　　And never did come to.   —KEITH PRESTON, *Epitaph*

I'm not a politician and my other habits are good.
　　　　　　　—ARTEMUS WARD, *Fourth of July Oration*

POLITICS

Man is a political animal.   —ARISTOTLE, *Politics, I*

All political parties die at last of swallowing their own
lies.　　　　　　—DR. ARBUTHNOT (quoted in Garnett,
　　　　　　　　　　　　　Life of Emerson)

In politics if thou wouldst mix,
　　And mean thy fortunes be,
Bear this in mind: Be deaf and blind,
　　Let great folks hear and see.
　　　　　　　—BURNS, *At the Globe Tavern*

We cannot safely leave politics to politicians, or political economy to college professors.

—HENRY GEORGE, *Social Problems*

I always voted at my party's call,
And never thought of thinking for myself at all!
I thought so little, they rewarded me
By making me the ruler of the Queen's navee!
—W. S. GILBERT, *H.M.S. Pinafore, I*

He serves his party best who serves the country best.
—RUTHERFORD B. HAYES, Address, March 5, 1877

If you wish the sympathy of broad masses, then you must tell them the crudest and most stupid things.
—ADOLF HITLER, *Mein Kampf*

You cannot adopt politics as a profession and remain honest.   —LOUIS MCHENRY HOWE, Address, Jan. 17, 1933

Public office is a public trust.
—W. C. HUDSON, Slogan for the Cleveland campaign, 1884

I tell you Folks, all Politics is Apple Sauce.
—WILL ROGERS, *The Illiterate Digest*

When quacks with pills political would dope us,
    When politics absorbs the livelong day,
I like to think about the star Canopus,
    So far, so far away!—BERT LESTON TAYLOR, *Canopus*

POORHOUSE

Over the hill to the poorhouse I'm trudgin' my weary way.   —WILL CARLETON, *Over the Hill to the Poorhouse*

POPPY

In Flanders fields the poppies blow
Between the crosses, row on row.
                        —JOHN McCRAE, *In Flanders Fields*

POSITIVE

To be positive: to be mistaken at the top of one's voice.
                        —AMBROSE BIERCE, *The Devil's Dictionary*

POSSESSION

Possession is nine points of the law.
                        —THOMAS FULLER, *Holy War, V*

Is it not lawful for me to do what I will with mine own?
                        —NEW TESTAMENT, *Matthew, XX, 15*

An ill-favoured thing, sir, but mine own.
                        —SHAKESPEARE, *As You Like It, V, 4*

He who says, what is mine is yours and what is yours is
yours, is a saint. He who says, what is yours is mine and
what is mine is mine, is a wicked man.
                        —BABYLONIAN TALMUD, *Aboth, V*

POSTERITY

People will not look forward to posterity, who never look
backward to their ancestors.
                        —EDMUND BURKE, *Reflections on Revolution in France*

POTOMAC

All quiet along the Potomac to-night,
    No sound save the rush of the river,
While soft falls the dew on the face of the dead—
    The picket's off duty forever.
                        —ETHEL L. BEERS, *All Quiet Along the Potomac*

POVERTY

There are only two families in the world, the Haves and
the Have Nots.   —CERVANTES, *Don Quixote, II*

To be poor and independent is very nearly an impossi-
bility.   —WILLIAM COBBETT, *Advice to Young Men*

Poverty is no vice, but an inconvenience.
                               —JOHN FLORIO, *Second Frutes*

Chill penury repressed their noble rage,
And froze the genial current of the soul.
          —GRAY, *Elegy Written in a Country Churchyard*

Let not Ambition mock their useful toil,
    Their homely joys and destiny obscure;
Nor Grandeur hear with a disdainful smile
    The short and simple annals of the poor.—GRAY, *Ibid.*

Stitch! stitch! stitch!
    In poverty, hunger, and dirt,
And still with a voice of dolorous pitch,
Would that its tone could reach the Rich,
    She sang this "Song of the Shirt!"
                    —THOMAS HOOD, *The Song of the Shirt*

This mournful truth is ev'rywhere confess'd,
Slow rises worth, by poverty depress'd.
                          —SAMUEL JOHNSON, *London*

Blessed be ye poor: for yours is the Kingdom of God.
                      —NEW TESTAMENT, *Luke, VI, 20*

For ye have the poor always with you.
                    —NEW TESTAMENT, *Matthew, XXVI, 2*

Rattle his bones over the stones!
He's only a pauper, whom nobody owns!
> —T. NOEL, *The Pauper's Drive*

He that hath pity upon the poor lendeth unto the Lord.
> —OLD TESTAMENT, *Proverbs, XIX, 17*

What mean ye that ye beat my people to pieces and
grind the faces of the poor?
> —OLD TESTAMENT, *Isaiah, III, 15*

The child was diseased at birth, stricken with a hereditary ill that only the most vital men are able to shake off. I
mean poverty—the most deadly and prevalent of all diseases.
> —EUGENE O'NEILL, *Fog*

Yes, we will do anything for the poor man, anything but
get off his back.   —TOLSTOY (quoted in Huntingdon's
> *Philanthropy and Morality*)

POWER

Power, like a desolating pestilence,
Pollutes whate'er it touches.
> —SHELLEY, *Queen Mab, III*

PRAISE

And hearts that once beat high for praise
Now feel that pulse no more.
> —THOMAS MOORE, *The Harp That Once
> Through Tara's Halls*

Approbation from Sir Hubert Stanley is praise indeed.
> —T. MORTON, *A Cure for the Headache, V, 2*

Out of the mouths of babes and sucklings thou hast per-
fected praise.   —NEW TESTAMENT, *Matthew, XXI, 16*

Damn with faint praise, assent with civil leer,
And, without sneering, teach the rest to sneer.
—POPE, *Epistle to Dr. Arbuthnot* (referring to Addison)

PRAYER

They never sought in vain that sought the Lord aright!
—BURNS, *The Cotter's Saturday Night*

Whoso will pray, he must fast and be clean,
And fat his soul, and make his body lean.
—CHAUCER, *The Somnour's Tale*

He prayeth well who loveth well
Both man and bird and beast.

He prayeth best who loveth best
All things both great and small;
For the dear God, who loveth us,
He made and loveth all.
—S. T. COLERIDGE, *The Ancient Mariner*

Ah! a seraph may pray for a sinner
But a sinner must pray for himself.
—CHARLES M. DICKINSON, *The Children*

Of course I prayed—
And did God care?
He cared as much
As on the air
A bird had stamped her foot
And cried "Give me!"   —EMILY DICKINSON, *Poems, V*

O Lord of Courage grave,
O Master of this night of Spring!
Make firm in me a heart too brave
To ask Thee anything.
—JOHN GALSWORTHY, *The Prayer*

And fools who came to scoff, remained to pray.
—GOLDSMITH, *The Deserted Village*

In prayer the lips ne'er act the winning part
Without the sweet concurrence of the heart.
—HERRICK, *The Heart*

I kneel not now to pray that thou
  Make white one single sin,—
I only kneel to thank thee, Lord,
  For what I have not been.   —HARRY KEMP, *A Prayer*

When the last sea is sailed and the last shallow charted,
  When the last field is reaped and the last harvest
    stored,
When the last fire is out and the last guest departed,
  Grant the last prayer that I shall pray, Be good to me,
    O Lord.   —MASEFIELD, *D'Avalos' Prayer*

Who rises from Prayer a better man, his prayer is answered.
—GEORGE MEREDITH, *The Ordeal of Richard Feverel*

  If by prayer
Incessant I could hope to change the will
Of him who all things can, I would not cease
To weary him with my assiduous cries.
—MILTON, *Paradise Lost, XI*

Now I lay me down to sleep
I pray the Lord my soul to keep;
If I should die before I wake,
I pray the Lord my soul to take.
—NEW ENGLAND PRIMER

Every one that asketh receiveth; and he that seeketh
findeth.   —NEW TESTAMENT, *Matthew, VII, 8*

Watch and pray.
> —NEW TESTAMENT, *Matthew, XXVI, 41*

What things soever ye desire, when ye pray, believe that ye receive them, and ye shall receive them.
> —NEW TESTAMENT, *Mark, XI, 24*

SOCRATES: O beloved Pan and all ye other gods of this place, grant to me that I be made beautiful in my soul within, and that all external possessions be in harmony with my inner man. . . .   —PLATO, *Phaedo* (conclusion)

Father of all! in ev'ry age,
   In ev'ry clime ador'd
By saint, by savage, and by sage,
   Jehovah, Jove, or Lord!   —POPE, *Universal Prayer*

Common people do not pray; they only beg.
> —BERNARD SHAW, *Misalliance*

My words fly up, my thoughts remain below:
Words without thoughts never to heaven go.
> —SHAKESPEARE, *Hamlet, III, 3*

For what are men better than sheep or goats
That nourish a blind life within the brain,
If, knowing God, they lift not hands of prayer
Both for themselves and those who call them friend.
> —TENNYSON, *Morte d'Arthur*

More things are wrought by prayer
Than this world dreams of.
> —TENNYSON, *The Passing of Arthur*

I am groping for the keys
Of the heavenly harmonies.
> —WHITTIER, *Andrew Rykman's Prayer*

When the gods wish to punish us they answer our prayers. —OSCAR WILDE, *An Ideal Husband, II*

PREACHER

A man he was to all the country dear,
And passing rich with forty pounds a year.
—GOLDSMITH, *The Deserted Village*

Skilful alike with tongue and pen,
He preached to all men everywhere
The Gospel of the Golden Rule,
The New Commandment given to men,
Thinking the deed and not the creed,
Would help us in our utmost need.
—LONGFELLOW, *Tales of a Wayside Inn,* Prelude

We dislike the man who tries
    To give us title clear
To any mansion in the skies
    An' grab our title here.
—DOUGLAS MALLOCH, *Behind a Spire*

I won't take my religion from any man
who never works except with his
mouth and never cherishes any memory except
the face of the woman on the American
silver dollar.
—CARL SANDBURG, *To a Contemporary Bunkshooter*
                    (i.e., Billy Sunday)

Do not, as some ungracious pastors do,
Show me the steep and thorny way to heaven;
Whiles, like a puff'd and reckless libertine,
Himself the primrose path of dalliance treads,
And recks not his own rede.
—SHAKESPEARE, *Hamlet, I, 3*

PREACHING

He preaches well who lives well.
(*Bien Predica quien bien vive.*)
—CERVANTES, *Don Quixote, II*

Sir, a woman preaching is like a dog walking on his hind legs. It is not done well: but you are surprised to find it done at all. —JOHNSON (Boswell's *Life* for the year 1763)

Practice yourself what you preach.
(*Facias ipse quod faciamus suades.*)
—PLAUTUS, *Asinaria, III, 3*

If to do were as easy as to know what were good to do, chapels had been churches and poor men's cottages princes' palaces. It is a good divine that follows his own instructions: I can easier teach twenty what were good to be done, than be one of the twenty to follow mine own teaching.
—SHAKESPEARE, *Merchant of Venice, I, 2*

PREJUDICE

A prejudice is a vagrant opinion without visible means of support. —AMBROSE BIERCE, *The Devil's Dictionary*

Prejudice is the child of ignorance.
—WILLIAM HAZLITT, *Sketches and Essays*

It is never too late to give up your prejudices.
—THOREAU, *Walden*

PREPAREDNESS

Ef you want peace, the thing you've gut to du
Is jes' to show you're up to fightin', tu.
—J. R. LOWELL, *Biglow Papers, II*

We have had the lesson before us over and over again—

nations that were not ready and were unable to get ready
found themselves overrun by the enemy.

—FRANKLIN D. ROOSEVELT, *Message to Congress,*
May, 1940

Speak softly and carry a big stick; you will go far.

—THEODORE ROOSEVELT, *Address, 1901 (quoted as an*
African proverb)

To be prepared for war is one of the most effectual means
of preserving peace.

—GEORGE WASHINGTON, *Address to Congress, 1790*

PRESENT, THE

Trust no Future, howe'er pleasant!
Let the dead Past bury its dead!
Act—act in the living Present!
Heart within, and God o'erhead!

—LONGFELLOW, *A Psalm of Life*

Ah, take the Cash, and let the Credit go,
Nor heed the rumble of a distant Drum!

—OMAR KHAYYÁM, *Rubáiyát* (FitzGerald trans.)

PRESS, THE

Then hail to the Press! chosen guardian of freedom!
Strong sword-arm of justice! bright sunbeam of truth!

—HORACE GREELEY, *The Press*

Were it left to me to decide whether we should have a
government without newspapers, or newspapers without a
government, I should not hesitate a moment to prefer the
latter.   —THOMAS JEFFERSON, *Writings, VI*

The liberty of the press is the *palladium* of all the civil,
political, and religious rights of an Englishman.

—"JUNIUS," *Letters,* Dedication

The gallery in which the reporters sit has become a fourth estate of the realm.
> —MACAULAY, *Essays: Hallam* . . .

Blessed are they who never read a newspaper, for they shall see Nature, and through her, God.
> —THOREAU, *Essays and Other Writings*

An Ambassador is a man of virtue sent to lie abroad for his country; a news-writer is a man without virtue who lies at home for himself.
> —SIR HENRY WOTTON, *Reliquae Wottonianae*

PRICE

Still as of old, men by themselves are priced—
For thirty pieces Judas sold himself, not Christ.
> —HESTER H. CHOLMONDELEY (quoted
> in *Diana Tempest*)

Earth gets its price for what Earth gives us;
  The beggar is taxed for a corner to die in,
The priest hath his fee who comes and shrives us,
  We bargain for the graves we lie in;
At the devil's booth are all things sold,
Each ounce of dross costs its ounce of gold.
> —J. R. LOWELL, *Vision of Sir Launfal*, Prelude I

All those men have their price.
> —SIR R. WALPOLE (in Coxe's *Memoirs of Walpole*)

PRIDE

Of all the lunacies earth can boast,
The one that must please the devil most
Is pride reduced to the whimsical terms
Of causing the slugs to despise the worms.
> —ROBERT BROUGH, *The Tent-Maker's Song*

And the Devil did grin, for his darling sin
  Is pride that apes humility.
          —S. T. COLERIDGE, *The Devil's Thoughts*

Oh, why should the spirit of mortal be proud?
Like a swift-fleeting meteor, a fast-flying cloud,
A flash of the lightning, a break of the wave,
He passeth from life to his rest in the grave.
      —WILLIAM KNOX, *Oh, Why . . .* (Lincoln's
                         favorite hymn)

Pride goeth before destruction, and a haughty spirit before a fall.   —OLD TESTAMENT, *Proverbs, XVI, 18*

Of all the causes which conspire to blind
Man's erring judgment, and misguide the mind,
What the weak head with strongest bias rules,
Is Pride, the never-failing vice of fools.
              —POPE, *Essay on Criticism, II*

Too coy to flatter, and too proud to serve,
  Thine be the joyless dignity to starve.
                —SMOLLETT, *Advice*

PRIMROSE

A primrose by the river's brim
A yellow primrose was to him,
And it was nothing more. —WORDSWORTH, *Peter Bell, I*

PRINCE

Princes and lords may flourish, or may fade;
A breath can make them as a breath has made.
          —GOLDSMITH, *The Deserted Village*

Put not your trust in princes.
          —OLD TESTAMENT, *Psalms, CXLVI*

O how wretched,
Is that poor man that hangs on princes' favours!
                    —SHAKESPEARE, *Henry VIII, III, 2*

PRISON

Prisons are built with stones of Law, brothels with bricks
of Religion.   —BLAKE, *Proverbs of Hell*

In durance vile here must I wake and weep,
And all my frowsy couch in sorrow steep.
                    —BURNS, *Epistle from Esopus to Maria*

Stone walls do not a prison make,
    Nor iron bars a cage;
Minds innocent and quiet take
    That for an hermitage;
If I have freedom in my love,
    And in my soul am free,
Angels alone, that soar above,
    Enjoy such liberty.
                    —LOVELACE, *To Althea from Prison*

Sometimes they shut you up in jail—
    Dark, and a filthy cell;
I hope the fellows built them jails
    Find 'em down in hell.   —E. F. PIPER, *Bindlestiff*

Whilst we have prisons it matters little which of us occu-
pies the cells.—BERNARD SHAW, *Maxims for Revolutionists*

I know not whether Laws be right,
    Or whether Laws be wrong:
All that we know who lie in gaol
    Is that the wall is strong;
        .   .   .   .

The vilest deeds like poison weeds
    Bloom well in prison air:

It is only what is good in Man
        That wastes and withers there.
                            —OSCAR WILDE, *The Ballad of Reading Gaol*

PRIVACY

No more privacy than a goldfish.
                            Attributed to IRVIN S. COBB and to
                                "SAKI" (H. H. MUNRO)

PROCRASTINATION

The patient dies while the physician sleeps;
The orphan pines while the oppressor feeds;
Justice is feasting while the widow weeps;
Avarice is sporting while infection breeds.
                            —SHAKESPEARE, *The Rape of Lucrece*

Procrastination is the thief of time:
Year after year it steals, till all are fled,
And to the mercies of a moment leaves
The vast concerns of an eternal scene.
                            —EDWARD YOUNG, *Night Thoughts, I*

PROFIT

. . . children dying of pellagra must die because a profit
cannot be taken from an orange. And coroners must fill in
certificates—died of malnutrition—because the food must
rot, must be forced to rot.
                            —JOHN STEINBECK, *The Grapes of Wrath*

PROGRESS

Not enjoyment, and not sorrow,
    Is our destined end or way;
But to act, that each to-morrow
    Brings us farther than to-day.
                            —LONGFELLOW, *A Psalm of Life*

From lower to the higher next,
Not to the top, is Nature's text;

And embryo Good, to reach its stature,
Absorbs the Evil in its nature.
                    —J. R. LOWELL, *Festina Lente: Moral*

Every step of progress the world has made has been
from scaffold to scaffold and from stake to stake.
—WENDELL PHILLIPS, *Speech for Women's Rights* (1851)

Men, my brothers, men, the workers, ever reaping some-
    thing new:
That which they have done but earnest of the things
    that they shall do.   —TENNYSON, *Locksley Hall*

PROHIBITION

See Social Life and Glee sit down
    All joyous and unthinking,
Till, quite transmugrify'd, they're grown
    Debauchery and Drinking.
                    —BURNS, *Address to the Unco Guid*

Forbidden fruit a flavor has
    That lawful orchards mocks;
How luscious lies the pea within
    The pod that Duty locks!
                    —EMILY DICKINSON, *Poems, 1*

Our country has deliberately undertaken a great social
and economic experiment noble in motive and far-reaching
in purpose.
    —HERBERT HOOVER, Letter to Senator Borah, 1928

Stolen sweets are always sweeter:
Stolen kisses much completer;
Stolen looks are nice in chapels:
Stolen, stolen be your apples.
                    —THOMAS RANDOLPH, *Song of Fairies*

PROMISE

We promise according to our hopes, and perform according to our fears.   —LA ROCHEFOUCAULD, *Maxims, 38*

And be these juggling fiends no more believ'd,
That patter with us in a double sense:
That keep the word of promise to our ear,
And break it to our hope. —SHAKESPEARE, *Macbeth, V, 8*

PROOF

Prove all things; hold fast that which is good.
    —NEW TESTAMENT, *I Thessalonians, V, 21*

PROPERTY

Property has its duties as well as its rights.
—T. DRUMMOND, *Letter to Landlords of Tipperary* (1838)

Property is theft.
(*La propriété, c'est le vol.*)
    —P. J. PROUDHON, *Principle of Right*

Whether we force the man's property from him by pinching his stomach, or pinching his fingers, makes some difference anatomically; morally, none whatsoever.
    —RUSKIN, *The Two Paths, V*

Dosn't thou 'ear my 'erse's legs, as they canters awaäy?
Proputty, proputty, proputty—that's what I 'ears them
saäy.   —TENNYSON, *Northern Farmer, New Style*

PROPHECY

My gran'ther's rule was safer 'n 'tis to crow:
Don't never prophesy—onless ye know.
    —J. R. LOWELL, *Mason and Slidell*

Your sons and your daughters shall prophesy, your old men shall dream dreams, your young men shall see visions.
    —OLD TESTAMENT, *Joel, II, 28*

If you can look into the seeds of time,
And say which grain will grow and which will not,
Speak then to me, who neither beg nor fear
Your favours nor your hate.
—SHAKESPEARE, *Macbeth, I, 3*

PROPHET

A prophet is not without honour, save in his own country, and in his own house.
—NEW TESTAMENT, *Matthew, XIII, 57*

Beware of false prophets, which come to you in sheep's clothing, but inwardly they are ravening wolves.
—NEW TESTAMENT, *Matthew, VII, 15*

"Prophet!" said I, "thing of evil—prophet still, if bird or devil!"
—POE, *The Raven*

He'd rather choose that I should die
Than his prediction prove a lie.
—SWIFT, *On the Death of Dr. Swift*

PROVIDENCE

Are not two sparrows sold for a farthing? and one of them shall not fall on the ground without your Father.
—NEW TESTAMENT, *Matthew, XI, 29*

He that doth the ravens feed
Yea, providentially caters for the sparrow,
Be comfort to my age!
—SHAKESPEARE, *As You Like It, II, 3*

There's a divinity that shapes our ends,
Rough-hew them how we will.
—SHAKESPEARE, *Hamlet, V, 2*

PRUDENCE

Festination may prove precipitation; deliberating delay
may be wise cunctation. [*sic*]
　　　　　　　　　—SIR THOMAS BROWNE, *Christian Morals*

Observe the prudent; they in silence sit,
Display no learning, and affect no wit;
They hazard nothing, nothing they assume,
But know the useful art of *acting dumb*.
　　　　　　　　　—G. CRABBE, *Tales: The Patron*

Put your trust in God, my boys, and keep your powder
dry.　　　　　　　—OLIVER CROMWELL, before a battle

Who never wins can rarely lose,
Who never climbs as rarely falls.
　　　　　　　　　—WHITTIER, *To James T. Fields*

PRUDERY

Father is rather vulgar, my dear. The word Papa, be-
sides, gives a very pretty form to the lips. Papa, potatoes,
poultry, prunes and prism are all very good words for the
lips, especially prunes and prism. —DICKENS, *Little Dorrit*

What is prudery? . . .
'Tis a virgin hard of feature,
Old and void of all good nature;
Lean and fretful; would seem wise,
Yet play the fool before she dies.
　　　　　　　　　—POPE, *Answer to Mrs. Howe*

PUBLIC

There is not a more mean, stupid, dastardly pitiless, selfish, spiteful, envious, ungrateful animal than the public.
　　　　　　　　　—HAZLITT, *Table Talk*

The public be damned.
　　　　　　　　　—W. H. VANDERBILT, Reply to reporter, 1883

PUNISHMENT

All punishment is mischief. All punishment in itself is evil.
—JEREMY BENTHAM, *Principles of Morals and Legislation*

My object all sublime
I shall achieve in time—
To let the punishment fit the crime—
The punishment fit the crime.
                    —W. S. GILBERT, *The Mikado, II*

Men are not hanged for stealing horses, but that horses may not be stolen.   —LORD HALIFAX, *Works,* p. 229

But that two-handed engine at the door
Stands ready to smite once, and smite no more.
                    —MILTON, *Lycidas*

My father hath chastised you with whips, but I will chastise you with scorpions.   —OLD TESTAMENT, *I Kings XII, 2*

There needeth not the hell that bigots frame
To punish those who err: Earth in itself
Contains at once the evil and the cure.
                    —SHELLEY, *Queen Mab, III*

PUNS, FAMOUS

1. The Window has four Little Panes;
      But One have I—
   The Window Panes are in its Sash;
      I Wonder Why!   —GELETT BURGESS, *Panes*

2. My sense of sight is very Keen,
      My sense of hearing weak.
   One time I saw a mountain pass,
      But could not hear its peak.
                    —OLIVER HERFORD, *My Sense of Sight*

3. Ben Battle was a soldier bold,
   And used to war's alarms;
   But a cannon-ball took off his legs,
   So he laid down his arms.
   —THOMAS HOOD, *Faithless Nelly Gray*

4. His death, which happen'd in his berth,
   At forty-odd befell;
   They went and told the sexton, and
   The sexton toll'd the bell.
   —THOMAS HOOD, *Faithless Sally Brown*

5. We wanted Li Wing
   But we winged Willie Wong,
   A sad but excusable
   Slip of the Tong.
   —KEITH PRESTON, *Lapsus Linguae*

6. When the Rudyards cease from Kipling
   And the Haggards Ride no more.
   —J. K. STEPHEN, *Lapsus Calami*

PURITAN

A puritan is a person who pours righteous indignation
into the wrong things.
   —G. K. CHESTERTON, *N. Y. Times*, Nov. 21, 1936

The Puritan hated bear-baiting, not because it gave pain
to the bear, but because it gave pleasure to the spectators.
   —MACAULAY, *History of England, I*

The great artists of the world are never Puritans, and
seldom even ordinarily respectable.
   —H. L. MENCKEN, *Prejudices: First Series*

PURITY

Blessed are the pure in heart: for they shall see God.
   —NEW TESTAMENT, *Matthew, V, 8*

Unto the pure all things are pure.
—NEW TESTAMENT, *Titus, I, 15*

My good blade carves the casques of men,
My tough lance thrusteth sure,
My strength is as the strength of ten,
Because my heart is pure. —TENNYSON, *Sir Galahad*

PURPOSE

I live for those who love me, for those who know me
true;
For the heaven that smiles above me, and awaits my
spirit too.
For the cause that lacks assistance, for the wrong that
needs resistance,
For the future in the distance, and the good that I can
do. —G. L. BANKS, *My Aim*

Yet I doubt not thro' the ages one increasing purpose
runs,
And the thoughts of men are widen'd with the process
of the suns. —TENNYSON, *Locksley Hall*

PYRAMIDS

The mighty pyramids of stone
That wedge-like cleave the desert airs,
When nearer seen, and better known,
Are but gigantic flights of stairs.
—LONGFELLOW, *The Ladder of St. Augustine*

QUARREL

Those who in quarrels interpose,
Must often wipe a bloody nose. —GAY, *Fables, I*

Beware
Of entrance to a quarrel; but being in,
Bear't that the opposed may beware of thee.
—SHAKESPEARE, *Hamlet, I, 3*

. . . we quarrel in print, by the book; . . . The first, the
Retort Courteous; the second, the Quip Modest; the third,
the Reply Churlish; the fourth, the Reproof Valiant; the
fifth, the Countercheck Quarrelsome; the sixth, the Lie with
Circumstance; the seventh, the Lie Direct. All these you
may avoid but the Lie Direct; and you may avoid that too,
with an if. . . .   —SHAKESPEARE, *As You Like It, V, 4*

QUESTION

What songs the Sirens sang, or what name Achilles assumed when he hid himself among the women, though
puzzling questions, are not beyond all conjecture.

—SIR THOMAS BROWNE, *Hydriotaphia*

I keep six honest serving men
(They taught me all I know):
Their names are What and Why and When
And How and Where and Who.

—KIPLING, *The Serving Men*

"QUO VADIS"

Simon Peter said unto him, Lord whither goest thou?
(*Quo vadis, Domine?*) —NEW TESTAMENT, *John, XIII, 36*

QUOTATION

Some for renown, on scraps of learning dote,
And think they grow immortal as they quote.

—EDWARD YOUNG, *Love of Fame*

RAIN

The day is cold, and dark, and dreary;
It rains, and the wind is never weary;
The vine still clings to the mouldering wall,
But at every gust the dead leaves fall,
And the day is dark and dreary.

—LONGFELLOW, *The Rainy Day*

He sendeth rain on the just and on the unjust.
—NEW TESTAMENT, *Matthew, V, 45*

When that I was and a little tiny boy,
   With hey, ho, the wind and the rain,
A foolish thing was but a toy,
   For the rain it raineth every day.
—SHAKESPEARE, *Twelfth Night, V,* (end)

RAINBOW

The rainbow never tells me
That gust and storm are by;
Yet she is more convincing
Than philosophy.   —EMILY DICKINSON, *Further Poems*

I do set my bow in the clouds, and it shall be for a token
of a covenant between me and the earth.
—OLD TESTAMENT, *Genesis, IX, 13*

My heart leaps up when I behold
A rainbow in the sky.
—WORDSWORTH, *My Heart Leaps Up*

RAVEN

Ghastly, grim, and ancient Raven, wandering from the
   nightly shore,—
Tell me what thy lordly name is on the night's Plutonian
   shore?
   Quoth the Raven, "Nevermore!" —POE, *The Raven*

READING

Reading maketh a full man; conference a ready man;
and writing an exact man.
—FRANCIS BACON, *Essays: Of Studies*

A man may as well expect to grow stronger by always
eating as wiser by always reading.
—JEREMY COLLIER, *Of the Entertainment of Books*

The three practical rules, then, which I have to offer, are,—

1. Never read any book that is not a year old.
2. Never read any but the famed books.
3. Never read any but what you like.

—EMERSON, *Society and Solitude: Books*

The art of reading is to skip judiciously.

—P. G. HAMERTON, *The Intellectual Life*

I love to lose myself in other men's minds. When I am not walking, I am reading; I cannot sit and think. Books think for me.   —CHARLES LAMB, *Last Essays of Elia*

He that I am reading seems always to have the most force.   —MONTAIGNE, *Essays, II*

For men that read much and work little are as bells, the which do sound to call others, and they themselves never enter into a church.

—THOMAS NORTH, *Diall of Princes* (1557)

Who readeth much, and never meditates,
  Is like the greedy eater of much food,
Who so surcloys his stomach with his cates,
  That commonly they do him little good.

—JOSHUA SYLVESTER, *Tetrasticha*

Verily, when the day of judgment comes, we shall not be asked what we have read, but what we have done.

—THOMAS à KEMPIS, *Imitation of Christ*

Give a man a pipe he can smoke,
  Give a man a book he can read:
And his home is bright with a calm delight,
  Though the room be poor indeed.

—JAMES THOMSON, *Sunday Up the River*

REASON

He who will not reason, is a bigot; he who cannot is a fool; and he who dares not is a slave.
—SIR WILLIAM DRUMMOND, *Academical Questions*

His tongue
Dropt manna, and could make the worse appear
The better reason.   —MILTON, *Paradise Lost, II*

The heart has reasons of which reason has no knowledge.
—PASCAL, *Pensées,* 277

REBELLION

Rebellion to tyrants is obedience to God.
—ANON. (sometimes attributed to Benj. Franklin)

RECRUIT

Sez Corporal Madden to Private McFadden:
"Yer figger wants padd'n—
Sure, man, ye've no shape!
Behind ye yer shoulders
Stick out like two bowlders;
Yer shins are as thin
As a pair of pen-holders!"
—R. W. CHAMBERS, *The Recruit*

REDEEMER

I know that my redeemer liveth.
—OLD TESTAMENT, *Job, XIX,* 25

REFORM

Reform must come from within, not from without. You cannot legislate for virtue.
—CARDINAL GIBBONS, *Address,* 1909

Every reform movement has a lunatic fringe.
—THEODORE ROOSEVELT, *In re* Progressive Party, 1913

REGRET

I only regret that I have but one life to lose for my country.
　　—NATHAN HALE, *Speech before his execution, Sept. 22,*
　　　　　　　　　　　　　　　　　　　　　　　　1776

For of all sad words of tongue or pen,
The saddest are these: "It might have been."
　　　　　　　　　　　—WHITTIER, *Maud Muller*

RELATIVES

God gives us relatives; thank God we can choose our friends.　　—ADDISON MIZNER, *The Cynic's Calendar*

RELIEF

For this relief much thanks: 'tis bitter cold,
And I am sick at heart.　—SHAKESPEARE, *Hamlet, I, 1*

RELIGION

All religions must be tolerated . . . for . . . every man must get to heaven his own way.
　　—FREDERICK THE GREAT, *In re Catholic Schools, 1740*

Religion has reduced Spain to a guitar, Italy to a hand-organ and Ireland to exile.
　　—R. G. INGERSOLL, *Gov. Rollin's . . . Proclamation*

Religion . . . is the opium of the people.
　　—KARL MARX, *Introduction to Critique of . . . Hegel*

Pure religion and undefiled before God and the Father is this, To visit the fatherless and widows in their affliction, and to keep himself unspotted from the world.
　　　　　　　　　—NEW TESTAMENT, *James, I, 27*

We have just enough religion to make us hate, but not enough to make us love, one another.
　　　　　　—SWIFT, *Thoughts on Various Subjects*

REMEMBER

If I forget thee, O Jerusalem, let my right hand forget her cunning.

If I do not remember thee, let my tongue cleave to the roof of my mouth; if I prefer not Jerusalem above my chief joy.   —OLD TESTAMENT, *Psalms, CXXXVII, 5 and 6*

REMORSE

Farewell, remorse: all good to me is lost;
Evil, be thou my good.   —MILTON, *Paradise Lost, IV*

There are some people who are very resourceful
At being remorseful.
And who apparently feel that the best way to make friends
Is to do something terrible and then make amends.
     —OGDEN NASH, *Hearts of Gold*

Stop up the access and passage to remorse,
That no compunctious visitings of nature
Shake my fell purpose.   —SHAKESPEARE, *Macbeth, I, 5*

REPENTANCE

Joy shall be in heaven over one sinner that repenteth, more than over ninety and nine just persons, which need no repentance.   —NEW TESTAMENT, *Luke, XV, 7*

REPUBLIC

Republics end through luxury; monarchies through poverty.   —MONTESQUIEU, *Spirit of the Laws, VII*

REPUTATION

A good name is better than precious ointment.
     —OLD TESTAMENT, *Ecclesiastes, VII, 1*

Good name in man and woman, dear my lord,
Is the immediate jewel of their souls:

Who steals my purse steals trash; ...
But he that filches from me my good name
Robs me of that which not enriches him,
And makes me poor indeed.

> —SHAKESPEARE, *Othello, III, 3*

Seeking the bubble reputation
Even in the cannon's mouth.

> —SHAKESPEARE, *As You Like It, II, 7*

RESIGNATION

It's no use crying over spilt milk: it only makes it salty
for the cat. —ANON. (see W. S. Gilbert, *Foggerty's Fairy*)

Father, ... not my will, but thine, be done.

> —NEW TESTAMENT, *Luke, XXII, 42*

RESOLUTION

And thus the native hue of resolution
Is sicklied o'er with the pale cast of thought.

> —SHAKESPEARE, *Hamlet, III, 1*

RESPECTABILITY

The more things a man is ashamed of, the more respectable he is. —BERNARD SHAW, *Man and Superman, 1*

REST

When Earth's last picture is painted and the tubes are
    twisted and dried,
When the oldest colours have faded, and the youngest
    critic has died,
We shall rest, and, faith, we shall need it—lie down for
    an aeon or two. ....

> —KIPLING, *When Earth's Last Picture* ...

Come unto me, all ye that labour and are heavy laden,
and I will give you rest.

> —NEW TESTAMENT, *Matthew, XI, 28*

Beyond the last horizon's rim,
  Beyond adventure's farthest quest,
Somewhere they rise, serene and dim,
  The happy, happy Hills of Rest.
                    —A. B. PAINE, *The Hills of Rest*

Rest, rest, perturbed spirit! —SHAKESPEARE, *Hamlet, I, 5*

RESURRECTION

Earth to earth, ashes to ashes, dust to dust, in sure and certain hope of the resurrection.
                    —BOOK OF COMMON PRAYER

RETRIBUTION

Though the mills of God grind slowly,
  Yet they grind exceeding small.
—LONGFELLOW (trans. from the German of VON LOGAU)

And with what measure ye mete, it shall be measured unto you.   —NEW TESTAMENT, *Matthew, VII, 2*

Whatsoever a man soweth, that shall he also reap.
                    —NEW TESTAMENT, *Galatians, VI, 7*

Ye have heard that it hath been said, An eye for an eye, and a tooth for a tooth: But I say unto you, That ye resist not evil: but whosoever shall smite thee on thy right cheek, turn to him the other also.
                    —NEW TESTAMENT, *Matthew, V, 38-39*

Eye for eye, tooth for tooth, hand for hand, foot for foot.
                    —OLD TESTAMENT, *Deuteronomy, XIX, 31*

He that diggeth a pit shall fall into it.
                    —OLD TESTAMENT, *Ecclesiastes, X, 8*

They have sown the wind, and they shall reap the whirl-wind.   —OLD TESTAMENT, *Hosea, VIII, 7*

For 'tis sport to have the enginer
Hoist with his own petar.
                    —SHAKESPEARE, *Hamlet, III, 4*

Men must reap the things they sow,
Force from force must ever flow.
            —SHELLEY, *Lines . . . Among the Euganean Hills*

REVELRY

There was a sound of revelry by night,
And Belgium's capital had gather'd then
Her Beauty and her Chivalry, and bright
The lamps shone o'er fair women and brave men.
                    —BYRON, *Childe Harold, III*

REVENGE

Revenge is a kind of wild justice; which the more man's
nature runs to, the more ought law to weed it out.
                    —FRANCIS BACON, *Essays: Of Revenge*

Vengeance is mine; I will repay, saith the Lord. Therefore if thine enemy hunger, feed him; if he thirst, give him
drink: for in so doing thou shalt heap coals of fire on his
head.   —NEW TESTAMENT, *Romans, XII, 19, 20*

If a Jew wrong a Christian, what is his humility? Revenge. If a Christian wrong a Jew, what should his suf-
france be by Christian example? Why, revenge. The vil-
lainy you teach me, I will execute, and it shall go hard
but I will better the instruction.
                    —SHAKESPEARE, *Merchant of Venice, III, 1*

If I can catch him once upon the hip,
I will feed fat the ancient grudge I bear him.
                    —SHAKESPEARE, *Merchant of Venice, I, 3*

REVOLUTION

Arise, ye prisoners of starvation,
    Arise, ye wretched of the earth,
For justice thunders condemnation—
    A better world's in birth. —ANON., *The Internationale*

Every revolution was first a thought in one man's mind.
                            —EMERSON, *Essays: History*

Sire, it is not a revolt,—it is a revolution.
                —DUC DE LA ROCHEFOUCAULD-LIANCOURT,
                        To Louis XVI, July, 1789

If by the mere force of numbers a majority should de-
prive a minority of any clearly written constitutional right,
it might, in any moral point of view, justify revolution— . . .
            —LINCOLN, First Inaugural Address, 1861

The proletarians have nothing to lose but their chains.
They have a world to win. Workers of the world, unite!
                —MARX AND ENGELS, *Communist Manifesto*

RHINE

The river Rhine, it is well known,
Doth wash your city of Cologne;
But tell me, Nymphs, what power divine
Shall henceforth wash the river Rhine?
                        —S. T. COLERIDGE, *Cologne*

The Rhine! the Rhine! the German Rhine!
Who will be the guardian of the stream?
(Zum Rhein, zum Rhein, zum deutschen Rhein!
Wer will des Stromes Hüter sein?)
            —MAX SCHNECKENBURGER, *Die Wacht am Rhein*

RICHES

Lay not up for yourself treasure upon earth; where the
rust and moth doth corrupt.   —BOOK OF COMMON PRAYER

And tempts by making rich, not making poor.
But Satan now is wiser than of yore,
—Pope, *Moral Essays, III*

A man is rich in proportion to the number of things he can afford to let alone.   —Thoreau, *Where I Lived . . .*

RICH MAN

He frivols through the livelong day,
  He knows not Poverty, her pinch.
His lot seems light, his heart seems gay;
  He has a cinch. —Franklin P. Adams, *The Rich Man*

The man who dies rich dies disgraced.
—Andrew Carnegie, *The Gospel of Wealth*

It is easier for a camel to go through the eye of a needle,
than for a rich man to enter into the kingdom of God.
—New Testament, *Matthew, XIX, 24*

RIDDLE

'Twas in heaven pronounced, and 'twas muttered in hell,
And echo caught faintly the sound as it fell;
On the confines of earth 'twas permitted to rest,
And the depth of the ocean its presence confessed. . . .
—Catherine Fanshawe, *Riddle on the Letter H*

What animal goes on four legs in the morning, two at noon, and three in the evening?
—The Riddle of the Sphinx, solved by Oedipus

RIGHT

I would rather be right than President.
—Henry Clay, To Preston of Kentucky, 1850

He will hew to the line of right, let the chips fly where they may.
>—ROSCOE CONKLING, Speech, 1880 (referring to U. S. Grant)

Be sure you are right, then go ahead.
>—DAVID CROCKETT, Motto during War of 1812

They are slaves who dare not be
In the right with two or three.
>—J. R. LOWELL, *Stanzas on Freedom*

Every man has by the law of nature a right to such a waste portion of the earth as is necessary for his subsistence.
>—SIR THOMAS MORE, *Utopia, II*

I see the right, and I approve it too,
Condemn the wrong, and yet the wrong pursue.
(*Video meliora proboque, deteriora sequor.*)
>—OVID, *Metamorphoses, VII* (Garth trans.)

RIGHTEOUS

My son, these maxims make a rule,
    And lump them aye tegither:
The Rigid Righteous is a fool,
    The Rigid Wise anither.
>—BURNS, Motto for *Address to the Unco Guid*

Be not righteous overmuch, neither make thyself over wise.
>—OLD TESTAMENT, *Ecclesiastes, VII, 16*

The righteous shall flourish like the palm tree: he shall grow like a cedar of Lebanon.
>—OLD TESTAMENT, *Psalms, XCII, 12*

RISING

Up rose the sun, and up rose Emelye.
>—CHAUCER, *The Knight's Tale*

And winking Mary-buds begin
   To ope their golden eyes:
With everything that pretty bin,
   My lady sweet, arise.
—SHAKESPEARE, *Cymbeline, II, 3* (Song: "Hark, hark, the
                                                lark")

A birdie with a yellow bill
Hopped upon the window sill,
Cocked his shining eye and said:
"Ain't you 'shamed, you sleepy-head?"
                        —R. L. STEVENSON, *Time to Rise*

RIVERS

1. AFTON
    Flow gently, sweet Afton, among thy green braes!
    Flow gently, I'll sing thee a song in thy praise.
                 —BURNS, *Flow Gently Sweet Afton*

2. ALPH
    In Xanadu did Kubla Khan
       A stately pleasure-dome decree;
    Where Alph, the sacred river, ran
    Through caverns measureless to man
       Down to a sunless sea.
               —S. T. COLERIDGE, *Kubla Khan*

3. CHATTAHOOCHEE
    Out of the hills of Habersham,
       Down the valleys of Hall,
    I hurry amain to reach the plain;
       Run the rapid and reach the fall, . . .
         —SIDNEY LANIER, *Song of the Chattahoochee*

4. CONGO
    Then I saw the Congo, creeping through the black.
    Cutting through the jungle with a golden track.
            —VACHEL LINDSAY, *The Congo*

ROAD

Any road leads to the end of the world.
> —EDWARD FITZGERALD, *Polonius*

The road was a ribbon of moonlight over the purple moor.   —ALFRED NOYES, *The Highwayman*

ROCK OF AGES

Rock of Ages, cleft for me,
Let me hide myself in Thee!
> —A. M. TOPLADY, *Rock of Ages*

ROD

He that spareth the rod hateth his son.
> —OLD TESTAMENT, *Proverbs, XIII, 24*

ROME

I found Rome brick and left it marble.
> —CAESAR AUGUSTUS (in Suetonius' *Lives*)

Butchered to make a Roman holiday.
> —BYRON, *Childe Harold, IV*

The Niobe of nations! there she stands,
Childless and crownless, in her voiceless woe;
An empty urn within her wither'd hands,
Whose holy dust was scatter'd long ago.
> —BYRON, *Childe Harold, IV*

When they are in Rome, they do there as they see done.
> —BURTON, *Anatomy of Melancholy, III*

Rome was not built in a day. —CERVANTES, *Don Quixote*

All roads lead to Rome.   —LA FONTAINE, *Fables, XII*

Not that I loved Caesar less, but that I loved Rome more.   —SHAKESPEARE, *Julius Caesar, III, 2*

The Roman Senate and People
(*S.P.Q.R.—Senatus Populusque Romanus*)
                    —Motto of Rome on coins, statues, etc.

ROMEO

O Romeo, Romeo! wherefore art thou Romeo?
Deny thy father and refuse thy name:
Or if thou wilt not, be but sworn my love,
And I'll no longer be a Capulet.
                    —Shakespeare, *Romeo and Juliet, II, 2*

ROOSEVELT, THEODORE

Theodore, if there is one thing more than another for
which I admire you, it is your original discovery of the ten
commandments.
    —Thomas B. Reed (quoted in Robinson's *Life of Reed*)

Our hero is a man of peace,
    Preparedness he implores;
His sword within its scabbard sleeps,
    But mercy, how it snores!
                    —McLandburgh Wilson, *A Man of Peace*

ROSE

It never will rain roses: when we want
To have more roses we must plant more trees.
                    —George Eliot, *The Spanish Gypsy*

Roses at first were white,
    Till they co'd not agree
Whether my Sappho's breast
    Or they more white sho'd be

But being vanquisht quite,
    A blush their cheeks bespread:
Since which (believe the rest)
    The Roses first came red.
                    —Herrick, *How Roses Came Red*

Sweet as the rose that died last year is the rose that is
born to-day.   —COSMO MONKHOUSE, *A Dead March*

'Tis the last rose of summer,
  Left blooming alone;
All her lovely companions
  Are faded and gone;
No flower of her kindred
  No rose-bud is nigh,
To reflect back her blushes,
  Or give sigh for sigh.
              —THOMAS MOORE, *The Last Rose of Summer*

As rich and purposeless as is the rose:
Thy simple doom is to be beautiful.
                    —STEPHEN PHILLIPS, *Marpessa*

Baby said
  When she smelt the rose,
"Oh! what a pity
  I've only one nose!"
              —LAURA E. RICHARDS, *The Difference*

This world that we're a-livin' in
  Is mighty hard to beat;
You git a thorn with every rose,
  But *ain't* the roses *sweet!*
              —FRANK L. STANTON, *This World*

A Rose is a rose is a rose is a rose.
              —GERTRUDE STEIN, *Geography and Plays*

The fairest things have fleetest end:
  Their scent survives their close,
But the rose's scent is bitterness
  To him that loved the rose!
                    —FRANCIS THOMPSON, *Daisy*

Go, lovely rose—
Tell her that wastes her time and me,
　　That now she knows,
When I resemble her to thee,
How sweet and fair she seems to be.
　　　　　　　　—EDMUND WALLER, *Go, Lovely Rose*

Red Rose, proud Rose, sad Rose of all my days!
Come near me, while I sing the ancient ways.
　　　　　　　　—W. B. YEATS, *The Rose of Battle*

"RUM, ROMANISM, AND REBELLION"

We are Republicans, and we don't propose to leave our
party and identify ourselves with the party whose ante-
cedents have been rum, Romanism, and rebellion.
　　　　　—REV. S. D. BURCHARD, Speech, Oct., 1884 (which
　　　　　　　　　probably lost the presidency for Blaine)

RUMOR

　　　　　　　　Rumour is a pipe
Blown by surmises, jealousies, conjectures.
　　　　　　　　—SHAKESPEARE, *Henry IV, II*, Induction

RUST

It is better to wear out than to rust out.
　　　　　　　　—RICHARD CUMBERLAND (quoted in Boswell's
　　　　　　　　　　　　Tour of the Hebrides)

RUTH

Whither thou goest, I will go; and where thou lodgest, I
will lodge: thy people shall be my people, and thy God my
God: . . .　　　　　　　—OLD TESTAMENT, *Ruth, I, 16*

SABBATH

I do not love the Sabbath,
　　The soapsuds and the starch,

The troop of solemn people
  Who to Salvation march.
                —ROBERT GRAVES, *The Boy Out of Church*

The sabbath was made for man, and not man for the
sabbath.   —NEW TESTAMENT, *Mark, II, 27*

SAFETY

... out of this nettle, danger, we pluck this flower, safety.
                —SHAKESPEARE, *Henry IV, I, II, 3*

It is man's perdition to be safe when he ought to die for
the truth. —R. VINES, Sermon, 1642 (quoted by Emerson)

SAINT

Saint: a dead sinner revised and edited.
                —AMBROSE BIERCE, *The Devil's Dictionary*

The tears of Saints more sweet by far
Than all the songs of sinners are.   —HERRICK, *Tears*

Precious in the sight of the Lord is the death of his saints.
                —OLD TESTAMENT, *Psalms, CXVI, 15*

It is easier to make a saint out of a libertine than out of
a prig.   —GEORGE SANTAYANA, *Little Essays*

The only difference between the saint and the sinner is
that every saint has a past and every sinner has a future.
                —OSCAR WILDE, *A Woman of No Importance, III*

SALESMAN

... the Romantic Hero was no longer the knight, the
wandering poet, the cowpuncher, the aviator, nor the brave
young district attorney, but the great sales-manager, who
had an Analysis of Merchandizing Problems on his glass-
topped desk, whose title of nobility was "go-getter," ...
                —SINCLAIR LEWIS, *Babbitt*

"SALLY IN OUR ALLEY"

Of all the girls that are so smart
    There's none like pretty Sally;
She is the darling of my heart,
    And she lives in our alley.
          —HENRY CAREY, *Sally in Our Alley*

SALT

. . . a man must eat a peck of salt with his friend before
he knows him.   —CERVANTES, *Don Quixote*

I have eaten your bread and salt,
I have drunk your water and wine;
The deaths ye have died I have watched beside,
And the lives that ye led were mine.
          —KIPLING, *Departmental Ditties*

Ye are the salt of the earth: but if the salt have lost his
savour, wherewith shall it be salted?
          —NEW TESTAMENT, *Matthew, V, 13*

SATAN

High on a throne of royal state, which far
Outshone the wealth of Ormus and of Ind . . .
Satan exalted sat, by merit rais'd
To that bad eminence.   —MILTON, *Paradise Lost, II*

SATIRE

Satire or sense, alas! can Sporus feel?
Who breaks a butterfly upon a wheel?
          —POPE, *Epistle to Dr. Arbuthnot*

For who would be satirical
About a thing so very small?
          —SWIFT, *Dr. Delany's Villa*

Who, for the poor renown of being smart,
Would leave a sting within a brother's heart?
                    —EDWARD YOUNG, *Love of Fame*

SCANDAL

Assail'd by scandal and the tongue of strife,
His only answer was, a blameless life;
                              —COWPER, *Hope*

Tell it not in Gath, publish it not in the streets of
Askalon.   —OLD TESTAMENT, *II Samuel, 1, 20*

Mercy on me! here is the whole set! a character dead at
every word, I suppose.
              —SHERIDAN, *The School for Scandal, II*

How awful to reflect that what people say of us is true.
                    —L. P. SMITH, *Afterthoughts*

Swift flies each tale of laughter, shame or folly,
Caught by Paul Pry, and carried home to Polly.
                         —C. SPRAGUE, *Curiosity*

She is not old, she is not young,
The Woman with the Serpent's Tongue.
The haggard cheek, the hungering eye,
The poisoned words that wildly fly,
The famished face, the fevered hand—
Who slights the worthiest in the land,
Sneers at the just, contemns the brave,
And blackens goodness in its grave.
              —WILLIAM WATSON, *The Woman With*
                              the Serpent's Tongue

Have you heard of the terrible family They,
And the dreadful venomous things They say?
Why, half of the gossip under the sun,

If you trace it back, you will find begun
    In that wretched House of They.
                    —ELLA WHEELER WILCOX, *They Say*

SCHEMES

The best-laid schemes o' mice an' men
    Gang aft agley,
An' lea'e us nought but grief and pain,
    For promised joy!   —BURNS, *To a Mouse*

SCHOOL

But to go to school in a summer morn,
Oh, it drives all joy away!
Under a cruel eye outworn,
The little ones spend the day—
In sighing and dismay.   —BLAKE, *The Schoolboy*

SCHOOLBOY

The whining schoolboy, with his satchel
And shining morning face, creeping like snail
Unwillingly to school.
                    —SHAKESPEARE, *As You Like It, II, 7*

SCHOOLHOUSE

Still sits the school-house by the road,
    A ragged beggar sleeping;
Around it still the sumachs grow
    And blackberry-vines are creeping.
                    —WHITTIER, *In School-Days*

SCIENCE

Go, wondrous creature! mount where Science guides;

.   .   .   .

Go, teach Eternal Wisdom how to rule—
Then drop into thyself, and be a fool!
                    —POPE, *Essay on Man, II*

Science is vastly more stimulating to the imagination than are the classics. —J. B. S. HALDANE, *Daedalus*

True science teaches, above all, to doubt and to be ignorant. —MIGUEL DE UNAMUNO, *The Tragic Sense of Life*

SCORN

In heaven they scorn to serve,
  So now in hell they reign.
          —JOHN FLETCHER, *The Purple Land*

Nor sitteth in the seat of the scornful.
          —OLD TESTAMENT, *Psalms, I, 1*

SCOTLAND

My heart's in the Highlands, my heart is not here;
My heart's in the Highlands a-chasing the deer.
—ANON., *The Strong Walls of Derry* (later used by Burns)

O Scotia! my dear, my native soil!
  For whom my warmest wish to Heaven is sent!
Long may thy hardy sons of rustic toil
  Be blest with health, and peace, and sweet content!
          —BURNS, *The Cotter's Saturday Night*

Scots, wha hae wi' Wallace bled,
Scots, wham Bruce has aften led;
Welcome to your gory bed,
  Or to glorious victorie!
          —BURNS, *Bruce at Bannockburn*

If the Scotch knew enough to go in when it rained, they would never get any outdoor exercise.
          —SIMEON FORD, *My Trip to Scotland*

Oats: a grain which is generally given to horses, but in Scotland supports the people.
          —JOHNSON, definition in *Dictionary*

"SCRAP OF PAPER"

Just for a word, "neutrality," . . . just for a scrap of paper, Great Britain is going to make war on a kindred nation. . . .

  —T. VON BETHMANN-HOLLWEG, Dispatch, Aug. 4, 1914

SCULPTURE

With chiselled touch
The stone unhewn and cold
Becomes a living mould.
The more the marble wastes,
The more the statue grows.
  —MICHELANGELO, *Sonnet* (Mrs. Roscoe trans.)

SEA

Roll on, thou deep and dark-blue Ocean, roll!
Ten thousand fleets sweep over thee in vain;
Man marks the earth with ruin, his control
Stops with the shore; . . .
  —BYRON, *Childe Harold, IV*

The sea! the sea! the open sea!
The blue, the fresh, the ever free!
  —B. W. PROCTER, *The Sea*

We were the first that ever burst
Into that silent sea.
  —S. T. COLERIDGE, *The Ancient Mariner*

A wet sheet and a flowing sea—
 A wind that follows fast,
And fills the white and rushing sail,
 And bends the gallant mast,—
—ALLAN CUNNINGHAM, *A Wet Sheet and a Flowing Sea*

I must go down to the seas again, to the lonely sea and
 the sky,

And all I ask is a tall ship and a star to steer her by, . . .
—JOHN MASEFIELD, *Sea Fever*

All the rivers run into the sea; yet the sea is not full.
—OLD TESTAMENT, *Ecclesiastes, I, 7*

Deep calleth unto deep.
—OLD TESTAMENT, *Psalms, XLII, 7*

Ye gentlemen of England
    That live at home at ease,
Ah! little do you think upon
    The dangers of the seas.
—MARTIN PARKER, *Ye Gentlemen of England*

A life on the ocean wave,
    A home on the rolling deep,
Where the scattered waters rave,
    And the winds their revels keep!
—EPES SARGENT, *A Life on the Ocean Wave*

I will go back to the great sweet mother,
    Mother and lover of men, the sea.
I will go down to her, I and none other,
    Close with her, kiss her, and mix her with me.
—SWINBURNE, *The Triumph of Time*

Rocked in the cradle of the deep
I lay me down in peace to sleep;
Secure I rest upon the wave,
For thou, O Lord! hast power to save.
—EMMA HART WILLARD, *Rocked in the Cradle of the Deep*

SEEK

Seek, and ye shall find; knock, and it shall be opened
unto you.   —NEW TESTAMENT, *Matthew, VII, 7*

SELF-KNOWLEDGE

As I walk'd by myself, I talk'd to myself,
    And myself replied to me;
And the questions myself then put to myself,
    With their answers, I give to thee.
                    —BERNARD BARTON, *Colloquy With Myself*

O wad some Pow'r the giftie gie us
To see oursels as ithers see us!
It wad frae monie a blunder free us. . . .
                    —BURNS, *To a Louse* . . .

Just stand aside and watch yourself go by,
Think of yourself as "he" instead of "I."
            —STRICKLAND GILLILAN, *Watch Yourself Go By*

I have to live with myself, and so
I want to be fit for myself to know;
I want to be able as days go by,
Always to look myself straight in the eye.
                        —EDGAR A. GUEST, *Myself*

Know then thyself, presume not God to scan;
The proper study of mankind is Man.
                    —POPE, *Essay on Man, II*

Know thyself.   —Attributed to THALES

Great God, I ask thee for no meaner pelf
Than that I may not disappoint myself.
                        —THOREAU, *My Prayer*

SELF-LOVE

He that falls in love with himself, will have no rivals.
        —FRANKLIN, *Poor Richard's Almanac* for 1739

Self-love is the greatest of all flatterers.
                —LA ROCHEFOUCAULD, *Maxims, 2*

To love oneself is the beginning of a life-long romance.
—OSCAR WILDE, *An Ideal Husband, III*

SELF-PRESERVATION

Self-preservation is the first law of nature.
—S. BUTLER, *Remains (c.* 1675)

SELF-SACRIFICE

It is a far, far better thing that I do, than I have ever done; it is a far, far better rest that I go to, than I have ever known.   —DICKENS, *A Tale of Two Cities*

He weren't no saint—but at jedgment
    I'd run my chance with Jim,
'Longside of some pious gentlemen
    That wouldn't shook hands with him.
He seen his duty, a dead-sure thing,—
    And went for it thar and then;
And Christ ain't a-going to be too hard
    On a man that died for men.—JOHN HAY, *Jim Bludso*

Self-sacrifice enables us to sacrifice other people without blushing.   —BERNARD SHAW, *Maxims for Revolutionists*

SELFISHNESS

The least pain in our little finger gives us more concern and uneasiness, than the destruction of millions of our fellow-beings.   —WILLIAM HAZLITT, *Works, Vol. X*

The wretch, concentred all in self,
Living, shall forfeit fair renown,
And, doubly dying, shall go down
To the vile dust from whence he sprung,
Unwept, unhonoured, and unsung.
—SCOTT, *Lay of the Last Minstrel*

The primary and sole foundation of virtue or of the proper conduct of life is to seek our own profit.

—SPINOZA, *Ethics*

SERENITY

Serene I fold my hands and wait,
  Nor care for wind or tide nor sea;
I rave no more 'gainst time or fate,
  For lo! my own shall come to me.

—JOHN BURROUGHS, *Waiting*

SERVICE

All service is the same with God,
With God, whose puppets, best and worst,
Are we: there is no last nor first.

—R. BROWNING, *Pippa Passes*

Well done, thou good and faithful servant: thou hast been faithful over a few things, I will make thee ruler over many things.   —NEW TESTAMENT, *Matthew, XXV, 21*

Had I but served my God with half the zeal
I served my king, he would not in mine age
Have left me naked to mine enemies.

—SHAKESPEARE, *Henry VIII, III, 2*

O good old man, how well in thee appears
The constant service of the antique world,
When service sweat for duty, not for meed!

—SHAKESPEARE, *As You Like It, II, 3*

Small service is true service while it lasts:
Of humblest Friends, bright Creature! scorn not one;
The Daisy, by the shadow that it casts,
Protects the lingering dew-drop from the Sun.

—WORDSWORTH, *To a Child*

SEX

> Amoebas at the start
>> Were not complex
> They tore themselves apart
>> And started Sex. —ARTHUR GUITERMAN, *Sex*

> Breathes there a man with soul so tough
> Who says two sexes aren't enough?
>> —SAMUEL HOFFENSTEIN, *The Sexes*

> . . . Men, women, and clergymen. —SYDNEY SMITH

> . . . Men, women, and professors. —J. E. SPINGARN

> . . . Saints, sinners, and Beechers. —LEONARD BACON

SHADOW

> We are but dust and shadow.
> (*Pulvis et umbra sumus.*) —HORACE, *Odes, IV*

> Some there be that shadows kiss;
> Such have but a shadow's bliss.
>> —SHAKESPEARE, *Merchant of Venice, II, 9*

> I have a little shadow that goes in and out with me,
> And what can be the use of him is more than I can see.
>> —R. L. STEVENSON, *My Shadow*

SHAKESPEARE

> Others abide our question. Thou art free.
> We ask and ask; Thou smilest and art still,
> Out-topping knowledge.
>> —MATTHEW ARNOLD, *Shakespeare*

> Shakespeare!—to such names sounding, what succeeds
> Fitly as silence? —R. BROWNING, *The Names*

Shake was a dramatist of note;
He lived by writing things to quote.
—H. C. BUNNER, *Shake, Mulleary and Go-ethe*

Our *myriad-minded* Shakespeare—a phrase . . . which
belongs to him, *de jure singulari, et ex privilegio naturae.*
—S. T. COLERIDGE, *Biographia Literaria*

Subtract from many modern poets all that may be found
in Shakespeare, and trash will remain.
—C. C. COLTON, *Lacon*

But Shakespeare's magic touch could not copied be;
Within that circle none durst walk but he.
—DRYDEN, Prologue to his version of *The Tempest*

There is an upstart Crow, beautified with our feathers,
that with his *Tygers heart wrapt in a Players hide* supposes
he is as well able to bumbast out a blanke verse as the best
of you; and being an absolute *Johannes factotum,* is, in
his own conceit, the onely Shake-scene in a countrie. . . .
—ROBERT GREENE, *Groatsworth of Wit* . . . (1592)

I remember, the players have often mentioned it as an
honour to Shakespeare, that in his writing (whatsoever he
penn'd) he never blotted out a line. My answer hath been,
would he had blotted out a thousand.
—BEN JONSON, *Explorata*

And Hamlet how boring, how boring to live with,
So mean and self-conscious, blowing and snoring
His wonderful speeches, full of other folks' whoring.
—D. H. LAWRENCE, *When I Read Shakespeare*

. . . sweetest Shakespear, fancy's child,
Warble his native wood-notes wild. —MILTON, *L'Allegro*

What needs my Shakespear for his honour'd bones,
The labour of an age in piled stones,
Or that his hallow'd reliques should be hid
Under a star-y pointing pyramid?
—MILTON, *On Shakespear*

Shakespeare (whom you and every playhouse bill
Style the divine! the matchless! what you will),
For gain, not glory, wing'd his roving flight,
And grew immortal in his own despite.
—POPE, *Imitations of Horace*

Shakespeare is a savage with sparks of genius which
shine in a dreadful darkness of night.
—VOLTAIRE, *Irène* (preliminary letter)

Good frend for Jesvs sake forbeare,
To digg the dust encloased heare.
Bles be ye man yt spares thes stones.
And curst be he yt moves my bones.
—Epitaph on Shakespeare's tombstone in Stratford

SHAME

There smites nothing so sharp, nor smelleth so sour
As shame. —WILLIAM LANGLAND, *Piers Plowman*

He was not born to shame:
Upon his brow shame is ashamed to sit.
—SHAKESPEARE, *Romeo and Juliet, III, 2*

I never wonder to see men wicked, but I often wonder
not to see them ashamed.
—SWIFT, *Thoughts on Various Subjects*

SHEEP

Little Bo-Peep has lost her sheep,
And can't tell where to find them;

Leave them alone, and they'll come home,
   Wagging their tails behind them.
                              —ANON., Nursery Rhyme

My name is Norval; on the Grampian hills
My father feeds his flock; a frugal swain,
Whose constant cares were to increase his store,
And keep his only son, myself, at home.
                              —JOHN HOME, *Douglas, II, 1*

And before him shall be gathered all nations: and he
shall separate them one from another, as a shepherd divid-
eth his sheep from his goats.
                              —NEW TESTAMENT, *Matthew, XXV, 32*

The mountain sheep are sweeter,
But the valley sheep are fatter;
We therefore deemed it meeter
To carry off the latter.
                              —T. L. PEACOCK, *War Song of Dinas Vawr*

I am a tainted wether of the flock,
Meetest for death.
                              —SHAKESPEARE, *Merchant of Venice, IV, 1*

My flocks feed not,
My ewes breed not,
My rams speed not,
All is amiss. —SHAKESPEARE (?), *The Passionate Pilgrim*

SHELLEY, PERCY BYSSHE

". . . a beautiful and *ineffectual* angel, beating in the
void his luminous wings in vain."
                              —MATTHEW ARNOLD, *Literature and Dogma*

Ah, did you once see Shelley plain,
   And did he stop and speak to you,

And did you speak to him again?
  How strange it seems and new!
                    —R. BROWNING, *Memorabilia*

Shelley, lyric lord of England's lordliest singers, here
  first heard
Ring from lips of poets crowned and dead the Prome-
  thean word
Whence his soul took fire, and power to outsoar the
  sunward-soaring bird. —SWINBURNE, *Eton: An Ode*

SHEPHERDESS

She walks—the lady of my delight—
  A shepherdess of sheep.
Her flocks are thoughts. She keeps them white;
  She guards them from the steep.
She feeds them on the fragrant height,
  And folds them in for sleep.
                    —ALICE MEYNELL, *The Shepherdess*

SHIP

A capital ship for an ocean trip
  Was "The Galloping Window-blind."
No gale that blew dismayed her crew
  Or troubled the captain's mind.
              —C. E. CARRYL, *Davy and the Goblin*

For she *is* such a smart little craft,
Such a neat little, sweet little craft—
    Such a bright little,
    Tight little,
    Slight little,
    Light little,
Trim little, slim little craft.
                    —W. S. GILBERT, *Ruddigore, II*

The Liner she's a lady, an' she never looks nor 'eeds—
The Man-o'-War's 'er 'usband, an' 'e gives 'er all she
    needs,
But, oh, the little cargo-boats, that sail the wet seas roun',
They're just the same as you an' me a-plyin' up an' down!
                    —KIPLING, *The Liner She's a Lady*

Build me straight, O worthy Master!
    Stanch and strong, a goodly vessel
That shall laugh at all disaster,
    And with wave and whirlwind wrestle.
                —LONGFELLOW, *The Building of the Ship*

SHIPWRECK

Let us think of them that sleep,
Full many a fathom deep,
By thy wild and stormy steep,
    Elsinore!   —THOMAS CAMPBELL, *Battle of the Baltic*

"We are lost!" the captain shouted,
    As he staggered down the stairs.
                    —T. J. FIELDS, *Ballad of the Tempest*

And fast through the midnight dark and drear,
    Through the whistling sleet and snow,
Like a sheeted ghost. the vessel swept
    Tow'rds the reef of Norman's Woe.
                —LONGFELLOW, *The Wreck of the Hesperus*

Down, down beneath the deep,
That oft in triumph bore him,
He sleeps a sound and peaceful sleep,
With the salt waves dashing o'er him.
                    —H. F. LYTE, *The Sailor's Grave*

It was that fatal and perfidious bark,
Built in th' eclipse, and rigg'd with curses dark,
That sank so low that sacred head of thine.
                    —MILTON, *Lycidas*

Methought I saw a thousand fearful wrecks;
Ten thousand men that fishes gnaw'd upon;
Wedges of gold, great anchors, heaps of pearl,
Inestimable stones, unvalued jewels,
All scattered in the bottom of the sea.
—SHAKESPEARE, *Richard III, I, 4*

SILENCE

There is a time of speaking and a time of being still.
—WILLIAM CAXTON, *Charles the Grete* (1485)

Let him now speak, or else for ever after hold his peace.
—BOOK OF COMMON PRAYER

Silence is the element in which great things fashion
themselves.   —CARLYLE, *Sartor Resartus*

These be
Three silent things:
The falling snow . . . the hour
Before the dawn . . . the mouth of one
Just dead.   —ADELAIDE CRAPSEY, *Triad*

Thou foster-child of Silence and slow Time.
—KEATS, *Ode on a Grecian Urn*

Even a fool, when he holdeth his peace, is counted wise.
—OLD TESTAMENT, *Proverbs, XVII, 28*

The rest is silence.   —SHAKESPEARE, *Hamlet, V, 2*

He had occasional flashes of silence, that made his conversation perfectly delightful.
—SYDNEY SMITH, referring to Macaulay

He knew the precise psychological moment when to say
nothing.   —OSCAR WILDE, *The Picture of Dorian Gray*

Some sipping punch, some sipping tea,
But, as you by their faces see,
All silent and all damn'd!
                    —WORDSWORTH, *Peter Bell* (in original edition)

SILVER LINING

every cloud
has its silver
lining but it is
sometimes a little
difficult to get it to
the mint   —DON MARQUIS, *certain maxims of archie*

SIMON LEGREE

And the Devil said to Simon Legree:
"I like your style, so wicked and free."
                    —VACHEL LINDSAY, *A Negro Sermon*

SIN

The sins that tarnish whore and thief
   Beset me every day.
My most ethereal belief
   Inhabits common clay.

                    —GAMALIEL BRADFORD, *Rousseau*

Owning her weakness,
Her evil behaviour,
And leaving with meekness,
Her sins to her Saviour!
                    —THOMAS HOOD, *The Bridge of Sighs*

The sins ye do by two and two ye must pay for one by
   one.   —KIPLING, *Tomlinson*

He that is without sin among you, let him cast the first
stone.   —NEW TESTAMENT, *John, VIII, 7*

The wages of sin is death.
                    —NEW TESTAMENT, *Romans, VI, 3*

Though your sins be as scarlet, they shall be white as snow.   —OLD TESTAMENT, *Isaiah, I, 18*

Woe unto them that draw iniquity with cords of vanity, and sin as it were with a cart rope.
                        —OLD TESTAMENT, *Isaiah, V, 18*

> I am a man
> More sinn'd against than sinning.
>   —SHAKESPEARE, *King Lear, III, 2*

> Man-like it is to fall into sin,
> Fiend-like it is to dwell therein,
> Christ-like it is for sin to grieve,
> God-like it is all sin to leave.
>   —F. VON LOGAU (Longfellow trans.)

> But the sin forgiven by Christ in Heaven
> By man is cursed alway.
>   —N. P. WILLIS, *Unseen Spirits*

SINNER

God be merciful to me a sinner.
                        —NEW TESTAMENT, *Luke, XVIII, 13*

SISTER

> My sister! my sweet sister! if a name
> Dearer and purer were, it should be thine.
>   —BYRON, *Epistle to Augusta*

> For the Colonel's Lady an' Judy O'Grady
>   Are sisters under their skins!   —KIPLING, *The Ladies*

SKIN

Can the Ethiopian change his skin, or the leopard his spots?   —OLD TESTAMENT, *Jeremiah, XIII, 23*

SKY

The spacious firmament on high,
With all the blue ethereal sky,
And spangled heavens, a shining frame,
Their great Original proclaim. —ADDISON, *Ode* (1712)

The sky
is that beautiful old parchment
in which the sun and the moon
keep their diary. —ALFRED KREYMBORG, *Old Manuscript*

And that inverted Bowl they call the Sky,
Whereunder crawling coop'd we live and die,
    Lift not your hands to *It* for help—for it
As impotently moves as you or I.
        —OMAR KHAYYÁM, *Rubáiyát* (FitzGerald trans.)

The heavens declare the glory of God, and the firmament sheweth his handywork.
                    —OLD TESTAMENT, *Psalms, XIX, 1*

I never saw a man who looked
    With such a wistful eye
Upon that little tent of blue
    Which prisoners call the sky,
And at every drifting cloud that went
    With sails of silver by.
            —OSCAR WILDE, *Ballad of Reading Gaol*

SLANDER

If for a tranquil mind you seek,
    These things observe with care:
Of whom you speak, to whom you speak
    And how, and when, and where.
                    —ANON., *A Rule of Conduct*

If slander be a snake, it is a winged one—it flies as well as creeps.   —DOUGLAS JERROLD, *Slander*

Whose edge is sharper than the sword, whose tongue
Outvenoms all the worms of Nile, whose breath
Rides on the posting winds and doth belie
All corners of the world: Kings, queens and states,
Maids, matrons, nay, the secrets of the grave
This viperous slander enters.
                    —SHAKESPEARE, *Cymbeline, III, 4*

Defaming and defacing, till he left
Not even Lancelot brave nor Galahad clean.
                    —TENNYSON, *Merlin and Vivien*

SLAVERY

Resolved: That the compact which exists between the
North and the South is a covenant with death and an
agreement with hell, involving both parties in atrocious
criminality, and should be immediately annulled.
    —WILLIAM LLOYD GARRISON, *Resolution* . . . (1843)

"A house divided against itself cannot stand." I believe
this government cannot endure permanently half-slave and
half-free.   —LINCOLN, Speech, Springfield, 1858

If slavery is not wrong, nothing is wrong.
                    —LINCOLN, Letter to A. G. Hodges, 1864

Men! whose boast it is that ye
Come of fathers brave and free,
If there breathe on earth a slave,
Are ye truly free and brave?
                    —J. R. LOWELL, *Stanzas on Freedom*

They set the slave free, striking off his chains . . .
Then he was as much of a slave as ever . . .
His slavery was not in his chains,
But in himself . . .
They can only set free men free . . .

And there is no need of that:
Free men set themselves free.

—JAMES OPPENHEIM, *The Slave*

Slavery is a flagrant violation of the institutions of America—direct government—over all the people, by all the people, for all the people.

—THEODORE PARKER, Sermon, (1858)

SLEEP

Hush-a-bye, baby, on the tree-top,
When the wind blows, the cradle will rock;
When the bough breaks, the cradle will fall
And down will come baby, cradle, and all.

—ANON., (written before 1630)

Now I lay me down to sleep,
I pray the Lord my soul to keep;
If I should die before I wake,
I pray the Lord my soul to take.

—NEW ENGLAND PRIMER (1737)

Sleep, sleep, beauty bright,
Dreaming in the joys of night;
Sleep, sleep; in thy sleep
Little sorrows sit and weep.

—BLAKE, *Cradle Song*

Blessings on him that first invented sleep!
—CERVANTES, *Don Quixote, II*

O sleep! it is a gentle thing,
Beloved from pole to pole!
To Mary Queen the praise be given!
She sent the gentle sleep from Heaven
That slid into my soul.

—S. T. COLERIDGE, *The Ancient Mariner*

Golden slumbers kiss your eyes,
Smiles awake you when you rise.
Sleep, pretty wantons, do not cry,
And I will sing a lullaby.
Rock them, rock them, lullaby.
—DEKKER, *Patient Grissil: Lullaby*

Wynken, Blynken, and Nod one night
  Sailed off in a wooden shoe—
Sailed on a river of crystal light
  Into a sea of dew.
—EUGENE FIELD, *Wynken, Blynken, and Nod*

O magic sleep! O comfortable bird,
That broodest o'er the troubled sea of the mind
Till it is hush'd and smooth!   —KEATS, *Endymion, I*

Dreams of the summer night!
  Tell her, her lover keeps
Watch! while in slumbers light
  She sleeps! My lady sleeps!
—LONGFELLOW, *The Spanish Student, I, 3*

    Sleep, baby, sleep!
Thy father's watching the sheep,
Thy mother's shaking the dreamland tree,
And down drops a little dream for thee,
    Sleep, baby, sleep!
—ELIZABETH PRENTISS, *Cradle Song*

Canst thou, O partial sleep, give thy repose
To the wet sea-boy in an hour so rude
And in the calmest and most stillest night,
With all appliances and means to boot,
Deny it to a king? Then happy low, lie down!
Uneasy lies the head that wears a crown.
—SHAKESPEARE, *Henry IV, II, III, 1*

Methought I heard a voice cry, "Sleep no more!
Macbeth doth murder sleep," the innocent sleep,
Sleep that knits up the ravell'd sleave of care,
The death of each day's life, sore labour's bath,
Balm of hurt minds, great nature's second course,
Chief nourisher of life's feast.

—SHAKESPEARE, *Macbeth, II, 2*

Not poppy nor Mandragora,
Nor all the drowsy syrups of the world
Shall ever medicine thee to that sweet sleep
Which thou ow'dst yesterday.

—SHAKESPEARE, *Othello, III, 3*

O sleep, O gentle sleep,
Nature's soft nurse, how have I frighted thee,
That now no more wilt weight my eyelids down
And steep my senses in forgetfulness?

—SHAKESPEARE, *Henry IV, II, III, 1*

O sleep, thou ape of death, lie dull upon her!
And be her sense but as a monument.

—SHAKESPEARE, *Cymbeline, II, 2*

How wonderful is Death,
Death and his brother Sleep!   —SHELLEY, *Queen Mab*

I am tired of tears and laughter,
    And men that laugh and weep
Of what may come hereafter
    For men that sow to reap:
I am weary of days and hours,
Blown buds of barren flowers,
Desires and dreams and powers,
    And everything but sleep.

—SWINBURNE, *Hymn to Proserpine*

SMILE

Her very frowns are fairer far
Than smiles of other maidens are.
> —HARTLEY COLERIDGE, *Song: She is Not Fair*

He smiled a kind of sickly smile and curled upon the
  floor,
And the subsequent proceedings interested him no more.
> —BRET HARTE, *The Society Upon the Stanislaus*

Why comes not death to those who mourn?
  He never smiled again.
> —FELICIA D. HEMANS, *He Never Smiled Again*

Eternal smiles his emptiness betray,
As shallow streams run dimpling all the way.
> —POPE, *Epistle to Dr. Arbuthnot*

One may smile, and smile, and be a villain.
> —SHAKESPEARE, *Hamlet, I, 5*

'Tis easy enough to be pleasant,
  When life flows along like a song;
But the man worth while is the one who will smile
  When everything goes dead wrong.
> —ELLA WHEELER WILCOX, *Worth While*

SMITH

Under a spreading chestnut-tree
  The village smithy stands;
The Smith, a mighty man is he,
  With large and sinewy hands;
And the muscles of his brawny arms
  Are strong as iron bands.
> —LONGFELLOW, *The Village Blacksmith*

SNAIL

The snail, which everywhere doth roam,
Carrying his own house still, still is at home.
—DONNE, *To Sir Henry Wotton*

SNEER

Who can refute a sneer?
—WILLIAM PALEY, *Moral Philosophy*

Damn with faint praise, assent with civil leer,
And without sneering, teach the rest to sneer.
—POPE, *Epistle to Dr. Arbuthnot*

SNOW

Whenever a snowflake leaves the sky,
It turns and turns to say "Good-by!
Good-by, dear clouds, so cool and gray!"
Then lightly travels on its way.
—MARY MAPES DODGE, *Snowflakes*

Where are the snows of yesteryear?
(*Oú sont les neiges d'antan?*)
—VILLON, *Ballade des dames du temp jadis*

Oh! the snow, the beautiful snow,
Filling the sky and the earth below;
—J. W. WATSON, *Beautiful Snow*

SOCIETY

Ermined and minked and Persian-lambed,
    Be-puffed (be-painted, too, alas!)
Be-decked, be-diamond—be-damned!
    The Women of the Better Class.
—OLIVER HERFORD, *The Women of the Better Class*

There are only about four hundred people in New York
Society.

—WARD MCALLISTER (1892: origin of "The Four
Hundred")

There is
One great society alone on earth:
The noble Living and the noble Dead.

—WORDSWORTH, *The Prelude, II*

SOLDIER

Malbrouck is off to the wars . . .
I don't know when he'll return.
(Malbrouck s'en va-t-en guerre;
  Mironton, mironton, mirontaine,
Malbrouck s'en va-t-en guerre,
Ne sait quand reviendra.) —ANON., (17th century)

When captains courageous, whom death could not daunt,
Did march to the siege of the city of Gaunt.

—ANON., *Ballad: Mary Ambree*
(Source of title of book by Kipling)

Lay him low, lay him low,
In the clover or the snow!
What cares he? he cannot know:
  Lay him low! —G. H. BOKER, *Dirge for a Soldier*

How sleep the brave, who sink to rest,
By all their country's wishes blest!

—WILLIAM COLLINS, *Ode Written in 1746*

Eh-oh, my little brother,
They rigged you up in state,
In khaki coat and gun to tote,
But you never could learn to hate.

—MARTIN FEINSTEIN, *In Memoriam*

Under the sod and the dew,
  Waiting the Judgment Day;
Love and tears for the Blue,
  Tears and love for the Gray.
                —F. M. FINCH, *The Blue and the Gray*

Far and near and low and louder
  On the roads of earth go by
Dear to friends and food for powder,
  Soldiers marching, all to die.
              —A. E. HOUSMAN, *A Shropshire Lad*

Grant lies asleep in his great white tomb, where the
  Hudson tides run deep;
And Sheridan and Sherman lie on marble beds asleep;
          . . . .
But what of the men those heroes led: of Smith and
  Robinson?   —R. W. KAUFMAN, *Heroes of Yesterday*

So 'ere's *to* you, Fuzzy-Wuzzy, at your 'ome in the
  Soudan;
You're a pore benighted 'eathen but a first-class fightin'
  man.   —KIPLING, *Fuzzy-Wuzzy*

For it's Tommy this, an' Tommy that, an' "Chuck 'im
  out, the brute!"
But it's "Saviour of 'is country" when the guns begin to
  shoot.   —KIPLING, *Tommy*

Hail, ye indomitable heroes, hail!
Despite of all your generals, ye prevail.
                —LANDOR, *The Crimean Heroes*

The brave men, living and dead, who struggled here,
have consecrated it far above our poor power to add or
detract. The world will little note, nor long remember,
what we say here, but it can never forget what they did
here.   —LINCOLN, Gettysburg Address

Ninepunce a day fer killin' folks comes kind o' low fer
murder.   —J. R. LOWELL, *The Biglow Papers, I*

Take up our quarrel with the foe:
To you from failing hands we throw
   The torch; be yours to hold it high.
   If ye break faith with us who die
We shall not sleep, though poppies grow
   In Flanders fields.
                         —JOHN McCRAE, *In Flanders Fields*

A soldier of the Legion lay dying in Algiers,
There was lack of woman's nursing, there was dearth of
   woman's tears; . . .
                    —CAROLINE NORTON, *Bingen on the Rhine*

The muffled drum's sad roll has beat
   The soldier's last tattoo;
No more on life's parade shall meet
   The brave and fallen few.
On Fame's eternal camping-ground
   Their silent tents are spread,
And Glory guards, with solemn ground,
   The bivouac of the dead.
             —THEODORE O'HARA, *The Bivouac of the Dead*

Soldiers are citizens of death's grey land,
Drawing no dividend from time's to-morrows.
             . . . .
Soldiers are dreamers; when the guns begin
They think of firelit homes, clean beds, and wives.
                         —SIEGFRIED SASSOON, *Dreamers*

Soldier rest! thy warfare o'er,
Dream of fighting fields no more;
Sleep the sleep that knows not breaking,
Morn of toil, nor night of waking.
                    —SCOTT, *The Lady of the Lake, I*

A soldier,
Full of strange oaths and bearded like the pard,
Jealous in honour, sudden and quick in quarrel,
Seeking the bubble reputation
Even in the cannon's mouth.

      —SHAKESPEARE, *As You Like It, II, 7*

Sleep sweetly in your humble graves,
Sleep, martyrs of a fallen cause.   —H. TIMROD, *Ode*

Not in the Abbey proudly laid
   Find they a place or part;
The gallant boys of the old Brigade,
   They sleep in Old England's heart.

      —F. E. WEATHERLY, *The Old Brigade*

Not a drum was heard, not a funeral note,
   As his corse to the rampart we hurried;
Not a soldier discharged his farewell shot
   O'er the grave where our hero we buried.

    —CHARLES WOLFE, *The Burial of Sir John Moore*

SOLITUDE

Alone, alone, all, all alone,
Alone on a wide wide sea!

      —S. T. COLERIDGE, *The Ancient Mariner*

Oh solitude! where are the charms
   That sages have seen in thy face?
Better dwell in the midst of alarms
   Than reign in this horrible place.

    —COWPER, *Verses supposed to be written by*
                Alexander Selkirk

O Solitude! if I must with thee dwell,
Let it not be among the jumbled heap
Of murky buildings: climb with me the steep,—
Nature's observatory; . . .   —KEATS, *Sonnet: O Solitude*

I feel like one who treads alone
Some banquet-hall deserted,
Whose lights are fled, whose garlands dead,
And all but he departed!
> —THOMAS MOORE, *Oft, in the Stilly Night*

Avoid the reeking herd,
Shun the polluted flock,
Live like that stoic bird
The eagle of the rock.
> —ELINOR WYLIE, *The Eagle and the Mole*

I will arise and go now, and go to Innisfree,
And a small cabin build there, of clay and wattles made:
Nine bean-rows will I have there, a hive for the honey-
   bee,
And live alone in the bee-loud glade.
> —W. B. YEATS, *The Lake Isle of Innisfree*

SON

There is no prince or prelate
   I envy—no, not one.
No evil can befall me—
   By God, I have a son!
> —CHRISTOPHER MORLEY, *Secret Laughter*

What is the price of a thousand horses against a son
where there is one son only.
> —J. M. SYNGE, *Riders to the Sea*

O lord, my boy, my Arthur, my fair son!
My life, my joy, my food, my all the world!
My widow-comfort, and my sorrow's cure!
> —SHAKESPEARE, *King John, III, 4*

A wise son maketh a glad father.
> —OLD TESTAMENT, *Proverbs, X, 1*

SONG

Sing a song of sixpence, a pocket full of rye,
Four-and-twenty blackbirds baked in a pie.

—ANON., Old nursery rhyme

I cannot sing the old songs
 I sang long years ago,
For heart and voice would fail me
 And foolish tears would flow.

—CHARLOTTE A. BARNARD, *I Cannot Sing the Old Songs*

Sing me the songs I delighted to hear
 Long, long ago, long ago.

—T. H. BAYLY, *The Long Ago*

That which is not worth saying is sung.

—BEAUMARCHAIS, *Barber of Seville*

A wandering minstrel I—
 A thing of shreds and patches,
 Of ballads, songs, and snatches,
And dreamy lullaby.   —W. S. GILBERT, *The Mikado, I*

It's the song of a merryman, moping mum,
Whose soul was sad, and whose glance was glum,
Who sipped no sup, and who craved no crumb
 As he sighed for the love of a ladye.

—W. S. GILBERT, *Yeomen of the Guard, I*

Because the road was steep and long
 And through a dark and lonely land,
God set upon my lips a song
 And put a lantern in my hand.

—JOYCE KILMER, *Love's Lantern*

Or bid the soul of Orpheus sing
Such notes as, warbled to the string,
Drew iron tears down Pluto's cheek.

—MILTON, *Il Penseroso*

In Heaven a spirit doth dwell
   Whose heart-strings are a lute;
None sing so wildly well
As the angel Israfel.

—POE, *Israfel*

I think that life is not too long,
   And therefore I determine,
That many people read a song,
   Who will not read a sermon.

—W. M. PRAED, *Chant of the Brazen Head*

Our sweetest songs are those which tell of saddest
   thought.   —SHELLEY, *To a Skylark*

Singing is sweet, but be sure of this,
Lips only sing when they cannot kiss.

—JAMES THOMSON ("B. V."), *Sunday Up the River*

SONGS, OLD AND POPULAR

Abdul the Bulbul
   The sons of the prophet are brave men and bold,
      And quite unaccustomed to fear,
   But the bravest by far in the ranks of the Shah
      Was Abdul the Bulbul Amir.

—ANON. (college song in America)

After the Ball
   Many a heart is aching, if you could read them all,
   Many the hopes that have vanished, after the ball.

—CHARLES K. HARRIS (1892)

Bananas
   Yes, we have no bananas,
   We have no bananas today.

—F. SILVER AND I. COHEN (1923)

The Band Played On

 Casey would waltz with the strawberry blonde,
  And the band played on. —J. F. PALMER (1894)

Ben Bolt

 Don't you remember sweet Alice, Ben Bolt,—
  Sweet Alice whose hair was so brown,
 Who wept with delight when you gave her a smile,
  And trembled with fear at your frown.
       —THOMAS DUNN ENGLISH (1843)

Bring Back My Bonnie to Me

 My Bonnie lies over the ocean,
  My Bonnie lies over the sea,
 My Bonnie lies over the ocean,
  Oh, bring back my Bonnie to me.—ANON. (1882)

The Camptown Races

 De Camptown ladies sing dis song
  Doodah! doodah!
 De Camptown race track five miles long
  Oh! doodah-day!

 I come down dah wid my hat caved in
  Doodah! doodah!
 I go back home wid a pocket full o' tin
  Oh! doodah-day!

 Gwine to run all night!
 Gwine to run all day!
 I'll bet my money on de bobtail nag,
 Somebody bet on de bay.
        —STEPHEN C. FOSTER

Captain Jinks

I'm Captain Jinks of the Horse Marines,
I often live beyond my means;
I sport young ladies in their teens,
    To cut a swell in the army.

—WILLIAM LINDGARD (1869)

Clementine

In a cavern, in a canyon,
    Excavating for a mine,
Dwelt a miner, forty-niner,
    And his daughter, Clementine.

Oh my darling, oh my darling,
Oh my darling Clementine
You are lost and gone forever
Oh my darling Clementine.

—PERCY MONTROSS (1880)

Come Home, Father

Father, dear Father, come home with me now!
    The clock in the steeple strikes one.
You said you were coming right home from the shop
    As soon as your day's work was done.

—HENRY CLAY WORK (1862)

The Curse of an Aching Heart

You made me what I am to-day,
    I hope you're satisfied . . .
        And though you're not true,
        May God bless you,
That's the curse of an aching heart.

—HENRY FINK (1913)

Dixie

I wish I was in the land of cotton,
Old times thar are not forgotten,
Look away, look away,
Look away, Dixie land.

In Dixie land whar I was born in,
Early on a frosty mornin'
Look away, look away,
Look away, Dixie land.

Den I wish I was in Dixie,
Hooray, hooray!
In Dixie land we'll take our stand
To lib and die in Dixie.

Away, away,
Away down South in Dixie
Away, away,
Away down South in Dixie.   —DAN EMMETT

The Erie Canal Song

I've got a mule, her name is Sal,
Fifteen miles on the Erie Canal,
She's a good old worker and a good old pal,
Fifteen miles on the Erie Canal.

We've haul'd some barges in our day,
Filled with lumber, coal and hay,
And we know every inch of the way
From Albany to Buffalo.

Low bridge, ev'ry body down
Low bridge, for we're going through a town,
And you'll always know your neighbor,
You'll always know your pal,
If you ever navigated on the Erie Canal.   —ANON.

Father And I Went Down to Camp
　　　　(Yankee Doodle)
　Father and I went down to camp
　Along with Captain Goodling,
　And there we saw the men and boys,
　As thick as hasty pudding.

　Yankee Doodle keep it up,
　Yankee Doodle dandy
　Mind the music and the step,
　And with the girls be handy.

　And there was Captain Washington
　Upon a slapping stallion,
　A-giving orders to his men;
　I guess there was a million.

　Yankee Doodle, keep it up,
　Yankee Doodle dandy,
　Mind the music and the step,
　And with the girls be handy.　　　　　—ANON.

Frankie and Albert (original version of *Frankie and Johnny*)
　Frankie and Albert were lovers, O Lordy, how they
　　could love!
　Swore to be true to each other, true as the stars above;
　　He was her man, and he done her wrong.
　　　　　　　　　　　　　　—ANON. (1899)

Go Down, Moses
　When Israel was in Egyp' Lan',
　Let my people go,
　Oppressed so hard they could not stan',
　Let my people go.　　　　　　　—ANON.

Goodnight Ladies

(Merrily We Roll Along)

Goodnight ladies, goodnight ladies,
Goodnight ladies we're gonna leave you now
Merrily we roll along, roll along, roll along,
Merrily we roll along, o'er the deep blue sea.—ANON.

Hail! Hail! (to a tune from *The Pirates of Penzance*)

Hail! Hail! the gang's all here,
What the hell do we care,
What the hell do we care?
Hail! Hail! we're full of cheer—
What the hell do we care, Bill!

—D. A. ESROM (1917)

Hallelujah, I'm a Bum

Oh, why don't you work like other men do?
How the hell can I work when there's no work to do?
Hallelujah, I'm a bum, hallelujah, bum again,
Hallelujah, give us a hand-out to revive us again.

—ANON. (1897; among I. W. W. to the tune of a
revival hymn)

Hello, Central! Give Me Heaven

Hello, Central! give me heaven,
For my mamma's there.

—CHARLES K. HARRIS (1901)

Home on the Range

Home, home on the range,
Where the deer and the antelope play;
Where seldom is heard a discouraging word,
And the skies are not cloudy all day.

—BREWSTER HIGLEY (1873; the original title was
The Western Home)

A Hot Time in the Old Town To-night

When you hear those bells go ting-a-ling, . . .
There'll be a hot time in the old town to-night.
—JOSEPH HAYDEN (1896)

I Don't Want to Play in Your Yard

I don't want to play in your yard,
    I don't like you any more;
You'll be sorry when you see me
    Sliding down our cellar door;

You can't holler down our rain-bar'l,
    You can't climb our apple-tree,
I don't want to play in your yard
    If you won't be good to me.
—PHILIP WINGATE (1894)

In the Evening by the Moonlight

In de ebening by de moonlight, you could hear us
    darkies singing,
In de ebening by de moonlight, you could hear de
    banjo ringing;   —JAMES A. BLAND (*c.* 1875)

It's the Syme the Whole World Over

It's the syme the whole world over,
It's the poor what gets the blyme,
While the rich 'as all the plysures.
Now ayn't that a blinkin' shyme?

She was a parson's daughter,
Pure, unstyned was her fyme,
Till a country squire come courtin',
And the poor girl lorst her nyme.

So she went aw'y to Lunnon,
Just to 'ide her guilty shyme.
There she met an Army Chaplain:
Ornst ag'yn she lorst her nyme.

In a cottage down in Sussex
Lives 'er parents old and lyme,
And they drink the wine she sends 'em,
But they never, never speaks 'er nyme.

In their poor and 'umble dwellin'
There 'er grievin' parents live,
Drinkin' champyne as she sends 'em
But they never, never can forgive.

It's the syme the whole world over,
It's the poor what gets the blyme,
While the rich 'as all the plysures.
Now ayn't it a bloody shyme?

—ANON.

I've Been Workin' on the Railroad
I've been workin' on the railroad,
All the live-long day,
I've been workin' on the railroad,
Just to pass the time away. . . . —ANON. (1894)

Little Brown Jug
My wife and I lived all alone
In a little brown shack we called our own
She loved beer and I loved rum
Tell you what it was, oh we had fun.

Chorus:

Ha, ha, ha, you and me,
Little Brown Jug how I love thee,
Ha, ha, ha, you and me,
Little Brown Jug how I love thee.

Had I a cow that gave such milk
I would dress her in the finest silk
Feed her on the choicest hay
And I'd milk her twenty times a day.

—JOSEPH E. WINNER

Chorus:

Loch Lomond

Oh, ye'll tak' the high road an' I'll tak' the low road,
An' I'll be in Scotland afore ye;
But I an' my true love will never meet again
On the bonnie, bonnie banks of Loch Lomond.

—ANON. (old Scotch ballad)

Mademoiselle from Armentières

A mademoiselle from Armenteers,
She hasn't been kissed in forty years,
Hinky, dinky, par-lee-voo.

—"RED" ROWLEY (during World War I)

The Man on the Flying Trapeze

Once I was happy, but now I'm forlorn,
Like an old coat that is tatter'd and torn,
Left in this wide world to fret and to mourn,
Betray'd by a maid in her teens.

Now this girl that I lov'd she was handsome,
And I tried all I knew her to please,
But I never could please her one quarter so well
Like the man on the flying trapeze.

He flies through the air with the greatest of ease,
This daring young man on the flying trapeze;
His figure is handsome, all girls he can please,
And my love he purloined her away.

—GEORGE LEYBOURNE (1860)

McGinty

Down went McGinty to the bottom of the say
He must be very wet, for he hasn't come up yet,
But they say his ghost comes round the dock before
    the break of day,
      Dressed in his best suit of clothes.

                  —JOSEPH FLYNN (1889)

Mulligan Guard

We shouldered arms and marched and marched away,
From Baxter street we marched to Avenue A;
The fifes and drums how sweetly they did play,
As we marched, marched, marched in the Mulligan
    Guard.   —EDWARD HARRIGAN (1873)

My Mother Was a Lady

My mother was a lady, like yours you will allow. . . .
                —E. B. MARKS (1896)

My Old Kentucky Home

    Weep no more, my lady,
    Oh! weep no more to-day!
We will sing one song for the old Kentucky Home,
    For the old Kentucky Home far away.
            —STEPHEN C. FOSTER (*c.* 1858)

Nelly

    Nelly was a lady,
      Last night she died,
Toll de bell for lubly Nell,
    My dark Virginny bride.
            —STEPHEN C. FOSTER (1849)

Nobody

I ain't never done nothin' to nobody;
I ain't never got nothin' from nobody;

And until I get somethin' from somebody, sometime,
I don't intend to do nothin' for nobody, no time.
—ALEX ROGERS (1905)

The Old Chisholm Trail

Come gather 'round me, boys, and I'll tell you a tale
All about my troubles on the old Chisholm trail.
Coma Ti Yi Yippi, Yippi Yay, Yippi Yay,
Coma Ti Yi Yippi, Yippi Yay.

I started up the trail October twenty-third,
Started up the trail with the two u herd.
Coma Ti Yi Yippi, Yippi Yay, Yippi Yay,
Ti Yi Yippi, Yippi Yay.

On a ten dollar hoss and a forty dollar saddle
Started up the trail just to punch some cattle,
Coma Ti Yi Yippi, Yippi Yay, Yippi Yay,
Coma Ti Yi Yippi Yippi Yay.
—ANON.

Old Folks At Home (Swanee River)

Way down upon the Swanee River,
Far, far away,
There's where my heart is turning ever,
There's where the old folks stay;

All up and down the whole creation
Sadly I roam,
Still longing for the old plantation,
And for the old folks at home.

All the world is sad and dreary
Ev'rywhere I roam;
Oh! darkies, how my heart grows weary,
Far from the old folks at home.
—STEPHEN C. FOSTER (*c.* 1850)

The Old Oaken Bucket

How dear to my heart are the scenes of my childhood
When fond recollections present them to view.
The orchard the meadow, the deep tangled wildwood
And each loving spot which my infancy knew.

The wide spreading pond and the mill that stood by it
The bridge and the rock where the cataract fell.
The Old Oaken Bucket, the ironbound bucket,
The moss covered bucket that hung in the well.

The cot of my father, the little house nigh it
And too the old bucket that hung in the well.
The Old Oaken Bucket, the ironbound bucket,
The moss covered bucket that hung in the well.

—SAMUEL WOODWORTH

Promise Me

Oh, promise me that some day you and I
Will take our love together to some sky
Where we can be alone and faith renew,
And find the hollows where those flowers grew. . . .

—CLEMENT SCOTT (1888)

Rosary

The hours I spent with thee, dear heart,
 Are as a string of pearls to me;
I count them over, every one apart,
 My rosary, my rosary. —R. C. ROGERS (*c.* 1900)

School-Days

School-days, school-days, dear old golden rule days,
Readin' and 'ritin' and 'rithmetic,
Taught to the tune of a hick'ry stick; . . .

—WILL D. COBB (1907)

Sidewalks of New York

> East side, West side, All around the town,
> The tots sing "Ring-a-Rosie, London Bridge is falling
>   down";
> Boys and girls together, Me and Mamie O'Rourke,
> Trip the light fantastic On the sidewalks of New York.
> —JAMES W. BLAKE (*c.* 1900)

Silver Threads Among the Gold

> Darling, I am growing old,
> Silver threads among the gold.
> —E. E. REXFORD (1873)

Summer Time (In The Good Old,)

> In the good old summer time,
> In the good old summer time,
> Strolling through the shady lanes,
> With your baby mine; . . .   —REN SHIELDS (1902)

Sweet Betsey From Pike

> Oh, don't you remember sweet Betsey from Pike,
> Who crossed the big mountains with her lover Ike,
> With two yoke of cattle, a large yellow dog,
> A tall shanghai rooster and one spotted hog.

Chorus:

> Singing tooral lal looral lal looral lal la,
> Singing tooral lal looral lal looral lal la,
> Sing tooral lal looral, sing tooral lal la,
> Singing tooral lal looral lal looral lal la.

> One evening quite early they camped on the Platte,
> 'Twas near by the road on a green shady flat,
> Where Betsey, sore-footed, lay down to repose—
> With wonder Ike gazed on that Pike County rose.
> —ANON.

Sweet Marie

Come to me, Sweet Marie, Sweet Marie come to me,
Not because your face is fair, love, to see,
But your soul, so pure and sweet,
Makes my happiness complete,
Makes me falter at your feet, Sweet Marie.

—CY WARMAN (1893)

Take Back Your Gold

Take back your gold, for gold can never buy me;
Take back your bribe, and promise you'll be true;
Give me the love, the love that you'd deny me,
Make me your wife, that's all I ask of you.

—M. H. ROSENFELD (1897)

Ta-ra-ra Boom-der-é

A sweet Tuxedo girl you see,
Queen of swell society,
Fond of fun as fond can be,
When she's on the strict Q.T.
Ta-ra-ra Boom-der-é. . . .   —H. L. SAYERS (1891)

Tramp! Tramp! Tramp!

Tramp! Tramp! Tramp! the boys are marching,
Cheer up, comrades, they will come,
And beneath the starry flag
We shall breathe the air again
Of the free land in our beloved home.

—GEORGE F. ROOT (1862)

White Wings

"White Wings," they never grow weary,
    They carry me cheerily over the sea;
Night comes, I long for my dearie,
    I'll spread out my "White Wings" and sail home
        to thee.   —BANKS WINTER (1882)

SORROW

Heavy the sorrow that bows the head
When love is alive and hope is dead.
— W. S. GILBERT, *H.M.S. Pinafore*

Who ne'er his bread in sorrow ate,
  Who ne'er the mournful midnight hours
Weeping upon his bed has sate,
He knows you not, ye Heavenly Powers.
(*Wer nie sein Brod mit Thranen ass, . . .*)
— GOETHE, *Wilhelm Meister* (Longfellow trans.)

To Sorrow I bade good morrow,
And thought to leave her far away behind;
  But cheerly, cheerly,
  She loves me dearly;
She is so constant to me, and so kind.
— KEATS, *Endymion, IV*

Into each life some rain must fall,
Some days must be dark and dreary.
— LONGFELLOW, *The Rainy Day*

Earth has no sorrow that Heaven cannot heal.
— THOMAS MOORE, *Come, Ye Disconsolate*

When sorrows come, they come not single spies,
But in battalions.   — SHAKESPEARE, *Hamlet, IV, 5*

SOUL

This soul, to whom Luther and Mahomet were
Prisons of flesh.   — DONNE, *Progress of the Soul*

Gentle little soul, hastening away, my body's guest and comrade, whither goest thou now, pale, fearful, pensive, not jesting, as of old?
(*Animula, vagula, blandula . . .*)
— HADRIAN, *Ad animam suam*

Out of the night that covers me,
 Black as the pit from pole to pole,
I thank what ever gods may be
 For my unconquerable soul.

. . . .

It matters not how strait the gate,
 How charged with punishments the scroll,
I am the master of my fate:
 I am the captain of my soul.—W. E. HENLEY, *Invictus*

Build thee more stately mansions, O my soul,
 As the swift seasons roll!
 Leave thy low-vaulted past! . . .
          —O. W. HOLMES, *The Chambered Nautilus*

Ah, what a dusty answer gets the soul
When hot for certainties in this our life!
          —GEORGE MEREDITH, *Modern Love*

For what is a man profited, if he shall gain the whole
world, and lose his own soul?
          —NEW TESTAMENT, *Matthew, XVI, 26*

Go, Soul, the Body's Guest,
 Upon a thankless arrant:
Fear not to touch the best,
 The truth shall be thy warrant:
Go, since I needs must die,
And give the World the lie.
          —SIR WALTER RALEIGH, *The Lie* (1592)

And the souls mounting up to God
Went by her like thin flames.
          —D. G. ROSSETTI, *The Blessed Damosel*

Thou almost makest me waver in my faith
To hold opinion with Pythagoras,

That souls of animals infuse themselves
Into the trunks of men.
—SHAKESPEARE, *Merchant of Venice, IV, 1*

My soul is a dark ploughed field
In the cold rain;
My soul is a broken field
Ploughed by pain.
—SARA TEASDALE, *The Broken Field*

What profits now to understand
The merits of a spotless shirt—
A dapper boot—a little hand—
If half the little soul is dirt.
—TENNYSON, *The New Timon and the Poets*

O my brave soul! O farther farther sail!
O daring joy, but safe! are they not all the seas of God?
O farther, farther, farther sail!
—WALT WHITMAN, *Passage to India*

SPAIN

A nation swoln with ignorance and pride,
Who lick yet loathe the hand that waves the sword.
—BYRON, *Childe Harold, I*

Well here's to the Maine, and I'm sorry for Spain,
Said Kelly and Burke and Shea.
J. I. C. CLARKE, *The Fighting Race*

SPARROW

Sparrow, my lady's pet, with whom she often plays,
(*Passer, deliciae meae puella, Quicum ludere*).
—CATULLUS, *Odes, II*

"SPEAK FOR YOURSELF"

Archly the maiden smiled, and, with eyes overrunning
with laughter,

Said in a tremulous voice, "Why don't you speak for
yourself, John?"
—LONGFELLOW, *The Courtship of Miles Standish*

SPEECH

Blessed is the man who, having nothing to say, abstains
from giving us wordy evidence of the fact.
—GEORGE ELIOT, *Theophrastus Such*

The true use of speech is not so much to express our
wants as to conceal them.
—GOLDSMITH, A paraphrase of S. Butler

Speech is civilization itself. The word, even the most
contradictory word, preserves contact—it is silence which
isolates. —THOMAS MANN, *The Magic Mountain*

Out of the abundance of the heart the mouth speaketh.
—NEW TESTAMENT, *Matthew, XII, 34*

And 'tis remarkable that they
Talk most who have the least to say. —PRIOR, *Alma, II*

Speak the speech, I pray you, as I pronounce it to you,
trippingly on the tongue. —SHAKESPEARE, *Hamlet, III, 2*

SPELLING

English orthography satisfies all the requirements of the
canons of reputability under the law of conspicuous waste.
It is archaic, cumbrous, and ineffective; its acquisition con-
sumes much time and effort; failure to acquire it is easy of
detection.—THORSTEIN VEBLEN, *Theory of the Leisure Class*

SPIDER

"Will you walk into my parlour?" said a Spider to a Fly;
" 'Tis the prettiest little parlour that ever you did spy."
—MARY HOWITT, *The Spider and the Fly*

SPINACH

"It's broccoli, dear."
"I say it's spinach, and I say the hell with it."
—E. B. WHITE, In *The New Yorker*

SPIRIT

Not of the letter, but of the spirit: for the letter killeth, but the spirit giveth life.
—NEW TESTAMENT, *II Corinthians, III, 6*

The spirit indeed is willing, but the flesh is weak.
—NEW TESTAMENT, *Matthew, XXVI, 41*

Spirits are not finely touch'd
But to fine issues.
—SHAKESPEARE, *Measure for Measure, I, 1*

SPOILS

They see nothing wrong in the rule that to the victor belong the spoils of the enemy.
—W. M. MARCY, Speech in U. S. Senate, 1832

SPRING

The year's at the spring
And day's at the morn;
Morning's at seven;
The hill-side's dew-pearled;
The lark's on the wing;
The snail's on the thorn;
God's in his heaven—
All's right with the world! —R. BROWNING, *Pippa Passes*

She comes with gusts of laughter,—
The music as of rills;
With tenderness and sweetness,
The wisdom of the hills.
—BLISS CARMAN, *Over the Wintry Threshold*

Came the Spring with all its splendor,
All its birds and all its blossoms,
All its flowers, and leaves, and grasses.

—LONGFELLOW, *Hiawatha*

Spring rides no horses down the hill,
But comes on foot, a goose-girl still
And all the loveliest things there be
Come simply so, it seems to me.

—EDNA ST. VINCENT MILLAY, *The Goose-Girl*

In those vernal seasons of the year, when the air is calm
and pleasant, it were an injury and sullenness against
Nature not to go out and see her riches, and partake in her
rejoicing with heaven and earth.

—MILTON, *Tractate of Education*

For, lo, the winter is past, the rain is over and gone; the
flowers appear on the earth; the time of the singing of birds
is come, and the voice of the turtle is heard in our land.

—OLD TESTAMENT, *Song of Solomon, II*

When daffodils begin to peer
With heigh! the doxy over the dale,
Why, then comes in the sweet o' the year;
For the red blood reigns in the winter's pale.

—SHAKESPEARE, *Winter's Tale, IV, 3*

When the hounds of Spring are on winter's traces,
The mother of months in meadow or plain
Fills the shadows and windy places
With lisp of leaves and ripple of rain.

—SWINBURNE, *Atalanta in Calydon*

Come, gentle Spring, ethereal mildness, come;
And from the bosom of yon dropping cloud,

While music wakes around, veiled in a shower
Of shadowing roses, on our plains descend.
—THOMSON, *The Seasons*

In the spring a livelier iris changes on the burnish'd dove;
In the spring a young man's fancy lightly turns to
thoughts of love.   —TENNYSON, *Locksley Hall*

SQUARE DEAL

If elected, I shall see to it that every man has a square
deal, no less and no more.
—THEODORE ROOSEVELT, Address, Nov., 1904

STABAT MATER

By the cross on which suspended,
With his bleeding arms extended,
  Hung that Son she so adored,
Stood the mournful Mother weeping,
She whose heart, its silence keeping,
  Grief had cleft as with a sword.
    (Stabat mater dolorosa
    Iuxta crucem lacrimosa,
      Dum pendebat filius,
      Cuius animam gementem,
      Contristantem et dolentem
        Pertransavit gladius.)
—JACOPANE DA TODI, *Stabat Mater*, D. F. MACCARTHY
                                                          trans.

STAGE

All the world's a stage,
And all the men and women merely players.
—SHAKESPEARE, *As You Like It, II, 7*

STANDARD

You cannot choose your battlefield,
The gods do that for you,

But you can plant a standard
Where a standard never flew.
                                    —NATHALIA CRANE, *The Colors*

STARS

Go and catch a falling star,
Get with child a mandrake root,
Tell me, where all past years are,
Or who cleft the Devil's foot.   —JOHN DONNE, *Song*

Teach me your mood, O patient stars!
    Who climb each night the ancient sky,
Leaving on space no shade, no scars,
    No trace of age, no fear to die.   —EMERSON, *The Poet*

Two things fill the mind with ever new and increasing
wonder and awe—the starry heavens above me and the
moral law within me.
            —KANT, *Critique of Pure Reason*, Conclusion

Stars in the summer night!
    Far in yon azure deeps
Hide, hide your golden light!
    She sleeps! My lady sleeps!
                    —LONGFELLOW, *The Spanish Student*

The stars
That Nature hung in Heav'n, and filled their lamps
With everlasting oil, to give due light
To the misled and lonely traveller.   —MILTON, *Comus*

Canst thou bind the sweet influence of Pleiades, or loose
the bands of Orion? —OLD TESTAMENT, *Job, XXXVIII, 32*

The morning stars sang together, and all the sons of God
shouted for joy.   —OLD TESTAMENT, *Job, XXXVIII, 7*

The stars in their courses fought against Sisera.
—OLD TESTAMENT, *Judges*, V, 20

There's husbandry in heaven;
Their candles are all out.—SHAKESPEARE, *Macbeth*, II, 1

Twinkle, twinkle, little star!
How I wonder what you are,
Up above the world so high,
Like a diamond in the sky!   —ANN TAYLOR, *The Star*

STATE

I am the State!
(*L'état, c'est moi!*)   —LOUIS XIV (1655)

It was only one life. What is one life in the affairs of a state?
—BENITO MUSSOLINI, after running down a child in his automobile (as reported by Gen. Smedley D. Butler in Address, 1931)

Something is rotten in the state of Denmark.
—SHAKESPEARE, *Hamlet*, I, 4

STATESMAN

A statesman is a successful politician who is dead.
—THOMAS B. REED (quoted by Sen. H. C. Lodge)

A ginooine statesman should be on his guard,
Ef he *must hev* beliefs, not to b'lieve 'em tu hard.
—J. R. LOWELL, *Biglow Papers*, II

In statesmanship get the formalities right, never mind about the moralities.
—MARK TWAIN, *Pudd'nhead Wilson's New Calendar*

STATION

O, let us love our occupations,
Bless the squire and his relations,
Live upon our daily rations,
And always know our proper stations.

—DICKENS, *The Chimes*

STATISTICS

There are three kinds of lies: lies, damned lies, and statistics.

—B. DISRAELI (attributed to him by Mark Twain in his *Autobiography*

Statistics are like alienists—they will testify for either side.   —F. H. LA GUARDIA in *Liberty*, May, 1933

STEALING

For de little stealin' dey gits you in jail soon or late. For de big stealin' dey makes you emperor and puts you in de Hall o' Fame when you croaks. If dey's one thing I learns in ten years on de Pullman cars listenin' to de white quality talk, it's dat same fact.

—EUGENE O'NEILL, *The Emperor Jones*

STEEL

Lay me on an anvil, O God.
Beat me and hammer me into a crowbar.
Let me pry loose old walls.
Let me lift and loosen old foundations.

—CARL SANDBURG, *Prayers of Steel*

STONE

The stone which the builders refused is become the headstone of the corner.

—OLD TESTAMENT, *Psalms, CXVIII, 22*

STORM

Blow, winds, and crack your cheeks! rage! blow!
You cataracts and hurricanes, spout
Till you have drench'd our steeples.

—SHAKESPEARE, *King Lear, III, 2*

STRENGTH

O, it is excellent
To have a giant's strength; but it is tyrannous
To use it like a giant.

—SHAKESPEARE, *Measure for Measure, II, 2*

STRENUOUS LIFE

I wish to preach not the doctrine of ignoble ease, but the doctrine of the strenuous life.

—THEODORE ROOSEVELT, Speech, 1899

STRIKE

There is no right to strike against the public safety by anybody, anywhere, anytime.

—CALVIN COOLIDGE, Letter to Gompers, 1919

STUDY

Studies serve for delight, for ornament, and for ability.

—FRANCIS BACON, *Essays: Of Studies*

STUPIDITY

Shadwell alone of all my sons is he
Who stands confirm'd in full stupidity.
The rest to some faint meaning make pretense,
But Shadwell never deviates into sense.

—DRYDEN, *MacFlecknoe*

Against stupidity the very gods
Themselves contend in vain.

—SCHILLER, *The Maid of Orleans, III, 6*

STYLE

The style is the man himself.
—BUFFON, *Discourse* (1750)

Proper words in proper places.
—SWIFT, *Definition of a Good Style*

SUBLIME

There is but one step from the sublime to the ridiculous.
—*Attributed to* NAPOLEON

SUCCESS

Eureka! Eureka! (I have found it! I have found it!)
—ARCHIMEDES (first quoted by Vitruvius)

In anguish we uplift
A new unhallowed song:
The race is to the swift;
The battle to the strong.—JOHN DAVIDSON, *War-Song*

Success is the sole earthly judge of right and wrong.
—ADOLF HITLER, *Mein Kampf*

If you can dream—and not make dreams your master, . . .
If you can fill the unforgiving minute
With sixty seconds' worth of distance run,
Yours is the Earth and everything that's in it,
And—which is more—you'll be a Man, my son!
—KIPLING, *If*—

The race is not to the swift nor the battle to the
strong. . . .   —OLD TESTAMENT, *Ecclesiastes, IX, 2*

SUFFERING

To each his suff'rings: all are men,
Condemn'd alike to groan;

The tender for another's pain,
Th' unfeeling for his own.
—GRAY, *Ode on a Distant Prospect of Eton College*

SUICIDE

One more Unfortunate,
Weary of breath,
Rashly importunate,
Gone to her death!
—THOMAS HOOD, *The Bridge of Sighs*

When the blandishments of life are gone,
The coward sneaks to death, the brave live on.
—MARTIAL, *Epigram* (trans. by Sewell)

I know some poison I could drink;
I've often thought I'd taste it;
But Mother bought it for the sink,
And drinking it would waste it.
—EDNA ST. VINCENT MILLAY, *The Cheerful Abstainer*

Razors pain you;
Rivers are damp;
Acids stain you;
And drugs cause cramp.
Guns aren't lawful;
Nooses give;
Gas smells awful;
You might as well live. —DOROTHY PARKER, *Résumé*

To be or not to be: that is the question:
Whether 'tis nobler in the mind to suffer
The slings and arrows of outrageous fortune,
Or to take arms against a sea of troubles,
And by opposing end them.
—SHAKESPEARE, *Hamlet, III, 1*

In church your grandsire cut his throat;
To do the job too long he tarried:

He should have had my hearty vote
  To cut his throat before he married.
                —SWIFT, *On an Upright Judge*

SUMMER

Sumer is icumen in,
  Lhude sing cuccul   —ANON., *Cuckoo Song* (c. 1225)

SUN

Oft did I wonder why the setting sun
  Should look upon us with a blushing face:
Is't not for shame of what he hath seen done,
  Whilst in our hemisphere he ran his race?
                —LYMAN HEATH, *On the Setting Sun*

Down sank the great red sun, and in golden glimmering
    vapors
Veiled the light of his face, like the Prophet descending
    from Sinai.   —LONGFELLOW, *Evangeline*

The sun shineth upon the dunghill and is not corrupted.
                —JOHN LYLY, *Euphues*

The great luminary
Aloof the vulgar constellations thick,
That from his lordly eye keeps distance due,
Dispenses light from afar. —MILTON, *Paradise Lost, IV*

Wake! for the Sun, who scatter'd into flight
The Stars before him from the Field of Night,
  Drives Night along with them from Heav'n, and strikes
The Sultan's Turret with a Shaft of Light.
    —OMAR KHAYYÁM, *Rubáiyát* (FitzGerald trans.)

God is at the anvil, beating out the sun;
  Where the molten metal spills,
    At His forge among the hills
He has hammered out the glory of a day that's done.
                —LEW SARETT, *God Is at the Anvil*

Hark, hark! the lark at heaven's gate sings,
And Phoebus 'gins arise.
—SHAKESPEARE, Cymbeline, II, 3

   The glorious sun
Stays in his course and plays the alchemist,
Turning with splendour of his precious eye
The meagre cloddy earth to glittering gold.
—SHAKESPEARE, King John, III, 1

When the sun shines let foolish gnats make sport,
But creep in crannies when he hides his beams.
—SHAKESPEARE, Comedy of Errors, II, 2

SUNDAY

   ... I saw a Puritane one
Hanging of his cat on Monday,
For killing of a mouse on Sunday.
—R. BRATHWAITE, Barnabee's Journal

Of all the days that's in the week
  I dearly love but one day—
And that's the day that comes betwixt
  A Saturday and Monday.
—HENRY CAREY, Sally in Our Alley

On Sunday heaven's gate stands ope;
Blessings are plentiful and rife,
  More plentiful than hope.
—GEORGE HERBERT, Sunday

SUNDIAL

I count only the hours that are bright.
(*Horas non numero nisi serenas.*)
—ANON., Old sundial inscription

I am a Shade: a Shadowe too arte thou:
—AUSTIN DOBSON, The Sundial

I mark my hours by shadow;
                —C. B. HILTON-TURVEY, *The Sundial*

SUPERIORITY

My mother was a superior soul
   A superior soul was she
Cut out to play a superior role
   In the god-damn bourgeoisie.
                —D. H. LAWRENCE, *Red Herring*

SUPERMAN

I teach you the Superman. Man is something which shall
be surpassed.   —NIETZSCHE, *Thus Spake Zarathustra*

SUPERSTITION

Crush the infamous thing!
(*Écrasez l'infâme!*) —VOLTAIRE (1760; later, his motto)

SURRENDER

. . . unconditional and immediate surrender.
                —U. S. GRANT, At Fort Donelson, 1862

Don't give up the ship!
—COMMANDER O. H. PERRY, Signal for battle of Lake Erie,
        1813 (also Capt. Mugford's dying words, 1776)

SWALLOW

When the swallows homeward fly,
When the roses scattered lie,
When from neither hill nor dale,
Chants the silvery nightingale: . . .
                —Trans. from German of K. HERRLOSSOHN

Swallow, my sister, O sister swallow,
How can thine heart be full of the spring?
A thousand summers are over and dead.

What hast thou found in the spring to follow?
What hast thou found in thy heart to sing?
What wilt thou do when the summer is shed?
                              —SWINBURNE, *Itylus*

SWAN

All the water in the ocean
Can never turn the swan's black legs to white,
Although she lave them hourly in the flood.
                    —SHAKESPEARE, *Titus Andronicus, IV, 2*

SWAP

. . . it was not best to swap horses while crossing the
river, and . . . I am not so poor a horse that they might not
make a botch of it in trying to swap.
            —LINCOLN, Address, 1864 (when up for re-election)

SWEARING

Thou shalt not take the name of the Lord thy God in
vain: —OLD TESTAMENT, *Exodus, XX, 7*

SWEAT

His brow is wet with honest sweat,
    He earns whate'er he can,
And looks the whole world in the face,
    For he owes not any man.
                    —LONGFELLOW, *The Village Blacksmith*

SWEETHEART

As one who cons at evening o'er an album all alone,
And muses on the faces of the friends that he has known,
So I turn the leaves of Fancy till, in shadowy design,
I find the smiling features of an old sweetheart of mine.
                    —J. W. RILEY, *An Old Sweetheart of Mine*

SWEETNESS

Sweet is the rose, but grows upon a brier;
Sweet is the juniper, but sharp his bough;
Sweet is the eglantine, but pricketh near;
Sweet is the firbloom, but his branches rough;
Sweet is the cypress, but his rind is tough;
Sweet is the nut, but bitter is his pill;
Sweet is the broom-flower, but yet sour enough;
And sweet is moly, but his root is ill.
So every sweet with sour is tempered still.
                    —SPENSER, *Amoretti*, Sonnet XXVI

SWEETNESS AND LIGHT

Instead of dirt and poison, we have rather chosen to fill our hives with honey and wax; thus furnishing mankind with the two noblest of things, which are sweetness and light.   —SWIFT, *The Battle of the Books*

SWORD

. . . all they that shall take the sword shall perish with the sword.   —NEW TESTAMENT, *Matthew*, XXVI, 52

SYMPATHY

No one is so accursed by fate,
No one so utterly desolate,
    But some heart, though unknown,
    Responds unto his own.   —LONGFELLOW, *Endymion*

And whoever walks a furlong without sympathy walks to his own funeral drest in his shroud.
                    —WALT WHITMAN, *Song of Myself*

TAILOR

Like to nine tailors, who, if rightly spell'd
Into one man are monosyllabel'd.
                    —JOHN CLEVELAND, *Poems* (1639)

TALE

Tell me the tales that to me were so dear,
  Long, long ago—long, long ago.
                    —T. H. BAYLY, *Long, Long Ago*

I could a tale unfold whose lightest word
Would harrow up thy soul. —SHAKESPEARE, *Hamlet, I, 5*

TALENT

Talents differ; all is well and wisely put;
If I cannot carry forests on my back,
Neither can you crack a nut.
      —EMERSON, *Fable: The Mountain and the Squirrel*

Talent is developed in retirement: character is formed
in the rush of the world.   —GOETHE, *Tasso, I, 2*

That one talent which is death to hide.
                    —MILTON, *Sonnet: On His Blindness*

TALK

"The time has come," the Walrus said,
  "To talk of many things:
Of shoes—and ships—and sealing wax—
  Of cabbages—and kings—
And why the sea is boiling hot—
  And whether pigs have wings."
          —LEWIS CARROLL, *Through the Looking-Glass*

They never taste who always drink;
They always talk who never think.
          —PRIOR, *On a Passage . . . in . . . Scaligeriana*

TASTE

There can be no disputing about taste.
(De gustibus non est disputandum.)
                    —ANON., Old Latin proverb

Well, for those who like that sort of thing I should think
that it is just about the sort of thing they would like.

—LINCOLN, to R. D. Owen, the spiritualist

Every one to his taste, as the woman said when she
kissed her cow.   —RABELAIS, *Pantagruel*

TAXES

The marvel of all history is the patience with which men
and women submit to burdens unnecessarily laid upon
them by their governments.

—WILLIAM E. BORAH, Speech in U. S. Senate

. . . in this world nothing is certain but death and taxes.

—FRANKLIN, Letter (in French) to Leroy, 1789

O that there might in England be
A duty on Hypocrisy,
A tax on humbug, an excise
On solemn plausibilities.

—HENRY LUTTRELL, *An Aspiration*

Taxation without representation is tyranny.

—JAMES OTIS, *Argument on . . . Writs of Assistance* (1769)

TEA

Tea! thou soft, thou sober, sage, and venerable liquid,
. . . thou female tongue-running, smile-smoothing, heart-
opening, wink-tippling cordial, . . .

—COLLEY CIBBER, *The Lady's Last Stake, I, 1*

Now stir the fire, and close the shutters fast,
Let fall the curtains, wheel the sofa round,
And, while the bubbling and loud hissing urn
Throws up a steamy column, and the cups,
That cheer but not inebriate, wait on each,
So let us welcome peaceful ev'ning in.

—COWPER, *The Task, IV*

Here, thou, great Anna! whom three realms obey,
Dost sometimes counsel take—and sometimes tea.
—POPE, *The Rape of the Lock, III*

TEACHER

A teacher affects eternity; he can never tell where his influence stops.
—HENRY ADAMS, *The Education of Henry Adams*

And gladly would he learn and gladly teach.
—CHAUCER, *Canterbury Tales,* Prologue

The schools became a scene
Of solemn farce, where Ignorance on stilts,
His cap well lin'd with logic not his own,
With parrot tongue perform'd the scholar's part,
Proceeding soon a graduated dunce.
—COWPER, *The Task, II*

There, in his noisy mansion, skill'd to rule,
The village master taught his little school; . . .
Full well they laugh'd, with counterfeited glee,
At all his jokes, for many a joke had he;
Full well the busy whisper, circling round,
Convey'd the dismal tidings when he frown'd.
—GOLDSMITH, *The Deserted Village*

Our American professors like their literature clear, cold, pure, and very dead.
—SINCLAIR LEWIS, Address, Swedish Academy, 1930

The average schoolmaster is and always must be essentially an ass, for how can one imagine an intelligent man engaging in so puerile an avocation?
—H. L. MENCKEN, *Prejudices, Series 3*

The Prussian schoolmaster won the battle of Sadowa.
—VON MOLTKE, Speech, 1874

Those having torches will pass them on to others.

—PLATO, *The Republic*

He who can, does. He who cannot, teaches.

—BERNARD SHAW, *Maxims for Revolutionists*

Delightful task! to rear the tender thought,
To teach the young idea how to shoot.

—THOMSON, *The Seasons*

TEARS

It is the wisdom of crocodiles, that shed tears when they
would devour.   —FRANCIS BACON, *Essays*

Every tear from every eye
Becomes a babe in eternity.

—BLAKE, *Auguries of Innocence*

So bright the tear in Beauty's eye,
Love half regrets to kiss it dry.

—BYRON, *The Bride of Abydos*

"I weep for you," the Walrus said:
   "I deeply sympathize."
With sobs and tears he sorted out
   Those of the largest size,
Holding his pocket-handkerchief
   Before his streaming eyes.

—LEWIS CARROLL, *Through the Looking-Glass*

Nothing is lost that's wrought with tears:
The music that you make below
Is now the music of the spheres.

—JOHN DAVIDSON, *A Ballad of Heaven*

Weep not, my wanton, smile upon my knee,
When thou art old there's grief enough for thee.

—ROBERT GREENE, Song from *Menaphon*

She would have made a splendid wife, for crying only
made her eyes more bright and tender.
—O. HENRY, *Options*

She by the river sat, and sitting there,
She wept, and made it deeper by a tear.
—HERRICK, *Upon Julia, Weeping*

My tears must stop, for every drop
Hinders needle and thread.
—THOMAS HOOD, *The Song of the Shirt*

If you would have me weep, you must feel grief yourself.
(*Si vis me flere, . . .*)   —HORACE, *Ars Poetica*

Thrice he assay'd, and thrice, in spite of scorn,
Tears, such as angels weep, burst forth.
—MILTON, *Paradise Lost, I*

If you have tears, prepare to shed them now.
—SHAKESPEARE, *Julius Caesar, III, 2*

Tears, idle tears, I know not what they mean,
Tears from the depth of some divine despair
Rise in the heart, and gather to the eyes,
In looking on the happy autumn-fields,
And thinking of the days that are no more.
—TENNYSON, *The Princess*

TEMPTATION

Why comes temptation but for man to meet
And master and make crouch beneath his foot,
And so be pedestaled in triumph?
—R. BROWNING, *The Ring and the Book*

What's done we partly may compute,
But know not what's resisted.
                    —BURNS, *Address to the Unco Guid*

Lead us not into temptation, but deliver us from evil.
                    —NEW TESTAMENT, *Matthew, VI, 13*

I can resist everything except temptation.
                    —OSCAR WILDE, *Lady Windermere's Fan*

TEXAS

If I owned Texas and Hell, I would rent out Texas and
live in hell.   —GEN. PHILIP H. SHERIDAN, Speech, 1855

THANKSGIVING DAY

Heap high the board with plenteous cheer, and gather
    to the feast,
And toast the sturdy Pilgrim band whose courage never
    ceased.
—ALICE W. BROTHERTON, *The First Thanksgiving Day*

Over the river and through the wood,
Now grandmother's cap I spy!
    Hurrah for the fun!
    Is the pudding done?
Hurrah for the pumpkin pie!
                    —LYDIA M. CHILD, *Thanksgiving Day*

THEOLOGY

He could raise scruples dark and nice,
And after solve 'em in a trice;
As if Divinity had catched
The itch, on purpose to be scratched.
                    —BUTLER, *Hudibras, I*

Any stigma will do to beat a dogma.
                    —PHILIP GUEDALLA, *Supers and Supermen*

Theology is an attempt to explain a subject by men who do not understand it. The intent is not to tell the truth but to satisfy the questioner.

—ELBERT HUBBARD, *The Philistine, XX*

My theology, briefly,
Is that the Universe
Was Dictated
But not Signed. —CHRISTOPHER MORLEY, *Safe and Sane*

So oft in theologic wars,
    The disputants, I ween,
Rail on in utter ignorance
    Of what each other mean,
And prate about an Elephant
    Not one of them has seen
—J. G. SAXE, *The Blind Men and the Elephant*

THIEF

'Twas a thief said the last kind word to Christ;
Christ took the kindness and forgave the theft.

—R. BROWNING, *The Ring and the Book*

Now Barabbas was a robber.*

—NEW TESTAMENT, *John, XVIII, 40*

*Now Barabbas was a publisher. —THOMAS CAMPBELL

He that prigs what isn't his'n,
When he's cotched 'll go to prison.

—"HAPPY" WEBB (quoted by Lord Wm. Lennox)

THIRST

Water, water, every where,
And all the boards did shrink;
Water, water, every where,
Nor any drop to drink.

—S. T. COLERIDGE, *The Ancient Mariner*

The thirst that from the soul doth rise,
  Doth ask a drink divine;
But might I of Jove's nectar sup,
  I would not change for thine. —BEN JONSON, *To Celia*

I drank at every vine.
  The last was like the first.
I came upon no wine
  So wonderful as thirst.

                    —EDNA ST. VINCENT MILLAY, *Feast*

THOUGHT

I think, therefore I am.
(*Cogito, ergo sum*) —DESCARTES, *Principles of Philosophy*

Men of thought, be up and stirring
  Night and day:
Sow and seed—withdraw the curtain—
  Clear the way.   —CHARLES MACKAY, *Clear the Way*

No thought without phosphorus.
          —JACOB MOLESCHOTT, *Lehre der Nahrungsmittel*

And which of you with taking thought can add to his
stature one cubit?   —NEW TESTAMENT, *Luke, XII, 25*

If I have done the public any service, it is due to patient
thought.   —SIR ISAAC NEWTON, Remark to Dr. Bentley

For my thoughts are not your thoughts, neither are your
ways my ways.   —OLD TESTAMENT, *Isaiah, LV, 8*

Man is but a reed, the weakest in nature, but he is a
thinking reed.   —PASCAL, *Pensées, VI*

It is clear that thought is not free if the profession of certain opinions make it impossible to earn a living.
                    —BERTRAND RUSSELL, *Sceptical Essays*

Give thy thoughts no tongue
Nor any unproportion'd thought his act.
—SHAKESPEARE, *Hamlet, I, 3*

There is nothing either good or bad but thinking makes
it so. —SHAKESPEARE, *Hamlet, II, 2*

Yond Cassius has a lean and hungry look;
He thinks too much: such men are dangerous.
—SHAKESPEARE, *Julius Caesar, I, 2*

Break, break, break,
On thy cold gray stones, O Sea!
And I would that my tongue could utter
The Thoughts that arise in me.
—TENNYSON, *Break, Break, Break*

Thoughts too deep to be expressed,
And too strong to be suppressed.
—GEORGE WITHER, *Mistress of Philarete*

To me the meanest flower that blows can give
Thoughts that do often lie too deep for tears.
—WORDSWORTH, *Intimations of Immortality*

THRONE

The throne is but a piece of wood covered with velvet.
—NAPOLEON (quoted by Thiers)

In that fierce light which beats upon a throne.
—TENNYSON, *The Coming of Arthur*

THRUSH

That's the wise thrush: he sings each song twice over
Lest you should think he never could recapture
The first fine careless rapture.
—R. BROWNING, *Home Thoughts from Abroad*

Sing clear, O throstle,
Thou golden-tongued apostle
And little brown-frocked brother
Of the loved Assisian!   —T. A. DALY, *To a Thrush*

And hark! how blithe the throstle sings!
He, too, is no mean preacher:
Come forth into the light of things,
⸗et Nature be your teacher.
                    —WORDSWORTH, *The Tables Turned*

TIDE

There is a tide in the affairs of men,
Which, taken at the flood, leads on to fortune.
                    —SHAKESPEARE, *Julius Caesar*, IV, 3

TIGER

Tyger! Tyger! burning bright
In the forests of the night,
What immortal hand or eye
Could frame thy fearful symmetry?—BLAKE, *The Tyger*

Or if some time when roaming round,
    A noble wild beast greets you,
With black stripes on a yellow ground,
    Just notice if he eats you.
This simple rule may help you learn
    The Bengal Tiger to discern.
                —CAROLYN WELLS, *How to Tell Wild Animals*

TIME

Alas! how swift the moments fly!
    How flash the years along!
Scarce here, yet gone already by,
    The burden of a song.
See childhood, youth, and manhood pass,
    And age with furrowed brow;

Time was—Time shall be—drain the glass—
  But where in Time is now?
                              —JOHN QUINCY ADAMS, *The Hour Glass*

Backward, turn backward, O Time, in your flight,
Make me a child again just for to-night!
                              —ELIZABETH A. ALLEN, *Rock Me to Sleep*

Time whereof the memory of man runneth not to the
contrary.   —BLACKSTONE, *Commentaries*

He said, "What's time? Leave Now for dogs and apes!
  Man has Forever."
                              —R. BROWNING, *A Grammarian's Funeral*

Time goes, you say? Ah no!
Alas, Time stays, *we* go.
                              —AUSTIN DOBSON, *The Paradox of Time*

Where's the use of sighing?
  Sorrow as you may,
Time is always flying—
Flying!—and defying
  Men to say him nay.   —W. E. HENLEY, *Villanelle*

Gather ye Rose-buds while ye may,
  Old Time is still aflying:
And this same flower that smiles today,
  To-morrow will be dying.
                              —HERRICK, *To the Virgins . . .*

Time, you old gipsy man,
Will you not stay,
Put up your caravan
Just for one day.
                              —R. HODGSON, *Time, You Old Gipsy Man*

Catch then, oh catch the transient hour;
  Improve each moment as it flies!
Life's a short Summer, man a flower;
  He dies—alas! how soon he dies.
                —SAMUEL JOHNSON, *Winter: An Ode*

To every thing there is a season, and a time to every purpose under the heaven: A time to be born, and a time to
die; a time to plant, and a time to pluck up that which is
planted. . . .   —OLD TESTAMENT, *Ecclesiastes, III, 1-8*

In the dark backward and abysm of time.
                —SHAKESPEARE, *The Tempest, I, 2*

Thus the whirligig of time begins in his revenges.
                —SHAKESPEARE, *Twelfth Night, V, 1*

Unfathomable Sea, whose waves are years;
  Ocean of Time, whose waters of deep woe
Are brackish with the salt of human tears!
                —SHELLEY, *Time*

A wonderful stream is the River Time,
  As it runs through the realm of Tears,
With a faultless rhythm, and a musical rhyme,
And a broader sweep, and a surge sublime,
  As it blends with the Ocean of Years.
                —B. F. TAYLOR, *The Long Ago*

God stands winding His lonely horn,
And time and the world are ever in flight;
And love is less kind than the grey twilight,
And hope is less clear than the dew of the morn.
                —W. B. YEATS, *Into the Twilight*

The years like great black oxen tread the world
And God, the herdsman, goads them on behind.
                —W. B. YEATS, *The Countess Cathleen*

TOBACCO

For this you've my word, and I never yet broke it,
So put that in your pipe, My Lord Otto, and smoke it.
—R. H. BARHAM, *The Lay of St. Odille*

Tobacco, divine, rare, superexcellent tobacco, which goes
far beyond all panaceas, potable gold and philosopher's
stones, a sovereign remedy to all diseases.
—BURTON, *Anatomy of Melancholy*

Pernicious weed! whose scent the fair annoys,
Unfriendly to society's chief joys,
Thy worst effect is banishing for hours
The sex whose presence civilizes ours.
—COWPER, *Conversation*

Tobacco is a dirty weed: I like it.
It satisfies no normal need: I like it.
It makes you thin, it makes you lean,
It takes the hair right off your bean;
It's the worst darn stuff I've ever seen:
  I like it.   —G. HEMMINGER, *Tobacco*

. . . A custom loathsome to the eye, hateful to the nose,
harmful to the brain, dangerous to the lungs, and in the
black stinking fume thereof nearest resembling the horrible
Stygian smoke of the pit that is bottomless.
—JAMES I OF ENGLAND, *A Counterblast to Tobacco*

. . . A woman is only a woman, but a good cigar is a
smoke.   —KIPLING, *The Betrothed*

For thy sake, Tobacco, I
Would do anything but die.
—CHARLES LAMB, *A Farewell to Tobacco*

What this country really needs is a good five-cent cigar.
—T. R. MARSHALL, Remark while presiding over
the U. S. Senate.

And when the pipe is foul within,
Think how the soul's defiled with sin;
To purge with fire it does require,
Thus think, and drink tobacco.
—GEORGE WITHER (?), *Tobacco* (1699)

TODAY

Out of Eternity the new Day is born;
Into Eternity at night will return. —CARLYLE, *To-day*

I've shut the door on yesterday
And thrown the key away—
To-morrow holds no fears for me,
Since I have found to-day.
—VIVIAN Y. LARAMORE, *To-day*

To-morrow, to-morrow, not to-day
Hear the lazy people say.
*(Morgen, Morgen, nur nicht Heute;
Sprechen immer träge Leute.)*
—WEISSE, *Der Aufschub*

TOLERANCE

Then gently scan your brother man,
Still gentler sister woman;
Tho' they may gang a kennin wrang,
To step aside is human.
—BURNS, *Address to the Unco Guid*

TOMORROW

To-morrow, and to-morrow, and to-morrow,
Creeps in this petty pace from day to day
To the last syllable of recorded time
—SHAKESPEARE, *Macbeth*, V, 5

TONGUE

A Slip of the Foot you may soon recover,
But a Slip of the Tongue you may never get over.
—FRANKLIN, *Poor Richard's Almanac* for 1747

A tart temper never mellows with age, and a sharp tongue is the only edged tool that grows keener with constant use.   —WASHINGTON IRVING, *Rip Van Winkle*

"They are fools who kiss and tell"—
    Wisely has the poet sung.
Man may hold all sorts of posts
    If he'll only hold his tongue.
—KIPLING, *Pink Dominoes*

Keep thy tongue from evil, and thy lips from speaking guile.   —OLD TESTAMENT, *Psalms, XXXIV, 13*

TRAVEL

They change their clime, not their disposition, who run beyond the sea.   —HORACE, *Epistles, I*

From going to and fro in the earth, and from walking up and down in it.   —OLD TESTAMENT, *Job, I, 7*

Ay, now I am in Arden: the more fool I; when I was at home, I was in a better place: but travellers must be content.   —SHAKESPEARE, *As You Like It, II, 4*

Home-keeping youth have ever homely wits . . .
I would rather entreat thy company
To see the wonders of the world abroad
Than, living dully sluggardized at home,
Wear out thy youth with shapeless idleness.
—SHAKESPEARE, *Two Gentlemen of Verona, I, 1*

See one promontory, one mountain, one sea, one river, and see all. —SOCRATES (Burton, *Anatomy of Melancholy*)

I pity the man who can travel from Dan to Beersheba, and cry, " 'Tis all barren!" —STERNE, *A Sentimental Journey*

It is not worth while to go around the world to count the cats in Zanzibar.   —THOREAU, *Walden*

The fool that far is sent,
  Some wisdom to attain,
Returns an idiot, as he went,
  And brings the fool again.
                —G. WHITNEY, *Emblems* (1586)

TREASON

Just for a handful of silver he left us,
Just for a riband to stick in his coat.
                —R. BROWNING, *The Lost Leader*

Treason doth never prosper, what's the reason?
For if it prosper none dare call it Treason.
        —SIR JOHN HARINGTON, *Epigrams: Of Treason*

Caesar had his Brutus; Charles the First, his Cromwell; and George the Third—["Treason!" cried the Speaker]— *may profit by their example.* If *this* be treason, make the most of it.
—PATRICK HENRY, Speech, in Virginia House of Burgesses

The traitor to humanity is the traitor most accursed;
Man is more than Constitutions; better rot beneath the
    sod,
Than to be true to Church and State while we are
    doubly false to God!
—J. R. LOWELL, *On the Capture of . . . Fugitive Slaves*

And from the extremest upward of thy head
To the descent and dust below thy foot,
A most toad-spotted traitor.
                —SHAKESPEARE, *King Lear*, V, 3

TREE

What do we plant when we plant the tree?
We plant the ship that will cross the sea,
We plant the mast to carry the sails,
We plant the planks to withstand the gales—
The keel, and keelson, and beam and knee—
We plant the ship when we plant the tree.
—HENRY ABBEY, *What Do We Plant*

I wonder about the trees:
Why do we wish to bear
Forever the noise of these
More than another noise
So close to our dwelling-place?
—ROBERT FROST, *The Sound of Trees*

I remember, I remember
The fir-trees dark and high;
I used to think their slender tops
Were close against the sky.
—THOMAS HOOD, *I Remember, I Remember*

What does he plant who plants a tree?
He plants the friend of sun and sky;
He plants the flag of breezes free;
The shaft of beauty towering high.
—HENRY C. BUNNER, *The Heart of the Tree*

Woodman, spare that tree!
  Touch not a single bough!
In youth it sheltered me,
  And I'll protect it now.   —G. P. MORRIS, *The Oak*

Spreading himself like a green bay tree.
—OLD TESTAMENT, *Psalms XXXVII, 35*

Under the greenwood tree
Who loves to lie with me,

And turn his merry note
Unto the sweet bird's throat,
Come hither, come hither, come hither:
Here shall he see
No enemy
But winter and rough weather.
—SHAKESPEARE, *As You Like It, II, 5*

TRIFLES

Little drops of water,
    Little grains of sand,
Make the mighty ocean
    And the pleasant land.
—JULIA F. CARNEY, *Little Things*

For the want of a nail the shoe was lost,
For the want of a shoe the horse was lost,
For the want of a horse the rider was lost,
For the want of a rider the battle was lost,
For the want of a battle the kingdom was lost—
And all for the want of a horseshoe-nail.
—FRANKLIN, *Poor Richard's Almanac* for 1758

TRIUMPH

Hail to the Chief who in triumph advances!
—SCOTT, *The Lady of the Lake, II*

TROUBLE

Better never trouble Trouble
    Until Trouble troubles you;
For you only make your trouble
    Double-trouble when you do.
—DAVID KEPPEL, *Trouble*

Man is born unto trouble, as the sparks fly upward
—OLD TESTAMENT, *Job, V, 7*

To take arms against a sea of troubles.
>   —SHAKESPEARE, *Hamlet, III, 1*

Though life is made up of mere bubbles,
  'Tis better than many aver,
For while we've a whole lot of troubles,
  The most of them never occur.
>   —NIXON WATERMAN, *Shreds and Patches*

TRUST

And this be our motto, "In God is our trust."
>   —FRANCIS SCOTT KEY, *The Star-Spangled Banner*

He's mad that trusts in the tameness of a wolf, a horse's health, a boy's love, or a whore's oath.
>   —SHAKESPEARE, *King Lear, III, 6*

TRUTH

A truth that's told with bad intent
Beats all the lies you can invent.
>   —BLAKE, *Auguries of Innocence*

'Tis strange but true; for truth is always strange,—
Stranger than fiction.   —BYRON, *Don Juan*

I like a look of agony,
Because I know it's true;
Men do not sham convulsion,
Nor simulate a throe.   —EMILY DICKINSON, *Poems, IV*

God offers to every mind its choice between truth and repose. Take which you please,—you can never have both.
>   —EMERSON, *Essays: Intellect*

Mine eyes have seen the glory of the coming of the Lord;
He is trampling out the vintage where the grapes of
  wrath are stored;

He hath loosed the fateful lightning of his terrible swift
    sword;
His truth is marching on.
        —JULIA WARD HOWE, *Battle Hymn of the Republic*

Once to every man and nation comes the moment to
    decide,
In the strife of Truth with Falsehood, for the good or
    evil side.   —J. R. LOWELL, *The Present Crisis*

Truth forever on the scaffold,
Wrong forever on the throne.
        —J. R. LOWELL, *The Present Crisis*

Man with his burning soul
Has but an hour of breath
To build a ship of Truth
In which his soul may sail
Sail on the sea of death
For death takes toll
Of beauty, courage, youth,
Of all but Truth.   —JOHN MASEFIELD, *Truth*

Servant of God, well done! well hast thou fought
The better fight, who single hast maintain'd
Against revolted multitudes the cause
Of truth.   —MILTON, *Paradise Lost, VI*

I speak truth, not so much as I would, but as much as I
dare; and I dare a little more as I grow older.
        —MONTAIGNE, *Essays, III*

Pilate saith unto him, What is truth? And when he had
said this, he went out again unto the Jews.
        —NEW TESTAMENT, *John, XVIII,* 38

Ye shall know the truth, and the truth shall make you
free.   —NEW TESTAMENT, *John, VIII,* 13

And oftentimes to win us to our harm,
The instruments of darkness tell us truths,
Win us with honest trifles, to betray 's
In deeper consequence.   —SHAKESPEARE, *Macbeth, I, 3*

> To thine own self be true,
And it must follow, as the night the day,
Thou canst not then be false to any man.
> —SHAKESPEARE, *Hamlet, I, 3*

My way of joking is to tell the truth. It's the funniest joke in the world.
> —BERNARD SHAW, *John Bull's Other Island, II*

Truth is the most valuable thing we have. Let us economize it.   —MARK TWAIN, *Pudd'nhead Wilson's Calendar*

If you shut up truth and bury it under the ground, it will but grow, and gather to itself such explosive power that the day it bursts through it will blow up everything in its way.   —EMILE ZOLA, *J'accuse*

TURKEY

Know ye the land where the cypress and myrtle
Are emblems of deeds that are done in their clime, . . .
> —BYRON, *The Bride of Abydos*

At midnight in his guarded tent,
   The Turk was dreaming of the hour
When Greece, her knee in suppliance bent,
   Should tremble at his power.
> —FITZ-GREENE HALLECK, *Marco Bozzaris*

We have on our hands a sick man,—a very sick man.
> —NICHOLAS I OF RUSSIA
> (Quoted by Sir George Seymour, 1853)

TYRANNY

I impeach him in the name of the people of India, whose
rights he has trodden under foot, and whose country he
has turned into a desert. Lastly, in the name of human
nature itself, in the name of both sexes, in the name of
every age, in the name of every rank, I impeach the common enemy and oppressor of all.

—EDMUND BURKE, *Impeachment of Warren Hastings*

Think'st thou there is no tyranny but that
Of blood and chains? The despotism of vice,
The weakness and the wickedness of luxury,
The negligence, the apathy, the evils
Of sensual sloth—produce ten thousand tyrants. . . .
—BYRON, *Sardanapalus, I, 2*

Nature has left this tincture in the blood,
That all men would be tyrants if they could.
—DEFOE, *The Kentish Petition*

Tremble, ye tyrants, for ye cannot die.
—JACQUES DELILLE, *L'Immortalité de l'âme*

Some village Hampden, that, with dauntless breast,
The little tyrant of his fields withstood.
—GRAY, *Elegy Written in a Country Churchyard*

Resistance to tyrants is obedience to God.
—THOMAS JEFFERSON, *Epigrams*

Fear not the tyrants shall rule forever,
Or the priests of the bloody faith;
They stand on the brink of that mighty river,
Whose waves they have tainted with death
—SHELLEY, *Rosalind and Helen*

UMBRELLA

The rain it raineth on the just
    And also on the unjust fella;
But chiefly on the just, because
    The unjust steals the just's umbrella.
                            —SIR GEORGE F. OWEN
                    (Quoted by Sichel in *Sands of Time*)

UNDERSTANDING

I shall light a candle of understanding in thine heart,
which shall not be put out.
                    —APOCRYPHA, *II Esdras, XIV, 25*

UNION

E pluribus unum.
(One from many.)
                    —AMERICAN MOTTO (taken from Virgil)

United we stand, divided we fall.
                    —MOTTO OF THE STATE OF KENTUCKY

One flag, one land, one heart, one hand,
    One nation, evermore!
    —O. W. HOLMES, *Voyage of the Good Ship Union*

Liberty and Union, now and forever, one and insepa-
rable!   —DANIEL WEBSTER, Speech, 1830

UNITY

All for one, one for all.
                    —DUMAS, *The Three Musketeers*

All your strength is in your union,
All your danger is in discord.
                    —LONGFELLOW, *Hiawatha*

UNIVERSE

To see the world in a grain of sand.
—BLAKE, Auguries of Innocence

All that is in tune with thee, O Universe, is in tune with me!
—MARCUS AURELIUS, Meditations

Ah love! could you and I with Him conspire
To grasp this sorry Scheme of Things entire,
    Would we not shatter it to bits—and then
Re-mould it nearer to the Heart's Desire?
—OMAR KHAYYÁM, Rubáiyát, (FitzGerald trans.)

This goodly frame, the earth, seems to me a sterile promontory; this most excellent canopy, the air, look you, this brave o'erhanging firmament, this majestical roof fretted with golden fire, why, it appears no other thing to me than a foul and pestilent congregation of vapours.
—SHAKESPEARE, Hamlet, II, 2

One God, one law, one element,
And one far-off divine event,
To which the whole creation moves.
—TENNYSON, The Two Voices

UNIVERSITY

The true University of these days is a Collection of Books.
—CARLYLE, Heroes and Hero-Worship

"D'ye think th' colledges has much to do with th' progress iv the wurruld?" asked Mr. Hennessy.

"D'ye think," said Mr. Dooley, " 'tis th' mill that makes th' water run?"
—F. P. DUNNE, Colleges and Degrees

A pine bench, with Mark Hopkins at one end of it and me at the other, is a good enough college for me!
—JAMES A. GARFIELD, Address, 1871

VAGABOND

A hobo is a man who builds palaces and lives in shacks,
He builds Pullmans and rides the rods . . .
He reaps the harvest and stands in the bread line.
    —G. Irwin, *American Tramp and Underworld Slang*

O the Raggedy Man! He works fer Pa;
An' he's the goodest man you ever saw!
                        —J. W. Riley, *The Raggedy Man*

Wealth I ask not, hope nor love,
    Nor a friend to know me;
All I ask, the heavens above,
    And the road below me.
                        —R. L. Stevenson, *The Vagabond*

VALENTINE

Roses are red,
    And violets are blue,
Sugar is sweet,
    And so are you.
    —Anon., American version of old Valentine inscription

To-morrow is Saint Valentine's day,
    All in the morning betime.
And I a maid at your window,
    To be your Valentine.
                        —Shakespeare, *Hamlet, IV, 5*

VANITY

And the name of that town is Vanity; and at the town
there is a fair kept, called Vanity Fair.
                        —Bunyan, *The Pilgrim's Progress*

Lo, all our pomp of yesterday
    Is one with Ninevah and Tyre!
                        —Kipling, *The Recessional*

Vanity of vanities; all is vanity.

—OLD TESTAMENT, *Ecclesiastes*, I, 2

Woe unto them that draw iniquity with cords of vanity, and sin as it were with a cart rope.

—OLD TESTAMENT, *Isaiah*, V, 18

Oh, Vanity of Vanities!
How wayward the decrees of Fate are;
How very weak the very wise,
How very small the very great are!

—THACKERAY, *Vanitas Vanitatum*

VARIETY

Variety's the very spice of life,
That gives it all its flavour.   —COWPER, *The Task*, II

Age cannot wither her, nor custom stale
Her infinite variety: other women cloy
The appetites they feed; but she makes hungry
Where most she satisfies.

—SHAKESPEARE, *Antony and Cleopatra*, II, 2

VENUS

Venus, a notorious strumpet, as common as a barber's chair.   —BURTON, *Anatomy of Melancholy*

Venus, thy eternal sway
All the race of men obey.

—EURIPIDES, *Iphigenia in Aulis*

Venus smiles not in a house of tears.

—SHAKESPEARE, *Romeo and Juliet*, IV, 1

Lo, this is she that was the world's delight;
The old grey years were parcels of her might;

The strewlings of the ways wherein she trod
Were the twain seasons of the day and night.
—SWINBURNE, *Laus Veneris*

VICAR OF BRAY

... And this is the law that I'll maintain
  Until my dying day, sir,
That whatsoever king shall reign,
  Still I'll be Vicar of Bray, sir.
—ANON., *The Vicar of Bray* (*c.* 1700)

VICE

Vice itself lost half its evil, by losing all its grossness.
—BURKE, *Reflections on the Revolution in France*

When our vices leave us, we flatter ourselves with the
credit of having left them.
—LA ROCHEFOUCAULD, *Maxims, 192*

Saint Augustine! well hast thou said,
  That of our vices we can frame
A ladder, if we will but tread
  Beneath our feet each deed of shame.
—LONGFELLOW, *The Ladder of St. Augustine*

Vice is a monster of so frightful mien,
As to be hated needs but to be seen;
Yet seen too oft, familiar with her face,
We, first endure, then pity, then embrace.
—POPE, *Essay on Man, II*

The gods are just, and of our pleasant vices
Make instruments to plague us.
—SHAKESPEARE, *King Lear, V, 3*

Virtue itself turns vice, being misapplied;
And vice sometimes by action dignified.
—SHAKESPEARE, *Romeo and Juliet, II, 3*

Could you hurt me, sweet lips, though I hurt you?
　　Men touch them, and change in a trice
The lilies and languors of virtue
　　For the roses and raptures of vice.
　　　　　　　　　　　　　　　—SWINBURNE, *Dolores*

VICE-PRESIDENT

Once there were two brothers. One ran away to sea, the
other was elected Vice-President, and nothing was ever
heard of either of them again.
　　　　　　　　　　　—THOMAS R. MARSHALL, *Recollections*

VICTORY

God how the dead men
Grin by the wall,
Watching the fun
Of the Victory Ball.   —ALFRED NOYES, *A Victory Dance*

Woe to the vanquished!
(*Vae victis!*)　　　　　　　　　　　—PLAUTUS, *Pseudolus*

Another such victory over the Romans, and we are un-
done.　　　　　　　　　—PYRRHUS (in Plutarch's *Lives*)

"But what good came of it at last?"
　　Quoth little Peterkin.
"Why that I cannot tell," said he
"But 't was a famous victory."
　　　　　　　　　　　—SOUTHEY, *The Battle of Blenheim*

Nothing except a battle lost can be half so melancholy
as a battle won.   —DUKE OF WELLINGTON, *Dispatch*, 1815

VILLAGE

Sweet Auburn! loveliest village of the plain,
　　Where health and plenty cheer'd the labouring swain,

Where smiling spring its earliest visit paid,
And parting summer's lingering blooms delay'd.
—GOLDSMITH, The Deserted Village

VILLAIN

O villain, villain, smiling, damned villain!
—SHAKESPEARE, Hamlet, I, 5

VILLON, FRANÇOIS

Prince of sweet songs made out of tears and fire,
A harlot was thy nurse, a god thy sire,
   Shame soiled thy song, and song assoiled thy shame,
But from thy feet now death has washed the mire,
Love reads out first, at head of all our choir,
   Villon, our sad bad glad mad brother's name.
—SWINBURNE, Ballade of François Villon

VIOLENCE

The very first essential for success is a perpetually constant and regular employment of violence.
—ADOLF HITLER, Mein Kampf

VIOLET

You are brief, and frail and blue—
Little sisters, I am too.
You are heaven's master-pieces—
Little loves, the likeness ceases.
—DOROTHY PARKER, Sweet Violets

      Lay her i' the earth:
And from her fair and unpolluted flesh,
May violets spring!   —SHAKESPEARE, *Hamlet, V, 1*

Then let me to the valley go,
   This pretty flower to see,
That I may also learn to grow
   In sweet humility.   —JANE TAYLOR, *The Violet*

A violet by a mossy stone
  Half hidden from the eye!
Fair as a star, when only one
  Is shining in the sky.
—WORDSWORTH, *She Dwelt Among the Untrodden Ways*

VIRTUE

I think mankind by thee would be less bored
If only thou wert not thine own reward.
—J. K. BANGS, *A Hint to Virtue*

Rags are royal raiment when worn for virtue's sake.
—B. T. CAMPBELL, *The White Slave, III*

Virtue is its own reward.   —CICERO, *De finibus*

'Tis virtue, and not birth, that makes us noble;
Great actions speak great minds, and such should govern.
—JOHN FLETCHER, *The Prophetess, II, 3*

I cannot praise a fugitive and cloistered virtue, unexercised and unbreathed, that never sallies out and sees her adversary, but slinks out of the race where that immortal garland is to be run for, not without dust and heat.
—MILTON, *Areopagitica*

Mortals that would follow me,
Love virtue; she alone is free;
She can teach ye how to climb
Higher than the sphery chime;
Or if virtue feeble were,
Heav'n itself would stoop to her.   —MILTON, *Comus*

Whatsoever things are true, whatsoever things are honest, whatsoever things are just, whatsoever things are pure, whatsoever things are lovely, whatsoever things are of good report: if there be any virtue, and if there be any praise, think on these things.
—NEW TESTAMENT, *Philippians, IV, 8*

When we are planning for posterity, we ought to remember that virtue is not hereditary.
                              —THOMAS PAINE, *Common Sense*

Know then this truth (enough for men to know),
"Virtue alone is happiness below."
                              —POPE, *Essay on Man, IV*

                    His virtues
Will plead like angels, trumpet-tongued, against
The deep damnation of his taking-off.
                              —SHAKESPEARE, *Macbeth, I, 7*

VISION

Was it a vision or a waking dream?
Fled is that music:—do I wake or sleep?
                              —KEATS, *Ode to a Nightingale*

And it shall come to pass afterward, that I will pour out my Spirit upon all flesh; and your sons and your daughters shall prophesy, your old men shall dream dreams, your young men shall see visions.—OLD TESTAMENT, *Joel, II, 28*

Where there is no vision, the people perish.
                              —OLD TESTAMENT, *Proverbs, XXIX, 18*

VOICE

He ceas'd; but left so pleasing on the ear
His voice, that list'ning still they seemed to hear.
                              —HOMER, *Odyssey, XIII* (Pope trans.)

The melting voice through mazes running,
Untwisting all the chains that tie
The hidden soul of harmony.   —MILTON, *L'Allegro*

His voice is as the sound of many waters.
                              —NEW TESTAMENT, *Revelation, I, 15*

The voice is Jacob's voice, but the hands are the hands of Esau.   —OLD TESTAMENT, *Genesis, XXVII, 22*

The voice of him that crieth in the wilderness.
    —OLD TESTAMENT, *Isaiah, XL, 3*

Her voice was ever soft,
Gentle, and low, an excellent thing in woman.
    —SHAKESPEARE, *King Lear, V, 3*

But O for the touch of a vanish'd hand,
And the sound of a voice that is still!
    —TENNYSON, *Break, Break, Break*

Two voices are there; one is of the sea,
One of the mountains; each a mighty Voice,
In both from age to age thou didst rejoice,
They were thy chosen music, Liberty!
    —WORDSWORTH, *Poems . . . to National Independence*

WAGES

S'pose you got a job a work an' there's jus' one fella wants the job. You got to pay 'im what he asts. But s'pose they's a hundred men wants that job. S'pose them men got kids an' them kids is hungry. S'pose a nickel 'll buy at leas' sompin for the kids. An' you got a hundred men. Jus' offer 'em a nickel—why, they'll kill each other fightin' for that nickel.   —JOHN STEINBECK, *The Grapes of Wrath*

WAGON

Hitch your wagon to a star.   —EMERSON, *Civilization*

WAITING

Serene I fold my hands and wait.—BURROUGHS, *Waiting*

Learn to labor and to wait.
    —LONGFELLOW, *A Psalm of Life*

They also serve who only stand and wait.
                    —MILTON, *Sonnet: On His Blindness*

Everything comes to those who can wait.
                    —RABELAIS, *Gargantua*

WANDERLUST

What care I for my house and my land?
    What care I for my money, O?
What care I for my new-wedded lord?
    I'm off with the wraggle-taggle gipsies, O.
                    —ANON., *The Wraggle-Taggle Gipsies*

We travel not for trafficking alone;
    By hotter winds our fiery hearts are fanned:
For lust of knowing what should not be known,
    We take the Golden Road to Samarkand.
                    —J. E. FLECKER, *Hassan*, V, 2

Beyond the East the sunrise, beyond the West the sea,
And East and West the wander-thirst that will not let
    me be.   —GERALD GOULD, *Wander-Thirst*

I am fevered with the sunset,
I am fretted with the bay,
For the wander-thirst is on me
And my soul is in Cathay.
                    —RICHARD HOVEY, *The Sea Gypsy*

It's little I know what's in my heart,
What's in my mind it's little I know,
But there's that in me must up and start,
And it's little I care where my feet go.
                    —EDNA ST. VINCENT MILLAY, *Departure*

Afoot and light-hearted I take to the open road,
Healthy, free, the world before me,

The long brown path before me leading wherever I
   choose.
Henceforth I ask not good-fortune, I myself am good-
   fortune,
Henceforth I whimper no more, postpone no more, need
   nothing,
Done with indoor complaints, libraries, querulous criti-
   cisms,
Strong and content I travel the open road.
              —WALT WHITMAN, *Song of the Open Road*

WANT

Man wants but little here below,
Nor wants that little long.   —GOLDSMITH, *The Hermit*

My belief is that to have no wants is divine.
              —SOCRATES (*Xenophon*, Memorabilia)

WAR

When civil dudgeon first grew high,
And men fell out, they knew not why;
When hard words, jealousies and fears,
Set folks together by the ears,
And made them fight, like mad or drunk,
For dame Religion as for punk; . . .
              —BUTLER, *Hudibras* (opening lines)

The Assyrian came down like the wolf on the fold,
And his cohorts were gleaming in purple and gold;
And the sheen of their spears was like stars on the sea,
When the blue waves roll nightly on deep Galilee.
        —BYRON, *The Destruction of Sennacherib*

And 'mid the tumult Kubla heard from far
Ancestral voices prophesying war.
              —S. T. COLERIDGE, *Kubla Khan*

By the rude bridge that arched the flood,
　　Their flag to April's breeze unfurled,
Here once the embattled farmers stood,
　　And fired the shot heard round the world.
　　　　　　　　　—EMERSON, *Concord Hymn*

Yes; quaint and curious war is!
　　You shoot a fellow down
You'd treat if met where any bar is,
　　Or help to half-a-crown.
　　　　　　　　　—THOMAS HARDY, *The Man He Killed*

They wrote in the old days that it is sweet and fitting to
die for one's country. But in modern war there is nothing
sweet nor fitting in your dying. You will die like a dog for
no good reason.
　　　　　　　　　—ERNEST HEMINGWAY, *Notes on the Next War*

The tumult and the shouting dies,
The captains and the kings depart.
　　　　　　　　　—KIPLING, *The Recessional*

Doughboys were paid a whole dollar a day
and received free burial under the clay.
And movie heroes are paid even more
shooting one another in a Hollywood war.
　　　　　　　　　—KREYMBORG, *What Price Glory*

There was laughter and loving in the lanes at evening;
Handsome were the boys then, and girls were gay.
But lost in Flanders by medalled commanders
The lads of the village are vanished away.
　　　　　　　　　—CECIL DAY LEWIS, *A Time to Dance*

Ez fer war, I call it murder,—
　　There you hev it plain an' flat;
I don't want to go no furder
　　Than my Testyment fer that;

God hez said so plump an' fairly,
  It's ez long ez it is broad,
An' you've gut to git up airly
  Ef you want to take in God.
                    —J. R. LOWELL, *The Biglow Papers, II*

War should be the only study of a prince. He should consider peace only as a breathing-time, which gives him leisure to contrive, and furnishes as ability to execute, military plans.   —MACCHIAVELLI, *The Prince*

War alone keys up all human energies to their maximum tension and sets the seal of nobility on those peoples who have the courage to face it.   —BENITO MUSSOLINI, *Fascism*

I still remember the effect I produced on a small group of Galla tribesmen massed around a man in black clothes. I dropped an aerial torpedo right in the center, and the group opened up like a flowering rose. It was most entertaining.
        —VITTORIO MUSSOLINI, In an account of his Ethiopian
                                          fighting

. . . and he smelleth the battle afar off, the thunder of the captains, and the shouting.
                    —OLD TESTAMENT, *Job, XXXIX, 25*

They shall not pass.
(Ils ne passeront pas)   —GENERAL PÉTAIN (1916)

Stand! the ground's your own, my braves!
Will ye give it up to slaves?
                    —JOHN PIERPONT, *Warren's Address*

From the Rio Grande's waters to the icy lakes of Maine,
Let all exult, for we have met the enemy again.
Beneath their storm old mountains we have met them in
    their pride,

And rolled from Buena Vista back the battle's bloody
tide.   —GEN. ALBERT PIKE, *The Battle of Buena Vista*

The terrible rumble, grumble and roar
Telling the battle was on once more—
  And Sheridan twenty miles away!
                              —T. B. READ, *Sheridan's Ride*

The American people will not relish the idea of any
American citizen growing rich and fat in an emergency of
blood and slaughter and human suffering.
         —FRANKLIN D. ROOSEVELT, Radio chat, May, 1940

Providence is always on the side of the big battalions.
              —MME. DE SÉVIGNÉ, Letter to her daughter

... Cry "Havoc," and let slip the dogs of war.
                   —SHAKESPEARE, *Julius Caesar, III, 1*

When the hurly-burly's done,
When the battle's lost and won.
                       —SHAKESPEARE, *Macbeth, I, 1*

There's many a boy here today who looks on war as all
glory, but, boys, it is all hell.
               —GEN. WILLIAM T. SHERMAN, Address, 1880

Not with dreams but with blood and iron,
Shall a nation be moulded at last.
                —SWINBURNE, *A Word for the Country*

Cannon to right of them,
Cannon to left of them,
Cannon in front of them
  Volley'd and thunder'd;
Storm'd at with shot and shell,
Boldly they rode and well,

Into the jaws of Death,
Into the mouth of hell
    Rode the six hundred.
        —TENNYSON, *The Charge of the Light Brigade*

WASHINGTON, GEORGE

The Father of his Country—We celebrate Washington!
We celebrate an Independent Empire.
        —ANON., An editorial in the *Pennsylvania Packet,*
                                        July 9, 1789

Where may the wearied eye repose
    When gazing on the great;
Where neither guilty glory glows,
    Nor despicable state?
Yes—one—the first—the last—the best—
    The Cincinnatus of the West, . . .
        —BYRON, *Ode to Napoleon Bonaparte*

O Washington!—thrice glorious name,
    What due rewards can man decree—
Empires are far below thy aim,
    And sceptres have no charms for thee.
—PHILIP FRENEAU, Occasioned by Washington's Arrival
                                        at Philadelphia

A citizen, first in war, first in peace, and first in the
hearts of his countrymen.
        —COL. HENRY LEE, Resolution in Congress, 1799

Oh, Washington! thou hero, patriot sage,
Friend of all climes, and pride of every age!
        —THOMAS PAINE, *Washington*

A Pharos in the night, a pillar in the dawn,
By his inspiring light may we fare on!
        —CLINTON SCOLLARD, *At the Tomb of Washington*

Washington—a fixed star in the firmament of great names, shining without twinkling or obscuration, with clear, beneficent light.—DANIEL WEBSTER, *Eulogy* (1826)

WATER

Water, water every where,
Nor any drop to drink.
> —S. T. COLERIDGE, *The Ancient Mariner*

Take the proverb to thine heart,
    Take and hold it fast—
"The mill cannot grind
    With the water that is past."
> —SARA DOUDNEY, *The Lesson of the Water-Mill*

We never know the worth of water till the well is dry.
> —THOMAS FULLER, *Gnomologia*, 5451

Here's to old Adam's crystal ale,
    Clear sparkling and divine,
Fair H_2O, long may you flow,
    We drink your health (in wine).
> —OLIVER HERFORD, *Toast: Adam's Crystal Ale*

The waters wear the stones.
> —OLD TESTAMENT, *Job, XIV, 19*

Smooth runs the water where the brook is deep.
> —SHAKESPEARE, *Henry VI, II, III, 1*

The old oaken bucket, the iron-bound bucket,
The moss-covered bucket that hangs in the well!
> —SAMUEL WOODWORTH, *The Old Oaken Bucket*

WATERLOO

The battle of Waterloo was won on the playing fields of Eton.
> —DUKE OF WELLINGTON, while watching a cricket match at Eton

WAVES

What are the wild waves saying,
    Sister, the whole day long,
That ever amid our playing
    I hear but their low, lone song?
    —J. E. CARPENTER, *What Are the Wild Waves Saying*

The breaking waves dash'd high
    On a stern and rock-bound coast,
And the woods against a stormy sky,
    Their giant branches toss'd.
        —FELICIA D. HEMANS, *The Landing of the Pilgrims*

WEALTH

Ill fares the land, to hastening ills a prey,
Where wealth accumulates, and men decay.
            —GOLDSMITH, *The Deserted Village*

Superfluous wealth can buy superfluities only. Money is
not required to buy one necessary of the soul.
            —THOREAU, *Walden: Conclusion*

WEATHER

It hain't no use to grumble and complain,
    It's jest as easy to rejoice;
When God sorts out the weather and sends rain,
    Why rain's my choice.
            —J. W. RILEY, *Wet-Weather Talk*

Everybody talks about the weather, but nobody does
anything about it.
—CHARLES D. WARNER, In *Hartford Courant* (*c.* 1890)

WEBSTER, DANIEL

So fallen! so lost! the light withdrawn
    Which once he wore!

The glory from his gray hairs gone
   For evermore.   —WHITTIER, *Ichabod*

WEED

A weed is no more than a flower in disguise,
Which is seen through at once, if love give a man eyes.
         —J. R. LOWELL, *A Fable for Critics*

O thou weed,
Who art so lovely fair and smell'st so sweet
That the sense aches at thee, would thou hadst ne'er
   been born!   —SHAKESPEARE, *Othello, IV, 2*

Once in a golden hour
I cast to earth a seed.
Up there came a flower,
The people said, a weed.   —TENNYSON, *The Flower*

WERTHER

Werther had a love for Charlotte
   Such as words could never utter;
Would you know how first he met her?
   She was cutting bread and butter.
         —THACKERAY, *The Sorrows of Werther*

WEST

Westward the course of empire takes its way.
—GEORGE BERKELEY, Bishop of Cloyne, *On the Prospect
       of Planting Arts and Learning in America*

Out where the handclasp's a little stronger,
Out where the smile dwells a little longer,
   That's where the West begins.
      —ARTHUR CHAPMAN, *Out Where the West Begins*

Go West, young man, and grow up with the country.
        —HORACE GREELEY, *Hints Toward Reform*

WHITMAN, WALT

W. W. is the Christ of the modern world—he alone redeems it, justifies it, shows it divine.

—JOHN BURROUGHS, Entry in *Journal,* 1892

Under the dirty clumsy claws of a harper whose plectrum is a muck-rake any tune will become a chaos of discords. —SWINBURNE, *Whitmania*

WHORE

The harlot's cry from street to street
Shall weave old England's winding-sheet.

—BLAKE, *Auguries of Innocence*

When dying sinners, to blot out their score,
Bequeath the church the leavings of a whore.

—EDWARD YOUNG, *Love of Fame*

WICKEDNESS

. . . he that hides a dark soul and foul thoughts
Benighted walks under the mid-day sun;
Himself his own dungeon. —MILTON, *Comus*

The wicked flee when no man pursueth: but the righteous are bold as a lion.

—OLD TESTAMENT, *Proverbs, XXVIII, 1*

There is no peace, saith the Lord, unto the wicked.

—OLD TESTAMENT, *Isaiah, XLVIII, 22*

'Cause I's wicked,—I is. I's mighty wicked, anyhow, I can't help it. —HARRIET B. STOWE, *Uncle Tom's Cabin*

WIDOW

A widow of doubtful age will marry almost any sort of a white man.—HORACE GREELEY, *Letter to Dr B Griswold*

Did you hear of the Widow Malone, Ohone!
Who lived in the town of Athlone, alone?
   Oh, she melted the hearts
   Of the swains in them parts,
So lovely the Widow Malone.
            —SAMUEL LOVER, *The Widow Malone*

WIFE

Wives are young men's mistresses, companions for middle age, and old men's nurses.
   —FRANCIS BACON, *Essays: Of Marriage and Single Life*

She is a winsome wee thing,
She is a handsome wee thing,
She is a lo'esome wee thing,
This sweet wee wife o' mine.
          —BURNS, *My Wife's a Winsome Wee Thing*

What a pity it is that nobody knows how to manage a wife, but a bachelor.
   —GEORGE COLMAN (THE ELDER), *The Jealous Wife,*
                                 IV, 1

Here lies my wife: here let her lie!
Now she's at rest, and so am I.
            —DRYDEN, *Suggested Epitaph*

The only comfort of my life
Is that I never yet had wife.   —HERRICK, *His Comfort*

Giving honour unto the wife, as unto the weaker vessel.
   —NEW TESTAMENT, *I, Peter, II, 7*

A virtuous woman is a crown to her husband.
         —OLD TESTAMENT, *Proverbs, XII, 4*

All other goods by Fortune's hands are given;
A wife is the peculiar gift of heaven.
              —POPE, *January and May*

A modernist married a fundamentalist wife,
And she led him a catechism and dogma life.
                    —KEITH PRESTON, *Marital Tragedy*

"A different cause," says Parson Sly,
   "The same effect may give:
Poor Lubin fears that he may die;
   His wife, that he may live."
                    —PRIOR, *A Reasonable Affliction*

WILLOW

On a tree by a river a little tom-tit
   Sang "Willow, titwillow, titwillow!"
And I said to him, "Dicky-bird, why do you sit
   Singing, 'Willow, titwillow, titwillow'?"
                    —W. S. GILBERT, *The Mikado, II*

We hanged our harps upon the willows in the midst
thereof.   —OLD TESTAMENT, *Psalms, CXXXVII, 2*

The poor soul sat sighing by a sycamore tree,
   Sing all a green willow;
Her hand on her bosom, her head on her knee,
   Sing willow, willow, willow:
The fresh streams ran by her, and murmur'd her moans;
   Sing willow, willow, willow;
Her salt tears fell from her, and soften'd the stones:
   Sing willow, willow, willow.
                    —SHAKESPEARE, *Othello, IV, 3*

WIND

The wind is awake, pretty leaves, pretty leaves,
Heed not what he says, he deceives, he deceives;
   Over and over to the lowly clover
He has lisped the same love (and forgotten it, too),
He'll be lisping and pledging to you.
                    —J. V. CHENEY, *The Way of It*

I have forgot much, Cynara! gone with the wind,
Flung roses, roses riotously with the throng.
—ERNEST DOWSON, *Non Sum Qualis Eram*

Have you heard the wind go "Yo-o-o-o"?
'Tis a pitiful sound to hear.
—EUGENE FIELD, *The Night Wind*

I hear the wind among the trees
Playing celestial symphonies;
I see the branches downward bent,
Like keys of some great instrument.
—LONGFELLOW, *A Day of Summer*

The wind bloweth where it listeth.
—NEW TESTAMENT, *John, III, 8*

The wind was a torrent of darkness among the gusty
trees. —NOYES, *The Highwayman*

For they have sown the wind, and they shall reap the
whirlwind. —OLD TESTAMENT, *Hosea, VIII, 7*

Who has seen the wind?
Neither you nor I:
But when the trees bow down their heads,
The wind is passing by.
—CHRISTINA ROSSETTI, *Who Has Seen the Wind*

Blow, winds, and crack your cheeks! rage! blow!
—SHAKESPEARE, *King Lear, III, 2*

Ill blows the wind that profits nobody.
—SHAKESPEARE, *Henry VI, III, II, 5*

O wild West Wind, thou breath of Autumn's being,
Thou, from whose unseen presence the leaves dead
Are driven, like ghosts from an enchanter fleeing,

Yellow, and black, and pale, and hectic red,
Pestilence-stricken multitudes.
—SHELLEY, *Ode to the West Wind*

Sweet and low, sweet and low,
    Wind of the western sea,
Low, low, breathe and blow,
    Wind of the western sea.   —TENNYSON, *The Princess*

WINE

Bronze is the mirror of the form; wine, of the heart.
—AESCHYLUS, Fragments, 384

And Noah he often said to his wife when he sat down to
    dine,
"I don't care where the water goes if it doesn't get into
    the wine."   —G. K. CHESTERTON, *The Flying Inn*

God made Man
    Frail as a bubble;
God made Love,
    Love made Trouble.
God made the Vine,
    Was it a sin
That Man made Wine
    To drown Trouble in?   —OLIVER HERFORD, *A Plea*

Drink wine, and live here blitheful while ye may;
The morrow's life too late is, live to-day.
—HERRICK, *To Youth*

O for a beaker full of the warm South,
Full of the true, the blushful Hippocrene,
With beaded bubbles winking at the brim,
And purple-stained mouth,
—KEATS, *Ode to the Nightingale*

Wine is a mocker, strong drink is raging.
                    —OLD TESTAMENT, *Proverbs, XX, 1*

Wine that maketh glad the heart of man.
                    —OLD TESTAMENT, *Psalms, CIV, 15*

I wonder often what the Vintners buy
One half so precious as the stuff they sell.
        —OMAR KHAYYÁM, *Rubáiyát* (FitzGerald trans.)

In wine there is truth.
  (In vino veritas.)   —PLINY, *Historia naturalis*

Come, thou monarch of the vine,
Plumpy Bacchus with pink eyne!
In thy fats our cares he drown'd,
With thy grapes our hairs be crown'd:
Cup us, till the world go round!
            —SHAKESPEARE, *Antony and Cleopatra, II, 7*

Who loves not women, wine, and song,
Remains a fool his whole life long.
*(Wer nicht liebt Weiber, Wein, und Gesang,
 Der bleibt ein Narr sein Leben lang.)*
            —JOHANN HEINRICH VOSS (wrongly ascribed to
                                Martin Luther)

WINTER

Winter lingered so long in the lap of Spring, that it occasioned a great deal of talk.   —BILL NYE, *Spring*

Winter is icummen in,
Lhude sing Goddamm,
Raineth drop and staineth slop,
And how the wind doth ramm!
  Sing: Goddamm.   —EZRA POUND, *Ancient Music*

When icicles hang by the wall,
    And Dick the shepherd blows his nail,
And Tom bears logs into the hall,
    And milk comes frozen home in pail,
When blood is nipp'd and ways be foul,
    Then nightly sings the staring owl,
        Tu-whit;
        Tu-who, a merry note
    While greasy Joan doth keel the pot.
        —SHAKESPEARE, *Love's Labour's Lost*, V, 2

If Winter comes, can Spring be far behind?
        —SHELLEY, *Ode to the West Wind*

WISDOM

A sadder and a wiser man,
He rose the morrow morn.
        —S. T. COLERIDGE, *The Ancient Mariner*

    To know
That which before us lies in daily life,
Is the prime wisdom; what is more is fume.
        —MILTON, *Paradise Lost*, VIII

Be ye therefore wise as serpents, and harmless as doves.
        —NEW TESTAMENT, *Matthew, X, 16*

The children of this world are in their generation wiser
than the children of light.—NEW TESTAMENT, *Luke, XVI, 8*

The wisdom of this world is foolishness with God.
        —NEW TESTAMENT, *I Corinthians, III, 19*

Wisdom is justified of her children.
        —NEW TESTAMENT, *Matthew, XI, 19*

The price of wisdom is above rubies.
        —OLD TESTAMENT, *Job, XXVIII, 18*

Woe unto them that are wise in their own eyes, and prudent in their own sight!—OLD TESTAMENT, *Isaiah, V, 21*

Knowledge comes, but wisdom lingers.
                                        —TENNYSON, *Locksley Hall*

Wisdom is not finally tested by the schools,
Wisdom cannot be pass'd from one having it to another
    not having it,
Wisdom is of the soul, is not susceptible of proof, is its
    own proof.—WALT WHITMAN, *Song of the Open Road*

WISH

I wish I hadn't broke that dish,
    I wish I was a movie-star,
I wish a lot of things, I wish
    That life was like the movies are.
        —A. P. HERBERT, *It May Be Life, But Ain't It Slow?*

WIT

Wit is the salt of conversation, not the food.
        —W. HAZLITT, *Lectures on English Comic Writers*

True wit is nature to advantage dress'd,
What oft was thought, but ne'er so well express'd.
                            —POPE, *Essay on Criticism, II*

You beat your pate, and fancy wit will come:
Knock as you please, there's nobody at home.
                        —POPE, *Epigram: An Empty House*

Better a witty fool than a foolish wit.
                    —SHAKESPEARE, *Twelfth Night, I, 5*

It is with wits as with razors, which are never so apt to cut those they are employed on as when they have lost their edge.   —SWIFT, *Tale of a Tub*, Preface

WOMAN

Here's to woman! Would that we could fall into her arms
without falling into her hands.

—AMBROSE BIERCE (quoted in Grattan's *Bitter Bierce*)

As Father Adam first was fool'd,
    A case that's still too common,
Here lies a man a woman rul'd:
    The Devil rul'd the woman.
        —BURNS, *Epitaph on a Hen-Pecked Country Squire*

Auld Nature swears, the lovely dears
    Her noblest work she classes, O:
Her prentice han' she tried on man,
    An' then she made the lasses, O.
        —BURNS, *Green Grow the Rashes*

A little while she strove, and much repented,
And whispering "I will ne'er consent"—consented.
        —BYRON, *Don Juan, I*

Believe a woman or an epitaph,
Or any other thing that's false.
        —BYRON, *English Bards and Scotch Reviewers*

Between a woman's Yes and No
There is not room for a pin to go.
(*Entre el Si y el No de la mujer,
No me atreveria yo á poner una punta de alfiler.*)
        —CERVANTES, *Don Quixote*

Women are only children of a larger growth.
        —LORD CHESTERFIELD, *Letters*, Sept. 1748

Heav'n has no rage like love to hatred turn'd,
Nor hell a fury like a woman scorn'd.
        —CONGREVE, *The Mourning Bride, III, 8*

Whoe'er she be,
That not impossible She,
That shall command my heart and me.
   —CRASHAW, *Wishes to His (Supposed) Mistress*

A woman, a dog, and a walnut-tree,
The more you beat 'em the better they be.
    —THOMAS FULLER, *Gnomologia*, 6404

The Eternal Feminine draws us upward.
(*Das Ewig-Weibliche zieht uns hinan.*)
    —GOETHE, *Faust*, II (last lines)

When lovely woman stoops to folly,
 And finds too late that men betray,
What charm can soothe her melancholy?
 What art can wash her guilt away?
The only art her guilt to cover,
 To hide her shame from every eye,
To give repentance to her lover,
 And wring his bosom, is—to die,
   —GOLDSMITH, *Song* (in *The Vicar of Wakefield*)

Women and music should never be dated.
   —GOLDSMITH, *She Stoops to Conquer*, III

If men knew how women pass the time when they are
alone, they'd never marry.
   —O. HENRY, *Memoirs of a Yellow Dog*

All that remains of her
Now is pure womanly.
   —THOMAS HOOD, *The Bridge of Sighs*

Then, my boy, beware of Daphne. Learn a lesson from
 a rat:
What is cunning in the kitten may be cruel in the cat.
   —R. U. JOHNSON, *Daphne*

I am very fond of the company of ladies; I like their beauty, I like their delicacy, I like their vivacity, and I like their *silence*.

      —SAMUEL JOHNSON (in Seward's *Johnsoniana*)

I met a lady in the meads,
    Full beautiful—a faery's child;
Her hair was long, her foot was light,
    And her eyes were wild.

      . . . .

I saw pale kings, and princes too,
    Pale warriors, death-pale were they all:
They cried—"La Belle Dame sans Merci
    Hath thee in thrall!"

      —KEATS, *La Belle Dame Sans Merci*

For the female of the species is more deadly than the
    male.   —KIPLING, *The Female of the Species*

Oh, the years we waste and the tears we waste
And the work of our head and hand
Belong to the woman who did not know
(And now we know that she never could know)
And did not understand.   —KIPLING, *The Vampire*

She knifed me one night 'cause I wished she was white,
And I learned about women from 'er!

      —KIPLING, *The Ladies*

The woman was not taken
    From Adam's head, we know,
To show she must not rule him—
    'Tis evidently so.
The woman she was taken
    From under Adam's arm,
So she must be protected
    From injuries and harm.

      —ABRAHAM LINCOLN, *Song* (written on
        the occasion of a friend's wedding)

To say why gals acts so or so,
    Or don't, 'ould be presumin';
Mebby to mean *yes* an' say *no*
    Comes nateral to women.
                                    —J. R. LOWELL, *The Courtin'*

I expect that woman will be the last thing civilized by
man.—GEORGE MEREDITH, *The Ordeal of Richard Feverel*

O woman, born first to believe us;
    Yea, also born first to forget;
Born first to betray and deceive us,
    Yet first to repent and regret!
                                    —JOAQUIN MILLER, *Charity*

My only books
Were woman's looks,
And folly's all they taught me.
            —THOMAS MOORE, *The Time I've Lost in Wooing*

God created woman. And boredom did indeed cease
from that moment—but many other things ceased as well.
Woman was God's *second* mistake.
                                    —NIETZSCHE, *The Antichrist*

O woman! lovely woman! Nature made thee
To temper man: we had been brutes without you.
                        —OTWAY, *Venice Preserved, I, 1*

Prince, a precept I'd leave for you,
    Coined in Eden, existing yet:
Skirt the parlor, and shun the zoo—
    Women and elephants never forget.
        —DOROTHY PARKER, *Ballade of Unfortunate Mammals*

Woman is as false as a feather in the wind.
    (*La donna è mobile
        Qual piuma al vento.*)
                —F. M. PIAVE, Libretto for Verdi's *Rigoletto*

When the candles are out all women are fair.
>   —PLUTARCH, *Conjugal Precepts*

Oh! say not Woman's love is bought
  With vain and empty treasure!
Oh! say not Woman's heart is caught
  By ev'ry idle pleasure!
When first her gentle bosom knows
  Love's flame, it wanders never,
Deep in her heart the passion glows;
  She loves, and loves forever!
>   —ISAAC POCOCK, *Song* (from *The Heir of Vironi*)

For never was it given to mortal man
To lie so boldly as we women can.
>   —POPE, *Wife of Bath's Prologue*

Give God thy broken heart, He whole will make it:
Give woman thy whole heart, and she will break it.
>   —E. PRESTWICH, *The Broken Heart*

Be to her virtues very kind;
Be to her faults a little blind;
Let all her ways be unconfin'd;
And clap your padlock—on her mind.
>   —PRIOR, *An English Padlock*

As for the women, though we scorn and flout 'em,
We may live with, but cannot live without 'em.
>   —FREDERIC REYNOLDS, *The Will, I, 1*

O Woman! in our hours of ease
Uncertain, coy, and hard to please,
And variable as the shade
By the light quivering aspen made;
When pain and anguish wring the brow,
A ministering angel thou!   —SCOTT, *Marmion, VI*

For women are as roses, whose fair flower
Being once display'd, doth fall that very hour.
—SHAKESPEARE, *Twelfth Night, II, 4*

Frailty, thy name is woman.
—SHAKESPEARE, *Hamlet, I, 2*

Who is Silvia? what is she,
    That all our swains commend her?
Holy, fair, and wise is she;
    The heaven such grace did lend her,
That she might admired be.
—SHAKESPEARE, *Two Gentlemen of Verona, IV, 2*

In the beginning, said a Persian poet,—Allah took a rose,
a lily, a dove, a serpent, a little honey, a Dead Sea apple,
and a handful of clay. When he looked at the amalgam—it
was a woman.
—WILLIAM SHARP, in *The Portfolio* for July, 1894

If all the harm that women have done
Were put in a bundle and rolled into one,
    Earth would not hold it,
    The sky could not enfold it,
It could not be lighted nor warmed by the sun.
—J. K. STEPHEN, *Lapsus Calami: A Thought*

Women are wiser than men because they know less and
understand more.   —JAMES STEPHENS, *The Crock of Gold*

Ten measures of speech descended on the world; women
took nine and men one.
—BABYLONIAN TALMUD, *Kiddushim*

The man that lays his hand on woman,
Save in the way of kindness, is a wretch
Whom 'twere gross flattery to name a coward.
—JOHN TOBIN, *The Honeymoon, II, 1*

Shall I, wasting in despair,
Die because a woman's fair?
Or make pale my cheeks with care
'Cause another's rosy are?
Be she fairer than the day,
Or the flow'ry meads in May,
If she think not well of me,
What care I how fair she be?
—GEORGE WITHER, *The Lover's Resolution*

She was a Phantom of delight
When first she gleamed upon my sight;
A lovely Apparition sent
To be a moment's ornament.
—WORDSWORTH, *She Was a Phantom of Delight*

WONDER

There be three things which are too wonderful for me,
yea, four which I know not: The way of an eagle in the air;
the way of a serpent upon a rock; the way of a ship in the
midst of the sea; and the way of a man with a maid.
—OLD TESTAMENT, *Proverbs, XXX, 18*

Wonder is the feeling of a philosopher, and philosophy
begins in wonder. —SOCRATES, *Plato,* Theœtetus

WOODS

The groves were God's first temples.
—BRYANT, *A Forest Hymn*

In the midway of this our mortal life,
I found me in a gloomy wood astray,
Gone from the path direct.
*(Nel mezzo del cammin di nostra vita
 Mi ritrovai per una selva oscura,
 Que la diritta via era smarita.)*
—DANTE, *Inferno* (opening lines)

Thick as autumnal leaves that strow the brooks
In Vallombrosa.   —MILTON, *Paradise Lost, I*

WOOING

Duncan Gray cam here to woo
  (Ha, ha, the wooing o't!)
On blythe Yule-Night when we were fou
  (Ha, ha, the wooing o't!).
Maggie coost her head fu' high,
Look'd asklent and unco skeigh,
Gart poor Duncan stand abeigh—
  Ha, ha! the wooing o't!   —BURNS, *Duncan Gray*

Barkis is willin'!   —DICKENS, *David Copperfield*

Ah fool! faint heart fair lady ne'er could win.
                —PHINEAS FLETCHER, *Britain's Ida*

A fool there was and he made his prayer
  (Even as you and I!)
To a rag and a bone and a hank of hair
(We called her the woman who did not care)
But the fool he called her his lady fair—
  (Even as you and I!)   —KIPLING, *The Vampire*

The time I've lost in wooing,
In watching and pursuing
  The light that lies
  In woman's eyes,
Has been my heart's undoing.
              —THOMAS MOORE, *The Time I've Lost . . .*

She's beautiful and therefore to be woo'd:
She's a woman, therefore to be won.
            —SHAKESPEARE, *Henry VI, I, V, 3*

WORDS

> God wove a web of loveliness
>   Of clouds and stars and birds,
> But made not any thing at all
>   So beautiful as words.
>
> —ANNA H. BRANCH, *Her Words*

> Your little words are hard and cold,
>   You try to use them as a sling
> As David did to slay the bold
>   Goliath—but they only sting!
>
> —MAY BRINKLEY, *Pebbles*

"The question is," said Alice, "whether you *can* make words mean so many different things."

"The question is," said Humpty Dumpty, "which is to be master—that's all."

> —LEWIS CARROLL, *Through the Looking-Glass*

Weasel words are words that suck all the life out of the words next to them, just as a weasel sucks an egg and leaves the shell.

> —STEWART CHAPLIN, *Stained-Glass Political Platform*
> (1900)

> The little *and,* the tiny *if,*
>   The ardent *ahs* and *ohs,*
> They haunt the lanes of poesy,
>   The boulevards of prose. —NATHALIA CRANE, *Alliances*

He had used the word in its Pickwickian sense . . . he had merely considered him a humbug in a Pickwickian point of view.   —DICKENS, *Pickwick Papers*

> Go put your creed into your deed,
> Nor speak with double tongue.
>
> —EMERSON, *Ode. Concord*

I am not yet so lost in lexicography as to forget that words are the daughters of the earth, and that things are the sons of heaven. —SAMUEL JOHNSON, *Dictionary*, Preface

We should have a great many fewer disputes in the world if words were taken for what they are, the signs of our ideas only, and not for things themselves.
—LOCKE, *Essay on Human Understanding*

By thy words thou shalt be condemned.
—NEW TESTAMENT, *Matthew, XII, 37*

Who is this that darkeneth counsel by words without knowledge?   —OLD TESTAMENT, *Job, XXXV, 16*

In words as fashions the same rule will hold,
Alike fantastic if too new or old:
Be not the first by whom the new are tried,
Nor yet the last to lay the old aside.
—POPE, *Essay on Criticism, II*

Words are like leaves, and where they most abound,
Much fruit of sense beneath is rarely found.
—POPE, *Essay on Criticism, II*

Thou art not so long by the head as honorificabilitudini-tatibus.   —SHAKESPEARE, *Love's Labour's Lost, V, 1*

Words, words, mere words, no matter from the heart.
—SHAKESPEARE, *Troilus and Cressida, V, 3*

On wings of deeds the soul must mount!
    When we are summoned from afar,
Ourselves, and not our words will count—
    Not what we said, but what we are!
—WILLIAM WINTER, *George Fawcett Rowe*

WORK

Blessed is he who has found his work; let him ask no other blessedness. —CARLYLE, *Past and Present*

Work—work—work
Till the brain begins to swim;
 Work—work—work
Till the eyes are heavy and dim

 . . . .

Sewing at once with a double thread
A Shroud as well as a Shirt.
 —THOMAS HOOD, *The Song of the Shirt*

And only the Master shall praise us, and only the Master
 shall blame;
And no one shall work for money, and no one shall work
 for fame;
But each for the joy of the working, and each, in his separate star,
Shall draw the Thing as he sees It, for the God of Things
 as They Are! —KIPLING, *The Seven Seas: L'Envoi*

For men must work, and women must weep,
And there's little to earn, and many to keep,
Though the harbour bar be moaning.
 —CHARLES KINGSLEY, *The Three Fishers*

Each morning sees some task begun,
 Each evening sees it close;
Something attempted, something done,
 Has earned a night's repose.
 —LONGFELLOW, *The Village Blacksmith*

From each according to his abilities, to each according
to his needs. —KARL MARX, *The German Ideology*

If any would not work, neither should he eat.
 NEW TESTAMENT, II *Thessalonians, III, 10*

In the sweat of thy face shalt thou eat bread.
—OLD TESTAMENT, *Genesis, III, 19*

WORLD

The created world is but a parenthesis in eternity.
—SIR THOMAS BROWNE, *Christian Morals*

For the world I count it not an inn, but an hospital, and
a place not to live, but to die in.
—SIR THOMAS BROWNE, *Religio Medici*

The world, which took but six days to make, is like to
take six thousand to make out.
—SIR THOMAS BROWNE, *Christian Morals*

This bad, twisted, topsy-turvy world,
Where all the heaviest wrongs get uppermost.
—E. B. BROWNING, *Aurora Leigh, V*

However, you're a man, you've seen the world—
The beauty and the wonder and the power,
The shape of things, their colours, lights and shades,
Changes, surprises—and God made it all!
—R. BROWNING, *Fra Lippo Lippi*

This world is but a thoroughfare full of woe,
And we but pilgrims passing to and fro.
Death is an end of every worldly sore.
—CHAUCER, *The Knight's Tale*

Good-bye, proud world! I'm going home.
I am going to my own hearth-stone,
Bosomed in yon green hills alone,—
—EMERSON, *Good-Bye*

The world!—it is a wilderness,
Where tears are hung on every tree.
—THOMAS HOOD, *Ode to Melancholy*

For to admire an' for to see,
 For to be'old this world so wide—
It never done no good to me,
 But I can't drop it if I tried!
                        —KIPLING, *For to Admire*

There's too much beauty upon this earth
 For lonely men to bear.
—RICHARD LE GALLIENNE, *Ballad of Too Much Beauty*

The world is a nettle; disturb it, it stings.
Grasp it firmly, it stings not. —OWEN MEREDITH, *Lucile*

O world, I cannot hold thee close enough!
             —EDNA ST. VINCENT MILLAY, *God's World*

Half the world does not know how the other half lives.
                        —RABELAIS, *Gargantua*

Great, wide, beautiful, wonderful World,
With the wonderful water round you curled,
And the wonderful grass upon your breast,
World, you are beautifully dressed.
                —W. B. RANDS, *The Wonderful World*

            All the world's a stage,
And all the men and women merely players:
They have their exits and their entrances;
And one man in his time plays many parts,
His acts being seven ages.
            —SHAKESPEARE, *As You Like It, II, 7*

How weary, stale, flat and unprofitable,
Seem to me all the uses of this world!
            —SHAKESPEARE, *Hamlet, I, 2*

Why, then the world's mine oyster,
Which I with sword will open.
                    —SHAKESPEARE, *Merry Wives of Windsor, II, 2*

The world is so full of a number of things,
I'm sure we should all be as happy as kings.
                    —R. L. STEVENSON, *Happy Thought*

. . . this world is a comedy to those that think, a tragedy
to those that feel— . . .
    —HORACE WALPOLE, Letter to Sir Horace Mann, 1769

The world is too much with us; late and soon,
Getting and spending, we lay waste our powers.
                    —WORDSWORTH, *Miscellaneous Sonnets*

WORTH

What is the worth of anything
But for the happiness 'twill bring?
                    —R. O. CAMBRIDGE, *Learning*

Slow rises worth, by poverty depress'd:
But here more slow, where all are slaves to gold,
Where looks are merchandise, and smiles are sold.
                    —SAMUEL JOHNSON, *London*

Worth makes the man, and want of it the fellow,
The rest is all but leather or prunella.
                    —POPE, *Essay on Man, IV*

WOUNDS

He jests at scars that never felt a wound.
                    —SHAKESPEARE, *Romeo and Juliet, II, 2*

WRATH

Nursing her wrath to keep it warm.
                    —BURNS, *Tam O' Shanter*

Let not the sun go down upon your wrath.
                    —New Testament, *Ephesians*, *IV*, *26*

A soft answer turneth away wrath:
                    —Old Testament, *Proverbs*, *XV*, *1*

WRINKLES

Wrinkles should merely indicate where smiles have been.
        —Mark Twain, *Pudd'nhead Wilson's New Calendar*

WRITER

A serious writer is not to be confounded with a solemn
writer. A serious writer may be a hawk or a buzzard or
even a popinjay, but a solemn writer is always a bloody
owl.   —Ernest Hemingway, *Death in the Afternoon*

No man but a blockhead ever wrote except for money.
                    —Johnson (Boswell's *Life* for 1776)

The incurable itch of writing possesses many.
(*Tenet insanabile multos scribendi cacoëthes.*)
                    —Juvenal, *Satire*, *VII*

God have mercy on the sinner
Who must write without a dinner,
    No gravy and no grub,
    No pewter and no pub,
    No belly and no bowels,
    Only consonants and vowels.
                    —J. C. Ransom, *Survey of Literature*

WRITING

. . . And this is the writing that was written, mene,
mene, tekel, upharsin.   —Old Testament, *Daniel*, *V*, *5*

Oh that . . . mine adversary had written a book.
                    —Old Testament, *Job*, *XXXI*, *35*

Such was the Muse whose rules and practice tell
"Nature's chief masterpiece is writing well."
                    —POPE, *Essay on Criticism, III*

True ease in writing comes from art, not chance,
As those move easiest who have learn'd to dance.
                    —POPE, *Essay on Criticism, II*

Let him be kept from paper, pen, and ink;
So may he cease to write and learn to think.
                    —PRIOR, *To a Person Who Writes Ill*

You write with ease to show your breeding,
But easy writing's curst hard reading.
                    —R. B. SHERIDAN, *Clio's Protest*

. . . Biting my truant pen, beating myself for spite:
Fool! said my Muse to me, look in thy heart and write.
                    —SIR PHILIP SIDNEY, *Astrophel and Stella*

YEAR

All sorts of things and weather
Must be taken in together,
To make up a year
And a sphere.
        —EMERSON, *Fable: The Mountain and the Squirrel*

Ring out, wild bells, to the wild sky,
    The flying cloud, the frosty light:
    The year is dying in the night,
Ring out, wild bells, and let him die.

Ring out the old, ring in the new,
    Ring, happy bells, across the snow:
    The year is going, let him go;
Ring out the false, ring in the true.
                    —TENNYSON, *In Memoriam*

YESTERDAY

>And all our yesterdays have lighted fools
>The way to dusty death.
>>—SHAKESPEARE, *Macbeth*, V, 5

YOUTH

>Oh, talk not to me of a name great in story;
>The days of our youth are the days of our glory;
>And the myrtle and ivy of sweet two-and-twenty
>Are worth all your laurels, though ever so plenty.
>>—BYRON, *Stanzas Written on the Road between*
>>*Florence and Pisa*

>'Tis not on youth's smooth cheek the blush alone, which
>   fades so fast,
>But the tender bloom of heart is gone, ere youth itself
>   be past.   —BYRON, *Stanzas for Music*

>"And youth is cruel, and has no remorse
>And smiles at situations which it cannot see."
>I smile, of course,
>And go on drinking tea. —T. S. ELIOT, *Portrait of a Lady*

>To maids and lads I sing.
>(*Virginibus puerisque canto.*)   —HORACE, *Odes, III*

>When I was one-and-twenty
>   I heard a wise man say,
>"Give crowns and pounds and guineas
>   But not your heart away;
>Give pearls away and rubies
>   But keep your fancy free."
>But I was one-and-twenty,
>   No use to talk to me.
>>—A. E. HOUSMAN, *A Shropshire Lad*

>When all the world is young, lad,
>   And all the trees are green;

And every goose a swan, lad,
    And every lass a queen;
Then hey, for boot and horse, lad,
    And round the world away;
Young blood must have its course, lad,
    And every dog his day.
                —CHARLES KINGSLEY, *Song* (from *Water Babies*)

Rejoice, O young man, in thy youth; and let thy heart
cheer thee in the days of thy youth.
                —OLD TESTAMENT, *Ecclesiastes, XI, 9*

O Youth with song and laughter,
    Go not so lightly by.
Have pity—and remember
    How soon thy roses die.
                —A. W. PEACH, *O Youth With Blossoms Laden*

Flaming youth has become a flaming question. And
youth comes to us wanting to know what we may propose
to do about a society that hurts so many of them.
                —FRANKLIN D. ROOSEVELT, Address, April, 1936

My salad days
When I was green in judgement: cold in blood.
                —SHAKESPEARE, *Antony and Cleopatra, I, 5*

Then come kiss me, Sweet-and-Twenty,
Youth's a stuff will not endure.
                —SHAKESPEARE, *Twelfth Night, II, 3*

Bliss was it in that dawn to be alive,
But to be young was very heaven!
                —WORDSWORTH, *The Prelude, XI*

There was a time when meadow, grove, and stream,
The earth, and every common sight,

To me did seem
Apparelled in celestial light,
The glory and the freshness of a dream.
—WORDSWORTH, *Intimations of Immortality*

ZEAL

The zeal of fools offends at any time,
But most of all the zeal of fools in rhyme.
—POPE, *Imitations of Horace, II*

ZEPHYR

Zephyr with Aurora playing,
As he met her once a-Maying,
There on beds of violets blue,
And fresh-blown roses wash'd in dew,
Fill'd her with thee, a daughter fair,
So buxom, blithe, and debonair. —MILTON, *L'Allegro*

ZEUS

Shakes his ambrosial curls, and gives the nod,
The stamp of fate, and sanction of the god.
—HOMER, *Iliad, I* (Pope trans.)

INDEX OF
AUTHORS

459